SONG MAN

SONG MAN

A Melodic Adventure,
or,
My Single-minded Approach to Songwriting

WILL HODGKINSON

Da Capo Press
A Member of the Perseus Books Group

Cataloging-in-Publication data for this book is available
from the Library of Congress.

First Da Capo Press edition 2007
Reprinted by arrangement with Bloomsbury Publishing, London
ISBN-13: 978-0-306-81581-2
ISBN-10: 0-306-81581-8

Published by Da Capo Press
A Member of the Perseus Books Group
www.dacapopress.com

Da Capo Press books are available at special discounts for bulk
purchases in the U.S. by corporations, institutions, and other organizations.
For more information, please contact the Special Markets Department
at the Perseus Books Group, 2300 Chestnut Street, Suite 200,
Philadelphia, PA, 19103, or call (800) 255-1514, or e-mail
special.markets@perseusbooks.com.

10 9 8 7 6 5 4 3 2 1

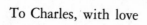
To Charles, with love

Contents

Introduction

It was the summer of 2005. I was in Brittany, France, with my wife, NJ. We had walked through a dark pine forest and down a gorse-dappled hill to reach a rock that jutted into a river. It had a plateau big enough to stretch out on, and you could dive from its edge into the deep water ten feet below. This part of the river was quiet and wide, with just a handful of small, empty boats along its banks and fields of corn and clover beyond them.

NJ crab-crawled down the side of the rock and glided into the river. I dived in with an inelegant splash and pushed through the water's depths, coming up to the surface to hear a dragonfly flapping past and to see NJ on the horizon, heading towards the middle of the river, her headscarf still dry.

'This is perfect,' said NJ after she came out of the river, drawing herself along the dry rock and its grassy patches. Our two young children were with her parents in a house about a mile away and, for the first time in a long while, all was calm. 'This is what I came here to do.'

'Me too,' I said. 'Although I told myself that I was going to come up with some songs while we were in France and I'm yet to write a word.'

A year earlier, aged thirty-four, I had learned guitar for the first time. The great thing about the guitar is that even someone with very little musical skill, knowledge, talent, taste or intelligence can make music with it fairly quickly. As such, it seemed like the ideal instrument for me to write songs with.

'What's stopping you?'

I looked around – at the water below us, at a little house on the far bank of the river – and could not think of an answer to her question. I could run through a few three- or four-chord songs on the guitar and execute some basic finger-picking patterns. But the best I had to offer the world in terms of original material was a song called 'Mystery Fox'. The words to the first verse were:

> Mystery Fox
> Get out of your box
> It's time for me
> To chase you up that tree, o mystery fox

My lyrical technique consisted of thinking of the name of an animal then finding something to rhyme with it.

Learning to play guitar had improved my life significantly, but to write a song felt like a nobler goal. The song is at the heart of humanity. It is the only art form that most of the planet has shared in. A percentage of people in the world have painted a picture, and significantly fewer have made a film, but almost everyone has sung a song and quite a lot of people have written one. From church hymns to national anthems to number one hits, songs are an encapsulation of what it means to be alive. Songs expose and articulate facets of human experience from birth to death and all points in between, and they thrive on simplicity. There are few better songs than 'Be My Baby' by The Ronettes, and that has a sentiment and a message that is as simple as it gets.

I had always told myself that, if only I had the time, I would surely write a few good songs. Now time stretched out like the river itself. I said that I needed inspiration. What could be more inspiring than this beautiful, silent place? It had been said many times, by many people, that I had a horrible voice and no sense of melody. That never stopped Bob Dylan.

Then there was the suspicion that songwriters were an elect few, a special breed touched with divine inspiration and a cavalcade of musical tricks and tools at their disposal. But the big news in the music industry that summer was the global success of MySpace, the website that allowed anyone, regardless of ability, financial situation or professional standing, to upload their songs onto their own site for the world to have access to. Some of the biggest bands in the country had got their first rung on the ladder through MySpace, while others knocked together songs and put them onto their computers in between going to school, going to work or picking up their pensions. The uncomfortable truth was that this simple, omnipresent art form, this three-minute creation made by everyone from children in their bedrooms to teenage rappers on street corners to millionaires in Hollywood mansions, was beyond me.

Anyone who has ever felt lonely can relate to Otis Redding as he sings 'Sitting On The Dock Of The Bay'. 'Wichita Lineman' by Jimmy Webb is filled with longing, mystery and melodic sophistication. Hearing a great song still affected me just as much as it did when, aged twelve and listening to the radio under the bed covers at night, I heard 'Hey Joe' by Jimi Hendrix for the first time. But I had no idea of how you go about creating these gems. I didn't know where melodies come from, or how you make words fit with music, or how you find the right style to express the mood you wish to convey. Anyone who has ever heard 'Mystery Fox' will be able to verify that.

We sat in silence on that rock for twenty minutes. NJ lay motionless with her eyes closed and I watched the river's ripples. I was thirty-five. It was far too late to take any professional songwriting ambitions seriously, and delusions of pop grandeur had died with my one and only attempt to be a singer, at a school talent competition. It was an avant-garde piece and I did a duet with a Hoover. The Hoover actually managed to get more votes than me.

But surely it was never too late to learn something new just for the hell of it, however much common sense and dignity might tell you otherwise. I remembered the excitement of friends in bands when we were in our early twenties, when boxes containing copies of their debut single would arrive from the record-pressing plant and they would stare at the slab of vinyl in their hands, marvelling at this sacred object. Those friends got older, their bands split up, they found jobs and had families, but that single would be rediscovered in attics, basements and charity shops, perhaps even cherished in a few record collections, and almost definitely have its ghost lifted onto the internet. It had a story of its own and it would, in one form or another, live on.

'I've got a new mission,' I told NJ. 'I'm going to learn how to write a song and record a single.'

She remained motionless. After a while she said: 'Is that wise?'

'Probably not. But I've let all these years pass, and spent so many hours hunting down records and marvelling at other people's efforts, that I've got to give it a go myself before it's too late. Even if only seventeen people get to hear it, at least it will exist.'

There could be a way of making it happen, too. ToeRag was a recording studio owned by a friend and former housemate of ours called Liam Watson. Everything in ToeRag was analogue and vintage – most of the equipment was culled from sixties studios – and Liam was one of the best producers in Britain. If I could just write some songs worthy of Liam's attention, and learn how to play a few well enough to justify their being recorded, perhaps he would allow me entry into this mysterious, glamorous world.

'So how are you going to approach this thing?' asked NJ.

'I guess I'll try and work out what it is that makes a great song,' I replied. 'And I'll get Doyle on the case – he's bound to come up with something.' Doyle was a slightly primitive friend, currently employed as a railway faults engineer, who had helped me learn to play guitar the year before. For some reason I had always envisioned him, despite the fact that he had never written a song in his life, as my songwriting partner. 'I'll try and find out if it really is true that anyone can write a song. And if it turns out that I'm wrong . . . there's always tribute bands.'

Chapter One

Lawrence

It was a Monday morning. We had been at our new house in Peckham, south London, for two weeks and Otto, our son, at his new school for one. It went uncharacteristically smoothly, although he was finding it difficult to come to grips with the concept of PE. He had already rebelled over the wearing of shorts, and had been the only child in his class to sit on the benches while the others climbed up ropes and jumped over vaulting horses, telling his teacher that, if she tried to force him, he would tear the school down, brick by brick. This sounded like a lot more effort than swinging on a rope, but Otto was adamant.

Now he was refusing to leave the house. So, that morning, I talked to him about how I hadn't liked PE at school either, and of how one day I had got over my fear of heights and climbed to the top of the rope, and how a huge sense of achievement followed. I also told him that, if he didn't get dressed and leave the house immediately, there would be no more sweets for the next twenty years. He finally agreed to go to school.

There had been plenty of people with children who had written songs, but I wondered how one combined songwriting with a normal life in which one goes to work, frets about the bills, and tries to make sure the kids get into bed at a reasonable time and leave the house before school is due to start. As life unfolds in its own parochial way, what creates the strong emotions and feelings that inspire a song?

Over the years I had heard about an eccentric songwriter called Lawrence. Having ditched his surname in his teens, Lawrence had formed a band called Felt at the beginning of the eighties. Felt made dreamy, rather fey music and built up a small but fervent cult following, but they didn't particularly interest me. Then, in the early nineties, Lawrence did an about-turn. His new band, Denim, drew their inspiration from seventies pop culture and the drab realities of growing up on a council estate in Birmingham. He had a way of cutting deep while apparently singing about the ephemeral. Denim had a song called 'The Osmonds' that starts off as a seemingly innocuous nostalgia piece about the seventies, referencing crushed-velvet flares, skinheads and 'lots of little Osmonds everywhere', before launching into the effects of the IRA bombing campaign in his hometown. 'Everybody knew some-one who died,' he sings, and the list of fun pop stuff that came before becomes tainted and tragic. Lawrence's very British wit became a blueprint later taken up by much more successful British bands, like Pulp and Blur. I couldn't understand why Denim weren't more famous.

Around the time that the album *Back In Denim* was released, I used to go to a nightclub in London called Smashing, where I would see a rake-thin man with a high forehead standing around the edge of the dance floor, looking like he might dissolve if water was poured on him. This was Lawrence, and, in our small subterranean microcosm, he was something of a star. Rumours circulated that his pathological fear of dirt meant that he couldn't stand bodily contact, that he would never so much as smoke a cigarette or drink a beer, and that Denim had made an album so expensive that it had caused their record company to collapse. When the sightings stopped, it was also rumoured that Lawrence had become a recluse, rarely venturing out of his flat, and that, in an about-turn of his clean-living ways, he had got mixed up with hard drugs.

I forgot about Lawrence for the next ten years until I heard his new album, which was recorded under the name of Go-Kart Mozart. A song called 'Um Bongo' managed to reference a popular children's fruit drink from the eighties and genocide in Rwanda. Another, 'Transgressions', was about a trend among British juvenile delinquents for spraying body deodorant onto their tongues for a cheap high. Tinny synthesisers and weedy guitars created an atmosphere of tawdry glamour. It was hard to believe, but nobody seemed to care any more about this uniquely gifted songwriter.

I decided that, since he was at the bottom of the career heap but at the top of the God-given talent one, Lawrence would be a good person to start with in my quest to learn to write a song. For a recluse, he was fairly easy to track down. One call to his record company resulted in a visit to a tiny flat in Victoria in central London, where a naked light bulb illuminated bare stained walls, a mattress, a television on the floor and a little record player. In his corridor were two storage cases under dust covers. One contained his collection of 'underground middle-of-the-road' records from the seventies and the other his favourite books: true-life accounts by junkies, anything by and about Andy Warhol, and Jack Kerouac's novels. The drab flat revealed the lack of logic typical of obsessive-compulsive behaviour. Lawrence was so worried about dust and fingerprints on his books and records that he insisted on visitors wearing surgical gloves before being allowed to touch them, but his bathroom looked like it hadn't been cleaned since he moved in five years earlier. As for the scene in the kitchen, I could only imagine.

'Don't go in there,' he warned. 'Nobody is allowed to go in there.'

Lawrence was living in near-total poverty. He hardly ever ate, believing that hunger was a necessary state for creative thought, but, if pushed, he would admit to snacking on the occasional sausage roll from a stand on Platform 8 of Victoria Station. He adhered to a minimalist, monk-like approach to life, of self-denial, and he dreamed of living in a prison cell and sleeping on a concrete bed that jutted out from a wall. At the same time he craved untold riches.

'When I have my number one hit,' he said, in his quiet Birmingham brogue, 'I'm going to buy a circular penthouse flat in Mayfair where I'll live by myself. I'll exist in a bubble of money and fame. I'll have a chauffeur waiting for me outside at all times – he can just sit in the car, smoking joints and perhaps the odd rock of crack. And there has to be a porter on the door of the building, because the last thing I want is for an axe murderer to come and chop me up in my sleep.'

Lawrence was forty-three years old and highly unlikely to have a number one hit, which wouldn't buy him a penthouse flat in Mayfair anyway, given the current parlous state of single sales. 'I'll never give up, ever,' he said, his small eyes staring straight at me. 'I don't care if I'm the first pensioner pop star. There is no other life for me than this one. I don't have any children and I never will. I never go anywhere because I haven't got any money. The only thing I care about is writing songs and living in the world of pop music, and I'm getting better all the time. I'm a slow learner. I couldn't tie my own shoelaces until I was twelve.'

He had an idea that he could make money by writing songs for the American Christian Midwest. 'It's a huge market,' he said, as he handed me one of his neat and tiny handwriting-filled notebooks. 'If you get a hit there, you'll make a million dollars.' He showed me his own attempt. It began: 'It's time that I confessed that I haven't got there yet, but it's getting easier to express that I like God.'

'I'm not sure if it comes across as entirely heartfelt,' I said.

'I don't really like God,' he said solemnly. 'But the point is that I'm trying to write the perfect song for those people in America.'

Lawrence held up Lou Reed as the ideal songwriter, as an example of someone who can raise descriptions of everyday life into high art. He also praised Lou Reed's simplicity – Reed's album *New York* consists of songs that are all made up of the same three chords: G, A and D.

'It takes time to get it right,' he said. 'Simplicity isn't easy. For one song called "Livin' On The Streets" I spent three-and-a-half years coming up with a single line. The rest of the words were written, but I couldn't think of the right word to end in an "o" sound. Then I was walking around a supermarket one day and they had a pile of Strongbow cider on special promotion. That was it. Strongbow. Rhymes with window. Finally the song was complete.'

I had been thinking about how to approach lyrics: whether to paint a recognisable picture and tell a story, as Ray Davies, Carole King and Lou Reed do, or to go for the Bob Dylan and Marc Bolan approach of mystery and imagery. 'Marc Bolan is brilliant at creating a poetic flow of gobbledygook, but he's also responsible for the atrocious lyrics of all the people who have copied him,' said Lawrence. 'My favourite lyric of all time is from Marc Bolan's song "Rock On": "Prophet pumped the car star, deeper only sweeter loves everyone." It's brilliant, but it can't have any meaning whatsoever. So words without meaning can be fantastic, but you have to have a creative and poetic mind to get away with it. When a band like Oasis do it, it's just plain bad.'

Lawrence was a believer in the eternal appeal of love songs, but I wondered where he found his material. He hadn't had a girlfriend in years. 'Love songs are good value for money, because love is one of the few true-life experiences that almost everyone can relate to,' he said. 'For much of the eighties and nineties nobody was looking forward to the new Bob Dylan album, yet he could always redeem himself with a good love song. I'm the same, although I need new inspiration. Right now I'm in the market for an extremely rich girl, because I can't go on living like this. She can be in her twenties or early thirties, and she doesn't have to be beautiful, but, if her dad's in *Who's Who*, that's a bonus.'

Even friendship was denied to Lawrence. 'This may surprise you,' he said, looking at me in a meaningful way, 'but I haven't got any friends. I want a buddy, like in those buddy films of the seventies, such as *Thunderbolt And Lightfoot*. Have you seen it? Clint Eastwood is the cool, aloof guy content to live the rest of his life in his own company. Then Jeff Bridges turns up and wants to be his friend. I want someone like that. I'm a lonely guy.'

The only thing Lawrence had in the way of social life was a weekly Narcotics Anonymous meeting. Taking place in Notting Hill, one of London's wealthiest neighbourhoods, this was not a place where street junkies hung out to get their fix, but a self-help group for the beautiful people. Lawrence had been astounded by the glamour of the weekly confessionals. He mentioned the names of an extremely famous rock star, a supermodel, and several habitués of the gossip pages who could best be described as minor celebrities. He described how nice everyone was; of how they tried to hug him as soon as he walked in, and of how they all said he could call them at any time of day or night if he was feeling depressed. Most at NA were taking the twelve-step regime to freedom from drug dependency and had put hard drugs behind them. The sessions were a chance to talk about their feelings, think positive, and look at the psychological reasons for taking drugs in the first place.

Lawrence had the job of Narcotic Anonymous tea boy. And he realised that, for all the talk of companionship, everybody left him to wash the cups without even stopping to say goodbye. 'Last week I didn't even have anyone to walk back to the tube with,' he sniffed. 'All I can say is that this is what feeds my songwriting.'

Drug addiction dictated Lawrence's lifestyle, but the creative process of writing songs gave his life meaning. He had plenty of advice for the aspiring songwriter. The first step, he told me, was to find a name that a boy of thirteen could proudly write on his satchel. 'Because, believe me, nobody is going to write "Will Hodgkinson" next to AC/DC or The Rolling Stones.'

'How about "Ultimate Cedric"?' I offered.

He reflected a little before shaking his head. 'You're limiting yourself to a niche market. If you want to only appeal to nerds, then you're on the right track, but I don't think it makes sound business sense.'

'I've got another one. "Sir Lord Will".'

He nodded. 'Sir Lord Will,' he said, rolling the words around his mouth like a ruminating cow. 'It aspires to regality, it's got a nice sound, and . . .', he tried writing it out, '. . . yes, it looks good on paper. You can put it inside a triangle with flames coming out of the side.'

'How about Double Fantasy?'

'Wasn't that the name of John Lennon's last album? Go for it — it's got a touch of ambiguity.'

We agreed that the next step was to come back to the flat with my guitar and show Lawrence the songs I had already written, which included the cosmic 'Mystery Fox' and a song about two friends having a one-night stand called 'Until Daylight'. In the meantime, I needed to get someone to actually sing these songs, since my own voice seemed to have the ability to clear rooms in seconds.

I liked the way my wife sang. She was shy, and too self-conscious even to sing in front of friends, but I had heard her harmonising along to her favourite songs in the car enough times to know that she could pull it off for our recording, if only she could be made to feel confident enough. But then there have been plenty of shy women who have somehow found it in themselves to get up on stage and sing. And my favourite person in this particular sub-group in the history of music was Nico, the former German model who sang on the first album by The Velvet Underground.

Nico was an inspiration, and my model of how I thought NJ could sing and present herself. When I was growing up and discovering The Velvet Underground, the articles I read about this New York band would paint Nico as a clownish figure, forever reduced to tears by Lou Reed's callous asides. The much-repeated story was that the band made her sing 'Femme Fatale', a song about a foolish but attractive woman, without telling Nico that it was based on her. And it's true that Lou Reed resented her. Nico claimed that this was because of what 'my people did to his people' – he was Jewish and she was German – but it seems that the real reason was a little less high-minded. He didn't like being pushed to stage left by a Teutonic beauty.

Nico was the best thing about The Velvet Underground. She was genuinely different – it was said that, when somebody asked

her a question, she would give an answer about five minutes later
– and her cold and stunning appearance was just one aspect of
what made her so compelling. She thrived on gloom and you
could hear that in her voice. Andy Warhol claimed that, when
she was stuck in a New York flat without electricity for a few
months in 1966 because the flat's owner had forgotten to pay the
bill, Nico spent her days indoors, in baths dimly lit by candles,
and she was the happiest she had ever been in her life.

After leaving The Velvet Underground, Nico spent a summer doing weekly performances at The Dom, the former Polish
social club that Andy Warhol and his gang had taken over. She
would sing alongside an enormous tape recorder that played the
backing tracks. Every night she was in tears because she would
get confused about which buttons to press. Eventually a bunch
of guitar players came to duet with her, including Jackson
Browne, Tim Hardin and Tim Buckley. In my romantic
delusion, that is how I imagined NJ and me: she in the
foreground, standing up, me in the background, sitting on a
chair, foot on knee, strumming a guitar.

Nico interpreted other people's songs on her first solo
album, 1968's *Chelsea Girl*, and she did it beautifully. She
sang three by Jackson Browne, then a young singer-songwriter
transposed from California to New York, who was her lover
for a while. The best of the three is 'These Days', a melancholic, wonderfully pretty song about not wishing to explore,
take risks or fall in love any more, but to just be, to live in a
state of unquestioning numbness. She also sang a couple by
John Cale and Lou Reed, Bob Dylan's 'I'll Keep It With
Mine', and one by Tim Hardin. *Chelsea Girl* is an album for
late nights and quiet Sunday mornings, with a reserved charm
that has little in common with the buoyant rebellion of
rock'n'roll. Once I had returned from France with a resolve

to understand how songs work, I kept going back to that record, to see how this woman, blessed not with a beautiful voice but one that draws you in through its curious, understated cadences, brought herself into these songs. On *Chelsea Girl* Nico is like a modern Marlene Dietrich, so completely out of step with the prevailing hippy dictum of the times that everybody must get stoned. A year later she made the leap from poised chanteuse to experimental hippy songwriter, unlocking a deep well of European suffering on her album *The Marble Index* in the process. But, for my purposes, it was that brief moment when she was a vehicle for the well-crafted three-minute song that mattered. NJ, with her silent ways and refined glamour, would make a very good Nico.

One evening, in the brief period between putting the kids to bed and falling asleep, NJ and I practised the half-formed songs I had already written. I didn't intend to record them at ToeRag, but they were the starting points from which, hopefully, I would move on to better things. We began with 'Until Daylight'. NJ had a great timbre to her voice, but she couldn't keep in time – I was sure that she was either going too fast or too slow.

'Why are you suddenly speeding up?' I said. 'Why can't you listen to the chord changes? They give you your cues about when to come in.'

'Because you keep changing the tempo,' she replied. 'And don't shout at me because remember that I'm doing you a favour here and, if you don't watch out, I might just refuse to do it.'

Lou Reed was said to have made Nico cry, yet it was Nico who had all the charm and charisma. I had better be careful. And I liked the way NJ sang the words – almost flat. When she tried to inject too much sexiness or feeling into them, they didn't work. 'This is a really hard song to do,' she said. 'The melody is weird and the timing is difficult to keep. There are too many words.'

She was already proving to be rebellious. She was claiming to be too tired to go through it one more time, even though all she had had to do that day was look after the kids, tidy up the house, deal with a grumpy neighbour, try to stop the gas from getting cut off and write up a report on vintage clothing – and that rebellion had to be stamped out fast. Before she halted entirely, I suggested we try 'Mystery Fox'. There isn't really any melody at all to this song, so I figured that the singer could get away with just speaking the words.

'You're not going to make me do this in front of anyone, are you?' she asked. 'It's not exactly difficult to sing, but I do think that a singer should feel comfortable with the words that they are conveying. And I'm not sure how possible it is to interpret a song called "Mystery Fox" with any degree of comfort. Can you imagine Nico doing it?'

I had an image of the never-smiling Nico, on stage in front of a crowd of New York sophisticates, dragging her gothic vowels over the words 'domestic caaaat, get out of your flaaaat' and concluded that, while plenty of lyricists have got away with all kinds of nonsense, I might possibly have to try a bit harder.

And there was another problem. It was only beginning to dawn on me that, with half of my life already used up, I knew less about how songs and music worked than the average child who has bothered to attend at least two piano lessons. Learning to play a sequence of chords on the guitar is one thing. Actually knowing how a song is structured using a verse, a chorus and a bridge (and I still didn't really know what a bridge was, beyond that James Brown took something there in his song 'Sex

Machine') is another. I had no idea how to write a song that told a singer's voice where to go, that actually had notes for the voice to follow. What I thought were self-penned songs were not songs at all: they were a random jumble of words and sort-of music. My singing voice was clearly horrific. In fact, the situation was about as bad as it could get. 'Mystery Fox' and 'Until Daylight' were proof that, musically speaking, I was in a special needs situation.

I needed to write some proper songs and I needed guidance. I called up Lawrence. He suggested that I accompany him to Narcotics Anonymous to understand how the reality of his life was reflected in his creative output. The next day I arrived at Ladbroke Grove Station to find him, close to translucent in the midday light, leaning against the railings, excited at the prospect of that day's outing.

'You're going to love it,' he told me, as we speeded towards the basement of the church hall where the weekly meeting was held. 'You get all sorts down there and everyone is dead friendly. You've got nothing to worry about.'

'But aren't they going to sniff me out as an impostor? It's obvious that I'm not a drug addict. Look at the glow in my cheeks.'

'You don't have to "share" if you don't want to, and you'll soon find out that you won't be able to get a word in edgeways because all these druggies are desperate to tell their story.'

When we arrived at the little room, the NA group leader was already there, setting out the chairs. I said hello. 'You haven't got a drug problem, have you?' he said by way of reply. I mumbled something about being there to support Lawrence. Then a large young man with wayward eyeballs came in and asked me who I was.

'My name's Will,' I said, almost adding, 'and I'm an addict', but somehow managing to stop myself. 'I'm a friend of Lawrence.'

'Oh right,' he said, looking at me with a sideways stare. 'So you've just come along for the ride, then?'

I panicked, and, in my panic, made up an enormous fib. 'Oh no, no,' I said quickly. 'I've had loads of problems in the past. A bit of everything, really . . . I must knock it on the head one of these days . . .'

He took a step back, staring at me. 'Do you mean to tell me that you're *still using?*'

'Good God, no!' I said, realising that I was digging myself a hole of lies that I had rapidly decreasing chances of climbing out of. 'I mean, I want to be totally clean. I don't even want to drink coffee. It gives me the jitters.'

His expression softened, and he smiled the smile of one religious convert to another. 'That's right, mate, total abstinence. It's the only way. Good luck, friend.'

Lawrence had been no help whatsoever during this sticky moment, apparently being too transfixed in removing the spot of grease he had found on a chipped teacup to intervene. I decided that the best thing to do was sit down in a corner and not say a word – after all, they couldn't *make* you share your problems with the group, could they? The group regulars filed in, hugging one another. Then the leader opened the group with the announcement: 'My name's ————— and I'm an addict', and going on to describe how reaching Step Six of the Twelve Step Program to an addiction-free life was almost like an out-of-body experience. Then he opened up the meeting to the floor and, sure enough, as soon as one person finished their story, another person jumped in with an ultra-quick 'My name's ————— and I'm an addict'. Drugs were hardly mentioned. It was all about overcoming fears, or difficult relationships, or the dangers of replacing one addiction with another, most often clothes shopping, oddly enough.

'Would any new members like to make themselves known to the group?' said the group leader. All eyes turned on me. I stared at the floor, my hand over my mouth, and tried to disappear into the chair. The silence, probably only half a minute long, was deafening.

Eventually he relented and the final stage of the session began: holding hands in a circle and thinking positive thoughts before ending up in a big group hug. Lawrence pulled me out before we got pulled in and dragged me towards the door.

'That was a bit of a disappointing one,' he said, as he walked at panic speed towards Ladbroke Grove underground station. 'There weren't any famous people and there was only one good-looking girl. Sorry about that.'

Although the NA meeting was a fairly terrifying experience, it did give me a little bit of insight into how Lawrence's songwriting mind worked. He had a song called 'Donna And the Dopeheads', which was about a mythical girl gang that went around New York selling heroin. Despite its cheery melody, it was a pretty bleak look at the life of the junkie, with its images of 'syringe kids fixing down by the Hudson River' and 'scenes of abject passive misery'.

'I met a girl called Donna, and I liked the old fifties books with the lurid covers that were about juvenile delinquency,' said Lawrence, as he attempted to remember the procedure for putting your travelcard through the ticket machine in order to get onto the London Underground. 'I wanted to write a druggy song that was bleak and existential, because you don't normally get that, and the whole thing was meant to be a work of fiction. But then, a few days before writing the second verse, I had to pawn my guitar because I was so desperate for money. So I wrote "I still want to be a star, but I've just pawned my guitar, and you know the way things are." Real life and personal experience creeps into your songs even when you try and write from a fictional perspective.'

Back at his airless, lightless, empty cell of a flat, Lawrence sat on the floor and smoked cigarettes while I sat on his bare, sheet-free mattress and played guitar. I began with 'Until Daylight'.

> Close the door, what do you say?
> Tonight we'll keep regrets at bay.
> I'll be yours and you'll be mine
> Until daylight
>
> I've boiled the rice, I've fried the fish,
> I'll let you eat straight from the dish.
> You know it's going to taste alright
> Until daylight
>
> *Chorus:*
> Well we've known each other for so long now
> That it's a strange thing to admit somehow.
> But the years have shown me how good you can be
> And tonight I'll know more intimately . . .

Three more verses and another chorus went on to describe chopping wood, building a fire, pouring whisky and generally setting up a scene conducive to rustic seduction while forgetting the outside world for a while. As I performed it for Lawrence, it felt like it was going quite well; at least I was playing guitar and the words were coming out of my mouth in the right order. But he stopped me after the first verse.

'Wow,' he said. 'You really can't sing.'

'Just try and ignore that and tell me if this song works.'

'I suppose it's quite nice,' he said dispiritedly, as I came to the end of the first verse. 'Nice and simple, at least. But you've got a really horrible note in there that's ruining everything. What is that?'

It was a high note that I had added to the song because I felt that it needed something extra. 'It's horrible!' repeated Lawrence. 'It's ghastly! Why are you playing it?'

'I'm trying to give the song an extra texture, that's all,' I said, sulkily.

'You're at the stage where you love trying out new things on the guitar, and you're really excited about learning new techniques,' he said. 'But I'm the opposite. I actually think of the guitar as my enemy. The goal now is to write really good songs that are going to live forever and the guitar gets in the way of that. I want everything to be on three chords or less these days, with all the technique being poured into the writing, not the playing. That's why I keep going back to Lou Reed as the perfect songwriter.'

I replaced the high note with a hammer-on, which changed one of the notes I was already using. 'That's better,' said Lawrence. 'But don't use the hammer-on every time, just once or twice. That gives it a special appeal and makes it stand out. Are you planning to play this song to other songwriters?'

'That's the idea,' I said, 'along with all the other compositions from my songbook. I want advice and input from the greats.'

He sighed and shook his head. 'One thing you're going to

have to remember is that songwriters hate to listen to songs by other people,' he said. 'Their goal in life is to have their songs heard by other people, not the other way round. It's all about ego. So you might find that some of those people get very impatient when you play them that song.'

'Are you telling me, in a roundabout way, that it's awful?'

'I wouldn't say that. Obviously you have to be careful of hurting people's feelings in situations like this.'

I explained to him how my wife, NJ, whom I thought sounded a little like Nico, would be my in-house singer. 'I *love* Nico,' he said. 'She's my favourite female singer – her or Jane Birkin. It's probably because they're both so thin and flat-chested. I like skinny girls. Go on then, let's hear the rest of it.'

'Until Daylight' went through quite a few chords and it followed the simple flat-picking style invented by the country music pioneer Maybelle Carter, in which a rhythm is kept on the treble strings while a melody is picked out on the bass notes. It creates an easy sound, but, for the choruses, the song changes completely, with a plucking of all the strings together over two chords. Lawrence was nodding along happily until I hit the first chorus. Then he looked as if a tiger had just run into his flat.

'Where the hell did that come from?' he shouted.

'What do you mean? That's the chorus.'

'It sounds like a completely different song! It's all wrong, and terrible, and horrible, and a complete disaster in terms of traditional songwriting. But, in a post-punk, independent sort of way, it's fun. Maybe its quaintness is part of its charm . . . well, get on with it.'

I carried on singing the verses as best I could. The second chorus came and, once again, Lawrence reacted with panic. His head darted from one direction to another, as if he had just been pulled out of a deep sleep by being hit with a mallet.

'Any proper songwriter would tell you to ditch that right away,' he said. 'And you keep calling it a chorus, but it's not. It's a weird bit that has no relation to anything else. Why did you add that? Did you think you needed it?'

'I thought I was creating a contrast,' I offered, weakly.

'That's one way of looking at it,' he said, taking a drag on his cigarette.

I still had my ace in the hole: 'Mystery Fox'. It didn't work when NJ sang it, but maybe it was a man's song. 'Good title,' Lawrence mused. Since I had to sing this tale of woodland activity myself, I decided that it needed the highest falsetto I could go to, as if a gorilla were squeezing my balls. It was only when I was about halfway through that I noticed Lawrence was letting out frantic, desperate squeals of laughter, as if about to collapse into uncontrollable sobs. I ignored him and carried on until I reached the final verse, which happened to be my favourite:

> Graceful bear
> With your curtain of hair
> You broke my arm with your gallons of charm
> O graceful bear . . .

Finally he collected himself enough to say, 'That's so evocative.' He brushed his forehead to mime a curtain of hair. 'Are you going to play that song to Ray Davies? Are you going to sing "Mystery Fox" to Hal David and Carole King?'

'I don't see why not,' I muttered, pouting at the guitar.

'They're going to think you've gone bonkers. Or they're going to think that you're taking the piss. Either way, they're going to be completely confused. Jesus Christ, imagine if you played "Mystery Fox" to Elton John!'

I felt that he was laying it on a bit thick. 'Why shouldn't I play it to those people?'

'It's not exactly "Leaving On A Jet Plane", is it?'

Maybe he realised that my feelings were hurt. He went on to say that it was idiosyncratic, but that, if I wanted to write a classic pop song, I was going the wrong way about it. 'Actually,' he said, 'it reminds me a bit of The Incredible String Band. Their songs jumped around and didn't sound like anything else. People always talk about finding an original voice and, if that's what you're after, I should say you've succeeded. But you may want to get rid of some of the verses. There are too many for the audience to remember and they'll get bored.'

'Why don't I just lop off the last two?' I suggested. 'That'll be the easiest thing to do.'

'You can't say that!' he screamed, his emaciated frame quivering with agitation. 'You're meant to be passionate about every moment in your song, and someone trying to tamper with it should be like cutting the arms and legs off your baby! Try not to be so slapdash.'

'But you just told me there were too many verses.'

'You're meant to fight to the end to keep your creation intact! You're going to have to learn how to craft if you ever want to write a great song. Think about the beginning, the middle and the end, and whether you need a middle eight or not.'

Lawrence stood up and started to pace around the little room. 'You need to define the intro, and work out what you're going to do for the coda, and look carefully at every section of the song,' he said. 'You need to make your decisions like a builder would, thinking about how the framework will support the whole. All of those Nico songs that you like so much have been perfectly constructed. That's why they can support her atrocious voice. Actually, you have a choice here. You could just write meandering hippy nonsense, or you could try and write a classic song like "Up, Up And Away". Which one do you want to do?'

I looked at him meaningfully, and said: 'I want to write an "Up, Up And Away".'

Lawrence told me to find a formula and stick to it. That's what the Motown hitmakers like Holland, Dozier, Holland, and the Brill Building songwriters of sixties New York, like Carole King and Gerry Goffin, did. They transposed a different set of lyrics to the same basic structure and a pop production line was the result.

There was one more thing to do before I left. Feeling that I hadn't impressed Lawrence sufficiently, I presented him with a display of my finger-picking guitar skills. Being able to make my thumb get a rhythm going by alternating between two bass strings was probably my proudest achievement on the guitar so far. I tried to sing a few hastily thrown-together words about being at the river in France over the top of the finger-picking guitar, but kept going out of time.

'Your problem is that you're trying to walk before you can run,' said Lawrence. 'You're doing all this fancy guitar work, which you can't really do very well, and consequently you're losing the essence of the song.'

'But the fancy guitar work *is* the essence of the song.'

'If you go up to Ray Davies and play him that he's not going to be interested in all your techniques. You could knock out a rhythm on a cardboard box for all he's going to care. What you should be thinking about now is the construction of the song, and its melody, and how well the lyrics work. All you're trying to show me is what you can do already. I understand that you've only just started playing and you're excited about it and all, but you're going to have to forget all of that for the time being and think about getting an actual song together.'

He was right, of course. I had gone to see Lawrence filled with pride for all of these songs that I had come up with, and he had quite rightly turned round and told me they were half-baked. If I did want to get better, I had to accept that I had a very long way to go.

Chapter Two

The Missing Melody

Where does the novice songwriter start? With only twelve notes to choose from, it has been said that there is nothing that hasn't been done before. Perhaps that doesn't matter? Modern pop music came of age in the sixties, after the bare bones of rock'n'roll were fashioned in the fifties, and one of the most primitive pop songs of them all, 'Louie Louie' by Richard Berry (performed by The Kingsmen), is also among the best. Thinking that I should take Lawrence's advice and aim to fashion a song out of the irreducible minimum of ingredients, I dug out my old 45 of The Kingsmen's 1963 smash hit and listened closely, to work out what went into it.

'Louie Louie' is remarkable for the fact that, while hearing it fills one with the raw energy of youth and the urge to both blow up the world and build a new one, it's totally meaningless. When The Kingsmen performed it, were the words are unfathomable, with the result that they could be about anything that the listener imagines. 'Louie Louie' reflected the FBI's natural tendency towards paranoia when the agency decided that, because the song was so good, it must be obscene. So a team was appointed to scrutinise the lyrics in order to find out whether it should be banned or not. They concluded that 'Louie Louie' was 'indecipherable at any speed', which any one of the thousands of teenagers who bought the record could have told them for free.

I knew enough about the guitar to play 'Louie Louie', which isn't much of a boast. (It's the first thing you learn.) The skill was the inspiration in coming up with it in the first place. That got me thinking about how much training you needed before you can start writing songs. Bob Stanley and Pete Wiggs, friends since their schooldays in Croydon, knew nothing about the rules of music whatsoever when they formed their band, St Etienne, in 1991 – and when I met Bob Stanley fifteen years later, he still didn't. Neither could play an instrument, they knew very little about music theory, and they certainly didn't know how to read sheet music. They came up with the ideas for the songs and got other people to make them a reality. And quite possibly, to the irritation of all those musicians who have spent years of their life in diligent study and pursuit of their craft, they have had a successful career as purveyors of thoroughly English, sixties-tinged electronic pop.

The paradox of being in a successful band while not being capable of doing anything musical was brought home to me when I went to see St Etienne in concert on an autumn evening a few weeks after meeting Lawrence. It was at the Barbican, one of London's most prestigious and stylishly modernist arts spaces, and there must have been over a thousand people in the sold-out, seated auditorium. The first half of the concert consisted of members of St Etienne's backing band providing a soundtrack to a film Bob Stanley had made about the Lea Valley, an underused area in east London that was about to be razed to make way for a stadium for the 2012 Olympics. In the second half, the backing musicians were joined by the band they were supposedly backing. St Etienne's singer, Sarah Cracknell, has a very good voice, and she held court centre stage, while behind her, Bob Stanley and Pete Wiggs stood behind trestle tables and computers with a few cables poking out of them, at which they stared intently. I think they may have been checking their emails.

Is it really possible to write melodic, hook-laden songs when you can't even play 'Happy Birthday' on a piano? I decided to find out by spending an evening with Bob Stanley. Songwriting has been good to him. He lives in High Point, a graceful minimalist block built in 1935 in Highgate, north London, by the modernist architect Lubetkin. The three-bedroom flat he shares with his sixties-dressed, wife Annelise, is a shrine to modern living. There is Dutch wooden furniture with elegant contours, obscure eastern European film posters, and a wall taken over by books that revealed an inquiring mind: coffee-table editions on the radical architects Archigram, biographies of the Regency dandy Beau Brummel and novels by the pub-fixated writer Patrick Hamilton. Bob's record collection is awarded its own room.

'From the word go I've been conscious that, if I knew how music worked, it would completely change the way I write songs and I've decided not to do that,' said Bob, polite, bright and rather awkward, as he sat on the edge of his orange sofa and poured us each a glass of wine. 'Pete [Wiggs] has learned how to operate a studio, but I don't even know that. I've kept on the same level all the time and my hope is that the songwriting can get better in spite of that.'

'How on earth can you write a song, then?' I asked.

'I structure our songs by basing them around other people's songs,' he replied. 'I'm a music fan, and I never wanted to be in a normal band that learns their instruments, goes out on the road, and then gets better over the years – I've never had the patience. I tried playing guitar once. It hurt my fingers.'

It was the democratising power of the sampler that allowed St Etienne to exist. In 1988 Bob Stanley and Pete Wiggs borrowed a Roland 303 keyboard and made a track that was, by his own admission, 'rubbish'. Two years later bands like The Happy Mondays and The Stone Roses were taking the beats and the energy of dance music and applying them to rock. Bob saw that something similar could be done with pop. Most hip-hop was based around a sample of somebody else's record, which was looped and used as a backing track for a rapper. There was no reason why pop couldn't be made in the same way.

'I wasn't exactly being cynical,' he said, 'but I did realise that, if I could find a singer, and get someone to do all the things I couldn't do, and then go into a studio with a bunch of records I liked and say to the engineer "make it sound like that", it might just work.'

In 1990 Bob and Pete convinced a friend of Pete's brother to sing a version of 'Only Love Can Break Your Heart' by Neil Young. Another friend came up with a bass line for the song. Then they went to a bedroom studio in Croydon with a stack of old records and made the track in two hours. They knew a promoter called Jeff Barrett, who was about to start a record label called Heavenly. Bob and Pete played the track to him and he suggested putting it out on his new label, and it was in the British Top Ten a few weeks later. 'The whole thing,' said Bob, 'was ridiculously easy.'

So it *was* possible for a non-musician to make a hit record, but Neil Young wrote 'Only Love Can Break Your Heart'. I asked Bob how he came to write a song himself. 'We knew we had to have a follow-up, and, at this point, we hadn't written a song in our lives. So we picked up structures from songs we loved, and we looked in the free ads papers and bought a keyboard. We couldn't actually play it, but we could make noises, and that, was enough.'

St Etienne's first self-written song was called 'Nothing Can Stop Us', which came into existence after they found a record by Gene Chandler called 'Nothing Can Stop Me'. They borrowed the melody from 'Eye Know', by the New York hip-hop band De La Soul, and took a sample from a song by Dusty Spring-field. From these elements they had their own song.

'I feel that I should apologise for borrowing the structure of somebody else's song,' said Bob, of the plagiarism that made 'Nothing Can Stop Us' come into existence. 'And, to this day, we're still making tracks by pilfering through our record collections. But then, what we produce ends up sounding completely different from what we were stealing from. That happens a lot. Apparently The Happy Mondays wanted to be like a cross between The Beatles and The Rolling Stones.'

Bob's sensibility, if not his musical ability, reminded me of Scott Walker. The Ohio-born singer fell in love with Europe and used the idea of it as his inspiration. Initially one third of The Walker Brothers, a semi-manufactured pop act trans-planted to England in the mid-sixties and marketed for a teenage audience, Scott rebelled against the industry he was in, took off at the height of his fame to stay in a monastery on the Isle of Wight, and came back a changed man. What followed were four astonishing solo albums that took in existentialism, English-language versions of the songs of the tormented Belgian singer Jacques Brel, ancient Christian spiri-tuality, and a portrait of Europe as a tragic but beautiful place where resignation and acceptance take the place of American optimism and vigour.

I had first heard Scott Walker's music when I was twenty-three. I was at a friend's house and he played *Scott 4*, the pinnacle of the singer's achievement and a commercial failure that resulted in his throwing in the towel and making his next release an

uninspiring collection of movie tunes. I had never heard anything
like it. It wasn't just the music, although that was wonderful:
deep, sweeping strings, dramatic trumpets, and Scott Walker's
sonorous, dramatic voice. And it wasn't just the lyrics: about the
Stalinist regime ('The Old Man's Back Again'); a game of chess
with death that describes the plot of Ingmar Bergman's film of the
same name ('The Seventh Seal'); and a tender ode to the monks
who had looked after Walker at the height of his fame-induced
confusion ('The Angels of Ashes') – it was the mood that these
songs created. They were miniature films, inviting you into a
world that would enrich and fascinate you.

The friend's girlfriend was a fashion person, quick to
name-drop, belittle her boyfriend and talk about her own
achievements. I remember her voice being like background
interference as *Scott 4* played on the stereo, and the two worlds
that these voices represented could not have been more different. It was after listening to *Scott 4* that I knew that time passed
too quickly not to get on with addressing the question of what
it means to be alive and see how fascinating the world can be.

'Scott Walker was a huge influence on me because he writes
about everyday things in a way that is vague but evocative,' said
Bob, uncorking a second bottle of wine. 'He uses words you
don't usually hear in songs, and, because he was an American
discovering European culture and art films and so on, he wrote
about Europe in a way that he felt it should be, which is a very
inspiring way to approach songs.'

Scott and *Scott 2* consist of a lot of cover versions by songwriters
like Jacques Brel and Tim Hardin, but a few originals, too: on *Scott
2*'s 'Plastic Palace People', Walker tells the story of Billy the
Balloon, 'a string tied to his underwear' as he floats over the houses
of the city at night after a boy lets go of him. And *Scott 3* is a
melancholic masterpiece featuring such redolent lines as 'I've

hung around too long, listening to the old landlady's hard-luck stories' (from 'It's Raining Today'); a romantic, idealistic ode to Copenhagen; and a moving story of a lonely transvestite called Big Louise ('didn't time sound sweet yesterday? In a world filled with friends, you lose your way').

'You can tell that Scott Walker reinterprets books and films by other people,' said Bob. 'That's where his inspiration comes from. The thing to learn from Scott Walker is that you shouldn't worry about writing a brilliant song that is relevant to everyone, and you shouldn't worry about sounding parochial – or that the American audience won't know what you're singing about. His songs are specific. That's why they work so well.'

It was getting late and it didn't look like Bob was going to give me anything to eat, which meant that the wine was going straight to my head and affecting my mental powers. Our house in Peckham was on the other side of London, but all I could think about was material for songs and the fact that Bob Stanley appeared to exist in an attractive, ideas-led world where everything looked right and sounded good. On top of all this, he was a socialist, apparently. So, when he suggested that we buy one more bottle of wine and that I stay the night, I agreed that this was an excellent idea.

Bob left before I woke. I emerged from the bathroom with a towel around my waist to see his wife, Annelise, talking to a smiling middle-aged lady who turned out to be the couple's cleaner. The bed in the middle of the living room floor had been cleared away, but there were still three empty bottles of wine by the sofa and my clothes randomly scattered around the room. The woman gave me an embarrassed smile and Annelise stuttered a quick response.

'This is Will,' said Annelise, her eyes moving rapidly from me to the cleaning lady. 'Bob and Will were here last night getting drunk while I wasn't even here at all. I hardly saw you, did I Will?'

'No, no you didn't,' I mumbled alcoholically, and the lady said: 'That's all right, I don't mind. Please don't mind me. I'll get started in the kitchen.' It was only after we left the flat that I realised Annelise was trying to make it clear to the cleaner that she hadn't just walked in on an affair. We made a quick exit, had breakfast in a greasy spoon on the Archway Road, and I thought about how grateful I was for an illumination into Bob Stanley's way of writing songs, even if it wasn't for me. As Hugh of St Victor said sometime in the twelfth century: 'Learn everything. It will all come in useful somewhere.'

Bob Stanley's approach to making music while knowing absolutely nothing about the rules of music whatsoever offered an entry point into songwriting, but I already did know something about music, albeit not very much. I needed to keep it simple and try to write a song that tapped into ageless aspects of human experience. So I decided to go back further. A lot further – all the way to the twelfth and thirteenth centuries, when a Bavarian monastery produced a collection of 228 profane and secular songs called the *Carmina Burana*.

The *Carmina Burana* comes from the wild student scene of twelfth-century Europe, when the inauguration of the earliest universities marked a shift from the spiritual and moral education of the cloistered monk to the training of a professional class to meet the new bureaucratic and legal demands of church and state. Students came from all over Europe to study in Paris (theology, arts and law), Bologna and Pavia (law), and Montpellier and Salerno (medicine), and they were united by their knowledge of Latin. The *Carmina Burana* was to reflect this new culture – a twelfth-century renaissance – in songs. They cover drinking, comradeship, satire, high-minded love (occasionally) and bordello lust (often).

Protected by king, pope and/or emperor, the students were a privileged section of society, free to travel throughout Europe and land the best jobs after their studies. The *Carmina Burana* was a product of the world of these gilded youth at the beginning of their careers, when they didn't know what Fortuna would have in store for them and satire was a good defence against insecurity. Not yet embroiled in the corrupt practices of the legal, clerical and ecclesiastical professions, the students were also in a position to parody their supposed betters. Walter of Chatillon's first poem in the *Carmina Burana* touched on this:

> Give and it shall be given unto you
> Thus says the text
> At the Curia it's the case
> That he who pays wins
> For the want of money
> Codrus loses his action.

The *Carmina Burana* was the protest music of its day and Walter of Chatillon was the era's Bob Dylan. Often the songs are more straightforward in their rebellion:

> Down with study! Books away!
> Come and learn a sweeter truth
> Finding pleasure in the play
> And the greenery of youth
> It's the pride of old professors
> To engage in serious things
> And the joy of youth (God bless us)
> To prefer venereous things.

And it wasn't just the students who were enjoying venereous things. There were reports of convents in twelfth-century Verdun in France where the nuns had given themselves up to prostitution to help pay the bills, while, in Canterbury in 1171, Clarembald, the abbot-elect, was discovered to have seventeen bastards in one village. The bawdy songs of the *Carmina Burana* were enjoyed by those inside the monasteries – and were even written by some of them, as there were only so many people literate in Latin – as much as those outside them.

Alongside the students and the clergy, the third group involved in the creation of the *Carmina Burana* were goliards; a brotherhood of wandering minstrels who sang its songs in taverns and town squares. The goliards were the bohemians of their day, standing outside of society and mocking its conventions while also bringing bawdy poetry to people otherwise tied up with survival, sin and church. One of the goliardic songs in the *Carmina Burana* is by a jealous lover who has lost his beloved.

> Tender in years,
> More radiant
> Than Venus's star,
> Weep for her mind's
> Dovelike sweetness then,
> Weep for her serpentine
> Bitterness now.
> Men who ask for love
> You drive off with a harsh word,
> Men who bring you gifts
> You warm in your bed.
> You order them to go away
> If you get nothing from them –

You welcome the blind and the lame
And delude illustrious men
With your poisoned honey.

The goliard has surely gone mad in his bitterness. Did the blind and the lame really have money for prostitutes in the twelfth century? How come his woman had dovelike sweetness when she was with him, but serpentine bitterness as soon as she was with others? The reason is that madness is at the heart of love and betrayal, and, as such, at the heart of the song. The goliard's song is so modern! It's exactly these sentiments that have been inspiring the vast bulk of the songs that make up the twentieth-century songbook. It became clear that inspirational material has essentially remained the same for the last 1,000 years, give or take the odd world-changing invention. This song by an unknown and probably drunken goliard has a similarly acerbic tone to Bob Dylan's 'Positively Fourth Street'. And the message is the same as 'I Heard It Through The Grapevine'. While Marvin Gaye sings of being 'about to lose my mind' through the rumours that have been circulating about the infidelities of his former lover, in a later stanza the goliard behind this song manages to give some advice to his estranged woman about keeping her affairs under wraps in the future: 'Whatever you do, do in darkness, from the lids of rumour's eyes.'

The best songs tap into an element of human nature that is universal, even if the details, as in Scott Walker's songs, might be specific. There are few adults on the planet who have not felt the sting of romantic rejection or betrayal, which is why songs on this subject are so enduring. The pain of heartbreak is even more intense and enveloping than being in love, and it is a fast-spreading disease that courses through the veins of the afflicted.

I was twenty-one and just out of university when my heart was first broken; a necessary rite of passage before one can go on to engage in a lasting and deeper relationship. We met when I was still an undergraduate and I had been rather blasé about this very attractive and intelligent girl, and her jealousy had been irritating. Then the tables turned as she made more friends, starred in plays, and generally became her own person. When she had arrived at university I had a room in Marble Arch and a ready-made social scene. Then I left university, got a job in a health-food shop, and moved in with my mum. The relationship collapsed soon after that.

A broken heart is the biggest inspiration in the history of song. You try to make sense of your feelings, as the person you loved becomes the fount of all that is wrong in the world. You were fine before you met them. Why can't you cope once they have been and gone? And, when you are heartbroken, you don't really think of your former lover as a real person, more a focus for the dark corners of your own identity. The goliardic song was a product of that conflict of emotions and it is part of a long and rich lineage. The poisoned honey of love will never run dry and people will never stop writing songs about the bitter taste it leaves.

I listened to Scott Walker's records that evening. Bob Stanley had told me that immersing oneself in interesting films, books, art and people was always going to provide inspiration, but I also wanted to add that depth of feeling that I heard in Scott Walker and the charm and personality that Nico and Lawrence had. Besides, the goal was to write and be able to play a song, and I needed some concrete advice on what worked and what didn't. Listening to Scott Walker's delivery, and the conviction he brought to the words he sang, made me realise that I needed to talk to a singer.

Good singers know whether words can be delivered or not, and whether a line scans properly, and how to write a song at the right pitch. As it happened, I had a friend who was making it as a professional singer. Mara Carlyle was writing her own songs and covering well-known ones in unusual styles. A few months earlier there had been a big hit called '1 Thing' by an African-American/Korean R&B singer called Amerie. She sings at the top of her range, giving her voice a frantic quality that works with the hysterical mood of the words. Mara had recorded a version of '1 Thing' in her poised English way, thereby turning the song into something entirely different. She lived an interesting life, too: when she wasn't performing live or making records, she worked in a homeless shelter in central London.

Mara was staying in a tiny flat at the top of a Georgian town house in Queen's Park, north-west London. She made porridge and tea and spoke a little about her life and music. Growing up in Shropshire, where her father was a musician and music teacher and her mother played piano, she was regularly hauled up on stage from the age of six onwards to sing in folk clubs and play violin in classical concerts.

'I'm one of those people who can get a note out of any instrument, but I'm not particularly good at any of them,' she said as she poured the kettle. 'I hate practising, and singing is the only thing I have really worked at.' The family did not play records at home but sang together from sheet music, and her two elder brothers formed bands before they were in their teens and Mara would beg to be allowed to sing with them. She had been deeply immersed in song, and had understood its language and world, for her entire life.

I asked Mara how much of her time was taken up with music. 'In my head, all of it,' she replied. 'But I have a day job, I don't have a manager, and I'm not ambitious in the conventional sense. I'm as happy getting drunk and singing madrigals with friends as I am being on stage.'

She had recently done a tour with Willy Mason, a very young singer-songwriter from Martha's Vineyard in Massachusetts, who had been getting a lot of attention, and the two of them had been talking about how so many musicians become jaded and end up hating what they are doing, but still do it anyway. 'I told Willy that if it ever gets to the point where it stops being enjoyable, jump off. Forget about success if you find yourself resenting the thing you once loved more than anything. Unfortunately, that's exactly what he did soon after we had that conversation. He abandoned the tour and nobody has heard of him since.' She sighed. 'And he was really going places, too.'

My main problem was melody. I don't think I really understood what it was.

'A melody can come from any number of places,' said Mara. 'I'll hear a bird song in a certain cadence and it triggers something. And one of the things I learned from classical training was the importance of how the words sound with the music, particularly from the singer's point of view.'

'Do you mean that you should write a song with a singer in mind?' I asked.

'No, more that you should be aware to never let words compromise the song. If it sounds awkward, get rid of it. I hate it when you hear lyrics that have been written beforehand and then they have been stuck onto a piece of music that clearly doesn't fit.'

I wasn't aware that there was any other way of writing songs than this. So far I had written some words, then played some sort of a tune, and then jammed the two together.

'Mozart was a total genius when he wrote for singers,' she

continued. 'He knew exactly which vowel sounds are easy to produce at what pitch. "Queen Of The Night" in *The Magic Flute* is very high, but it's really easy to sing because it's just a vocal exercise – if you had to say words over that it would be impossible, so Mozart made it wordless. He knew the voice so well that everything in his work can be sung. That is the sort of skill and understanding that is rare to find in modern song-writing.'

Mara explained how the classical composers would give the words extra meaning by putting the right emphasis on them. She cited Purcell's 'I Blame You Not', in which the line 'my heart is broken' is given tenderness and depth by the way the singer will elongate the vowel sounds on 'heart'.

'The music has to be right for the words, and the only people doing that in the modern age are the really good rappers,' she continued. 'They're not using melody, but they use rhythm in the same way, finding a way of delivering the language that gives it force. That's what I miss; that thoughtful marriage of the meaning of the words and they way the music expresses them.'

It seemed that the best songs, or at least the ones that become standards, are all about ease of delivery. 'The consummate songwriters, like Bacharach and David, Cole Porter and George and Ira Gershwin, wrote songs that anyone could sing,' Mara explained. 'David Bowie's songs haven't become standards, brilliant though they are, because they're designed around his own voice and they're hard to interpret. I have the feeling that I write songs for my own voice, too. But anyone can sing "Every Time I Say Goodbye" because it's just *there*.'

We had eaten our porridge and drunk our tea. Now seemed as good a time as any to foist 'Until Daylight' on her. I warned her that my singing might leave something to be desired; she bade me continue nonetheless. So I launched into the lilting tune. I finished it with a two-chord vamp and a strum.

'It sounds like you're going to have your wicked way with someone in a wood,' she said.

'Not in a wood, in a cottage!' I snapped, irritated that she had not instantly grasped the meaning of the words. 'It's a song from a woman's point of view. She's in the cottage boiling the rice, frying the fish, chopping the wood . . .'

'I'm glad she's frying the fish *and* chopping the wood,' said Mara. 'No gender stereotypes in this little cottage . . . What can I say?' She frowned. 'No, really, what can I say?'

As if she had just pulled out a chocolate in a jar full of empty wrappers, her face lit up. 'That's it – there's something casual about it. It goes up and down, rather like a Bob Dylan song, and some people could see that as quite charming.' Then she frowned. 'But the melody isn't well defined and the chorus bears no relation to the verse. You have this pleasant little tune going on and then this horrible chorus comes in out of nowhere and completely ruins the feeling.'

'But I wanted to have some sort of contrast,' I said, beginning to realise that, with this criticism mirroring what Lawrence had said, trying to defend the chorus was looking like a lost cause.

'Yes, but there either has to be a good segue or the two sections have to have a relationship with each other. There are certain keys that make sense against one another and others that don't. This falls into the latter. Why don't you explain the song to me a little more and we'll see if we can work it out.'

'OK. She's being flirtatious, and they're having a nice cosy time in this cottage, and the suggestion is that they will sleep together. She's saying, "How about it?" There is a hint of regret because they're doing something they probably shouldn't, but none of that will matter until daylight.'

'Right. That's really important in terms of emphasis. The first line is "Close the door, what do you say". So, to get the message across, you want to put the emphasis on "say".'

Mara said lyrics should be sung as they're spoken because inappropriate emphasis means that the song has no conviction. For this reason a songwriter must not cram too many words in, as it will make it impossible for a singer to get them across naturally. She said that I had a lot of words in 'Until Daylight'.

Mara agreed to sing it the whole way through anyway, and she did have a great voice. It seemed odd to have this rather unprofessional little song carried by a professional singer. I liked the way NJ sang it, but she was from my world and on my level, and, of course, she was my wife. When Mara sang 'Until Daylight', it didn't seem like mine any more. Which, come to think of it, was probably a good thing.

'Maybe it's not so bad after all,' she said, as we finished another round of the song. 'What I find fascinating is that you are not a singer – in fact, your voice is terrible – yet you did have the vague shape of a melody there and you knew what you wanted the singer to do. How can you not be able to sing something, and yet know where the melody should go?'

'I didn't think I did know where the melody should go.'

'But you obviously do, otherwise the song couldn't exist,' she said, looking perplexed. 'A song without a melody is not a song. It's very strange . . . I don't think I've met anyone who has a worse voice than you who has even attempted to write a song. You're trying to run before you can crawl and that's why your songs are coming out in strange ways. Most people spend years practising "Frère Jacques" on their guitars before they get to the stage of coming up with their own material.'

'I haven't got that much time left. I might be dead before I get to write my one great song.'

'We all might be dead before we do that, mightn't we?' she replied. 'I don't think this is your one great song. And I'm afraid I'm going to have to go.'

Three hours had passed and all we had come up with was a slightly better way to sing the words. Mara seemed to think that this was good going. 'Any piece of music that's good always takes ages to get right,' she said. 'You really to need patience if you're going to do this.'

And with that she began to prepare for a video shoot she was doing that afternoon. As she combed her black hair, she told me about her latest plan: to steal the song structure of the barcarolle from Offenbach's *Tales Of Hoffman* and play it in a country style on her ukulele. 'I might be nicking the whole thing,' she said, 'but it will be unrecognisable.'

Originality is an elastic concept. When I first picked up the guitar, many of the guitarists I spoke to claimed to have no knowledge of the rules of music, to be totally self-taught, to have never had a guitar lesson, and generally to have re-invented the wheel. But they knew which chords worked well together, based on laws of music that even humanity did not write.

'My ex-husband wouldn't listen to anything for months on end when he was recording an album for fear that he might be inadvertently influenced by what he heard,' said Mara, as she collected keys, travelcard and make-up and prepared to leave the flat. 'That confused me. How do you write if you're not surrounded by noise and sounds and music? Where does it come from? You are taught by what you listen to.'

We managed to get out of the door. Mara agreed to meet up again, and, before we went our separate ways, she asked me what I wanted for my song: to write a hit, or to write a song similar to the ones I like.

'To write a song similar to the ones I like,' I replied.

'Then you will be taught by what you listen to just as much as you will be by studying songwriting. That's my last piece of advice for the day: listen carefully to the music you love.'

Before going to bed that night, I wondered if anyone had ever written an entirely original song, or if, indeed, one existed. Led Zeppelin have been criticised for taking old blues songs and changing a word or two to claim them as their own, as have The Rolling Stones, but those bands created a unique sound and style even if their roots are derivative. And who knows where Muddy Waters or Mississippi Fred McDowell copped their tunes?

Thoughts of Led Zep and the Stones led me, just before sleep took over, to the great songwriting partnerships: Lennon and McCartney, Jagger and Richards, Page and Plant. It was time to look up an old friend who had been lying low for the past few months. But should it be Hodgkinson and Doyle, or Doyle and Hodgkinson?

Chapter Three

The Reluctant Partner

I had always wanted Doyle to be my songwriting partner, but the one and only time we had tried to write together had been a disaster. We got increasingly bellicose as we disagreed over the direction that our first co-write should take. Doyle wanted the song to be about an argument he had had with his girlfriend, but I felt that this loosely connected string of insults, 'She's A Goddam Bitch But I Love Her', lacked subtlety. I wanted the song to be about the time we went horse-riding in the Czech Republic, when Doyle's horse kept ignoring his commands in order to wander off down the hill and graze in a cornfield. 'You cannot control a horse that does not respect you,' the riding instructor kept telling him, solemnly. Doyle felt that the song I proposed, 'My Little Pony', was not sufficiently reverent of his equestrian skills.

Doyle didn't like putting his creative vision down onto paper. His unconventional worldview was expressed in the way he lived and the things he said. But I needed him, if only to inspire me to look at things in a different way. Andy Warhol feared that he wasn't a particularly interesting person, so he surrounded himself with interesting people generally incapable of working hard and doing something artistic themselves. I related to that. I suspected that I, too, might be rather boring, but unconventional people inspired me. NJ said that I collected freaks.

The problem now was that Doyle was attempting to deny his own feral nature and become bourgeois. He was working increasingly long hours for two reasons: to get the money together for a deposit on a flat, and to stop himself from getting drunk and picking a fight with the biggest thug in the bar. It was fair enough. There are only so many times that even Doyle could wake up, look in the mirror, and say: 'It's a shame. I happened to like that tooth.'

A side-effect of this new work ethic was that he wouldn't devote any time to something as inconsequential as writing songs with me. Ever since Double Fantasy, our mostly hypothetical band, played their first and last concert, Doyle's crazy work shifts had been starting some time in the late afternoon and ending the following morning. His sleeping patterns were erratic and you never knew if he was going to bite your head off for waking him up at seven in the evening, a few minutes after he had drifted off to sleep, or be pleased for the start-of-the-day call, having just finished his breakfast.

Then I picked up the phone on a Monday morning to hear Doyle's croaking voice. 'What are you doing on Wednesday afternoon?' he said.

'I'll be at work, I suppose.'

'I'm getting married. I was hoping you might be my, like, best man.'

I did a bit of work on Wednesday morning, changed into a suit, and went up to Islington Town Hall. The wedding party was sitting in a row outside the ceremonial hall. There was Doyle, his wild eyes, caveman's brow, Struwwelpeter hair and remaining teeth, tamed by a grey suit; his Japanese bride-to-be, Yukiko, looking very pretty in a red dress; Doyle's mother, who

looked like a sixty-year-old, female version of Doyle; his sister
Mary, who was sweet and nervous, with a habit of giggling at
everything; and his brother Bernard, who had even fewer teeth
than Doyle. It was too much to expect Doyle's father to be there.
A long-term alcoholic, he was living in a hospital and confined
to a wheelchair after a lifetime of erratic behaviour that was
destructive to both him and his family.

Everyone was subdued. 'Do you think it's going to be all
right?' asked Doyle. He kept making little bouncing moves,
like a rubber ball in the hands of a schoolboy. The registrar, a
smartly dressed middle-aged woman, arrived to show us into
the huge room. We filed in and all sat on one side of it. Yukiko
left the room and the registrar pressed a button on a big old tape
recorder. The traditional wedding march began. 'I was going to
bring some tunes but I forgot,' said Doyle. Yukiko came back
in. Five minutes later they were married.

'Does anybody want to take photographs?' asked the registrar. Doyle's mother, at the behest of Mary, raised a disposable
camera to her chest, pressed down the button once, and put it
back into her handbag.

The reception was in a Spanish bar called Bradley's in a
narrow alley behind Tottenham Court Road, in the heart of
London. Doyle and I have been going to Bradley's and getting
drunk there for as long as I have known him. It is a tiny
basement room plastered with curling, ancient posters for
Spanish holiday resorts in the seventies, and it is lined with
the kind of cheap mementos you might find in such places:
straw donkeys, little dolls with big eyes, knitted tableaux and
empty bottles of cognac encrusted with wax. The bar itself is
about a metre long and the walls are of curving stone, like a cave
interior. The jukebox appears to be unchanged since we first
went into the place fifteen years ago, with great songs we had

discovered as teenagers, like 'Itchycoo Park' by The Small Faces and 'All The Young Dudes' by Mott the Hoople. The wedding party sat around an oval formica table flanked by red velveteen banquette seating on one side and wobbling stools on the other. We loaded up the jukebox with songs and the table with beers.

'I didn't want to do some fancy wedding,' said Doyle, holding onto his pint firmly. 'I wanted to do something that was genuine.'

'You can't argue with Bradley's,' I added. 'It's got history.'

'I always told Richard not to get married,' said Doyle's mother, a cigarette in one hand and half a pint of beer in the other. 'He always said he never would. Now look at him.'

'But we didn't really think anyone would have him, did we Mum?' said Mary.

'She's Japanese. What do they talk about?' said Doyle's mother, who was Portuguese-Madeiran and came to England, with no knowledge of the language, in her early twenties, to marry an Irishman.

'You didn't speak English when you met Dad,' said Doyle. 'You couldn't understand a word he said.'

'I still can't,' she replied. 'But when I met him he tricked me. I thought he was drunk because he had been in the pub that afternoon. I thought he would be sober in the morning.'

Talk turned to the activities of the absent father. Mary remembered the time he attempted to rob his own electricity meter by prising it open to get the coins inside using a metal screwdriver, resulting in an electric shock powerful enough to propel him to the other side of the room. Bernard, a quiet boy with a love of classical music and science fiction, remembered having to stand at the door of the flat, at the age of eight, and make a human barricade to prevent the man from London Electricity collecting the coins from the meter that his dad had now spent on booze. Doyle recalled the shock of his dog being sold down the pub for a tenner.

'He used to spend our food money on drink, didn't he Mum?' said Mary. 'Then we'd just have to go hungry.'

'It was easy to look after you children,' said Doyle's mum. 'It was him that was the tough one.' At some point in the early evening, the wedding party left the basement bar and went two doors down to a Spanish restaurant where flamenco dancers stomped out a haughty performance to the strains of a virtuoso guitarist, despite the fact that we were the only people in there. An elderly waiter in a fraying red tuxedo hurriedly laid down a paper tablecloth and snapped his fingers at a slightly less elderly waiter to bring a carafe of wine. Doyle ordered champagne and then knocked over the bottle before anyone had a chance to pour it. Every time the creaking waiters brought another bottle its contents ended up making rivulets across the table. The food came, and that seemed to slow down Doyle's champagne-bashing activities somewhat. It must have been around eight or nine when he said: 'I've got an idea. The best man should sing a song.'

I didn't relish this proposal at all. Not only had the wedding party filled out – a handful of Doyle's friends had joined us – but the restaurant was full now and the flamenco players were in full swing.

'I'd better not,' I said, nervously, knowing so well that when Doyle gets an idea into his head it is almost impossible to shake it out again. It just rattles around in there until it is ultimately crushed by the weight of its own imprudence.

'Do you know "I Will Always Love You" by Whitney Houston?' said Mary.

'What about "D.I.V.O.R.C.E"?' said Doyle's mother.

'I don't think this is such a good idea . . .'

'Come on, don't be such a spoilsport!' someone shouted.

'I'm really not very good . . .'

But Doyle had already grabbed a waiter and asked him if, for a special wedding treat, the flamenco player could lend me his guitar. The waiter had asked the short, shiny-pated guitarist, who thought it such an excellent idea that he even told his dancers to accompany me.

The only song that I could think of to play was 'Mystery Fox'.

'You sing, we dance!' announced the flamenco couple with cheerful optimism.

'Get on with it, Elton John,' slurred Doyle.

By now it seemed like the whole restaurant was cheering and calling for me to get up there and do something. What did it matter, I said to myself – it was a wedding. You were meant to make a fool of yourself.

'OK, since it's Doyle's wedding day,' I said in an 'aw, shucks' kind of way, feeling a thrill at being the centre of attention. I took the guitar off the rather good flamenco player and started up the two-chord riff that begins 'Mystery Fox'. The dancers started to stomp out a haughty beat. People were clapping along. It was a fantastic moment! I closed my eyes and tried to give the words my all. I wanted the crowd to feel the music. They had to be part of the song, to live inside it.

I was lost in the grooves of 'Mystery Fox'. It was only by the third verse that I noticed what had been happening elsewhere. The flamenco dancers had stopped and were standing in front of me, arms crossed. Doyle's head was slumped on the table, submerged in a pool of champagne. Doyle's mother was staring blankly, a cigarette hanging from her mouth, nodding her head very slowly in a resigned, acceptant way. The other people in the restaurant were either conspicuously looking away or staring with horror-struck grimaces.

'That was the worst thing I have ever heard in my life,' said one loud-voiced city boy.

'Will, man,' drawled Doyle from the table, 'golden rule of showbusiness. Leave them wanting more.'

I looked down at the guitar. In my excitement, and not being used to the delicacies of a classical guitar, I had snapped three strings. The guitar's owner was staring at it in dismay, then rage. His eyes flashed. He fired an outstretched finger towards the door, and said: 'Get out! And never come back!' The flamenco dancers were standing with their backs to me, their arms crossed.

'I told you we should have gone to Nando's,' I heard someone say.

'This guy is a joke.'

'Imagine how small his penis must be.'

I slunk back to the wedding party, muttered a few goodbyes and thanks, and decided that it really was time to get some new material together.

'Clearly we can never let that happen again,' said Doyle when he came round to the house a few days later. 'We need to go to that place you're always talking about, so you can write a song *and* hold your head up in society.'

He had distributed the contents of the enormous Hamley's bag he was carrying to the children: a robot that turned into an articulated lorry for Otto and a large purple cat for Pearl. And the debacle of the flamenco fiasco at the wedding had the effect of instilling in him a desire to do something more than just work and watch daytime television; to leap to the rescue and save the day.

'What place?' I replied. 'New York? Paris? Rio?'

'Egg,' he said. 'The Island of Egg. That's the only place we can write songs at. Egg.'

He was talking about Eigg, a tiny island in the Inner Hebrides off the west coast of Scotland. Our father used to take my brother and me to Eigg when we were children. With around fifty inhabitants, one shop, and one boat with an outboard motor as its only link to the wider world, Eigg is a rough and remote patch of land dominated by a huge rock called the Sgirr, which rises from the centre of the island like a gnarled old bone sticking out of a grave. All the people I met who lived there were friendly, accepting and extremely work-shy. With no policeman, the untamed children were free to ride around on motorbikes, and the island van looked like it had been picked up by a crane, crushed in half, then put down again and persuaded to carry on working. Men stared at you wildly before thrusting a petrol can full of whisky and lemon juice in your face by way of a welcome – and that was at nine in the morning. None of the land on Eigg was farmed; the islanders claimed that it was too windswept to make anything grow. (On neighbouring Rhum, which has the same climatic conditions, there was an entire organic industry going on with brisk, middle-aged women cheerfully lugging sacks of potatoes while healthy-looking children clip-clopped by on ponies.)

'You can't write a song just like that,' said Doyle. 'Cosmic forces need to align themselves and the spirits must be consulted before inspiration blesses us. In other words, we've got to go to Egg.'

Doyle was adamant that he would not help me in my quest until I arranged a trip there. 'The water will not boil until the fire burns brightly,' he said, enigmatically.

It was with Doyle that I intended to fulfil a long-gestating dream of cutting a song onto vinyl, if only to live in hope that at least one person out there might experience the thrill I used to get from saving up my pocket money to spend 99p on a seven-inch disc of excitement at Harlequin Records, Richmond High Street, on a Saturday morning. We would record at ToeRag, the vintage studios owned by our friend, Liam Watson. Perhaps we would even find out what all those studio buttons and levers you see on documentary films of rock bands did.

We went upstairs and played 'If I Were A Carpenter' and 'The Red Balloon' by the American singer Tim Hardin, two songs that, although they sound very different, are made up of the same chords (D, C and G), with a few added notes to set them apart. 'That's what we need to do,' said Doyle. 'We need to write a song like "If I Were A Carpenter" that people can cover. Then we might even make some money and I'll be able to get the money together for a deposit on a flat.'

It seemed like the wedding might have been Doyle's last hurrah. I suspected that the drunken maniac of legend was receding into the mists of time.

Hodgkinson–Doyle (or maybe, after endless legal wrangles, Doyle–Hodgkinson) was never going to be Lennon–McCartney or Jagger–Richards, but, with his wit, his good taste and his musical sense, Doyle might help me get closer to writing one good song. After Doyle had gone home, I decided to listen to some music by other songwriting partnerships, to find out what could be made when two minds clicked and worked together.

I put on *Rubber Soul* by The Beatles, their 1966 album which captured that moment when they were still irreverent and funny but beginning to explore other worlds, and were yet to take themselves too seriously. My favourite song on *Rubber Soul* is 'Norwegian Wood'. As George Harrison plucks out a primitive sitar melody, John Lennon sings, in his best Bob Dylan impersonation, about a one-night stand going wrong. He throws a double meaning into the first line by telling the story of the night he had a girl, then conceding that she had him – it could be that she had sex with him, or pulled a trick on him, or both. (But he does go on to fall asleep in the bath, so it's probably the latter.) The proto-hippy freakout 'The Word' sounds like a bunch of sharp-suited mods discovering LSD, and 'In My Life' and 'Michelle' are simple, beautiful songs that anyone (or almost anyone, apparently) can sing.

The Beatles wrote songs that appear to have always existed. Like all the best ideas, you cannot imagine a world without them. And John and Paul (and George, when he was allowed) were so very young when they wrote these songs that you wonder where their wisdom and deep melodic understanding came from. The following decades proved that those songs were not just a product of Paul McCartney or of John Lennon, but of the parallel world that their relationship created, which is why both of them seemed so misguided when they argued over who did what.

John Lennon's post-Beatles songs are held up to be revolutionary, wild and brilliant; a product of a cynical mind that saw through everyone. But when you compare the wry wit of 1966's 'And Your Bird Can Sing' (about Mick Jagger, apparently; the 'bird' was Marianne Faithfull) with the sentimentality and transparency of 1975's 'Imagine', you realise that cuddly, conservative Paul McCartney was essential for Lennon to work with and against. And you realise that McCartney needed Lennon in his life to come up with such adventurously creative, poetic songs as 'She's Leaving Home', 'A Day in the Life' and 'Fixing a Hole' (all 1967), even if Lennon didn't have anything, ostensibly at least, to do with writing them.

Mick Jagger and Keith Richards were the same. One cannot foresee a song like 'Sympathy For The Devil' or 'Gimme Shelter' coming from Mick Jagger without Keith to argue about it with or vice versa. If you want evidence of this, just look at their solo albums.

It was the whole package that made Keith so iconic. He had turned a not exactly handsome face into a thing of jagged beauty with the aid of a good haircut, a casually humorous attitude and a character that imprinted itself ever more onto his skin as the years passed. The golden age of Keith's appearance was the early seventies, when he had been chiselled by rock'n'roll but not yet ravaged by it. And I always thought he was the best dressed of The Stones, particularly in their heyday. Brian Jones was too preposterous in his vanity, Charlie Watts and Bill Wyman too square, and Mick Jagger too aspirational. Keith was perfect just for his sheer Keithness, and, at his musical best, nobody can touch him. 1972's *Exile On Main Street* is my favourite album by The Rolling Stones because it, more than any other, is Keith's album. The elements of blues, soul and rock'n'roll are thrown together, rubbed around in the dirt, and turned into tarnished gold. The first time you hear *Exile on Main Street* you cannot believe that the biggest rock'n'roll group in the world could make such a derivative record with such terrible production. Then you keep on listening, and layers upon layers are revealed to you as you realise that the sheen of grime that is the first thing you notice is an integral part of this multi-faceted expression of humanity.

Every song on *Exile On Main Street* is great, but the stark version of Slim Harpo's 'Hip Shake Boogie', the romantic 'Sweet Black Angel' and the tobacco-stained anthem 'Sweet Virginia' are my own favourites. And, although I wouldn't like to get on the wrong side of him, you cannot help but feel that you would like Keith Richards. Who wouldn't want to hang out with him?

Then the opportunity came to meet the man himself, to find

out what went into that magical brew that was Jagger–
Richards. This was no casual thing. I had tried and failed on
numerous occasions to get a lesson from Keith Richards in my
quest to learn about the world of the guitar – he always seemed
to have better things to do, funnily enough – but then the call
came to say that he was in town and he was doing a few
interviews. I'd like to say that I jammed with Keith around a
log fire, but it wasn't quite like that. He was fulfilling his
promotional duties as a member of a gigantic capitalist en-
terprise – I think The Rolling Stones' tour he was on at the time
was being sponsored by American Express – and I had forty
minutes with him in a grand but sterile and rather fussy hotel
suite in the heart of London on a midweek afternoon. I was
ushered in to the room by his PR, offered a coffee, and told to sit
and wait. Fifteen minutes later Keith came in with a smile and
what looked like small bells hanging from his hair. He was well
into his sixties but still rake-thin and with a face that was
beaten but undefeated. He introduced himself, poured both of
us his favourite drink – vodka and orangeade – and sat down.

I wanted, of course, to get the secrets of songwriting from
him, to find out how he managed to get so many moods out of
so few chords with 'Wild Horses' simply by changing the order
in which they are played for the verse and the chorus, but
mostly he talked and I listened. I did manage to ask him about
how he discovered rock'n'roll and blues as a teenager, growing
up in London suburbs at a time (the fifties) when you were
unlikely to hear John Lee Hooker or Muddy Waters on the
Light Programme or Housewives' Choice.

'It wasn't easy,' he replied. 'You were lucky if you heard it on
Radio Luxembourg and maybe on the BBC once in a while,
played as a joke. I remember 'Long Tall Sally' and 'Heartbreak
Hotel' on Radio Luxembourg, and I can still remember the

signal, the song, and the ad for the Irish sweepstakes that
followed. Electrifying night for me – I was twelve, thirteen and
I was supposed to be in bed and not listening to the radio. Then
Bill Haley and Elvis made American music available, but we
didn't know anything about these cats. I thought Jerry Lee
Lewis was black. It was like a lightning bolt to kids of my
generation. You grew up in the aftermath of war and it was drab
and austere, although you didn't know it at the time. I hated
classical music back then, but I've learned to appreciate it now.
If only that Mozart had a good drummer . . .'

There was something about his manner that suggested that
the whole thing – The Rolling Stones, music, perhaps life itself
– really wasn't to be treated with too much reverence. 'When I
met Mick he had the Chess catalogue,' he said, talking of the
apocryphal time he bumped into his old childhood acquain-
tance as a teenager at Dartford rail station, Jagger having a stack
of hard-to-find blues records on the legendary Chicago label
Chess under his arm. 'So then you learn that, if a record is on
Sun or Chess, you should buy it. I liked the Chicago blues
players because they were rough-and-ready country boys that
had just got into town and were making the most of it, and they
were magnetic for me. And you begin to realise that the names
of the musicians on the Muddy Waters records are the same as
the ones on Bo Diddley, Chuck Berry . . . the house band. Then
you want to be one of them.'

So began Keith Richards' education in blues songwriting,
with him and Mick Jagger picking apart the finest moments in
the Chess back catalogue and learning how to play them. Then,
in 1964, when their young and eccentric manager, Andrew
Loog Oldham, locked them in a kitchen (or bathroom or toilet,
depending on who you talk to) at their flat in Mapesbury Road,
north-west London, to force them to write their own material,

they looked at the way their favourite songs were structured and acted accordingly. 'As Tears Go By' was the result.

'There came a point when we discovered that we could write songs,' he said of this moment. 'I'm eternally grateful to Andrew Oldham for locking us in the kitchen and not letting us out until we had a song, because six weeks later Marianne Faithfull was in the Top Ten with "As Tears Go By". Then Mick and I looked at each other and said: "Got any other ideas?" Slowly you learn that the songs come to you. You craft them a bit, but basically you stick your finger up and hope to catch it.'

It turned out that the number of songs Jagger and Richards have actually released is nothing compared to the ones they have written. 'What has come out of The Stones locker is the tip of the iceberg. There are hours and hours of grooves in there, from all different periods – all a bit unfinished but they're there,' he said, leaning back in the hotel room's rather fussy-looking chair. 'Being prolific is one thing, but you also have to write specifically for the band, which is why so much doesn't get used. First, I've got to get Mick's attention. Then I have to make sure that it's made for his voice, and get the right key. When Mick writes songs they're always in the same key. But I love him for that.'

The Rolling Stones, under the original leadership of Brian Jones, started out as a blues band. That's what they may well have remained had Andrew Loog Oldham not had other ideas. The first singles by the band were not heavy blues covers, but pop singles.

'We were a bit sheepish about putting on the black-and-white check jackets that Andrew made us wear, but, at the same time, we didn't really think the band would do anything,' said Keith, surprisingly. 'Then, all of a sudden, it's *Top Of The Pops*. So you think: "Oh no. That means we've got to do this bloody miming bullshit and wear this uniform, which is what we're totally doing this stuff not to do." And when you've got a hit record, the wave lasts eighteen months, maybe two years, so you have a feeling that it's the beginning of the end already and that was always the undercurrent of our success. But, at the same time, 3,000 screaming chicks and £50 a week meant that we swallowed our idealistic, snobbish bluesmen pride and said: "OK, it's rhythm'n'blues. And we couldn't get laid last week".'

'Wild Horses' was written at Keith's decadent mansion, Villa Noncote, a former Nazi headquarters in the South of France, during the band's stay down there as tax exiles. It was given to Gram Parsons, one of the guests down at Villa Noncote and a great songwriter himself, to record with his band, The Flying Burrito Brothers, before it made it onto Rolling Stones vinyl. Keith met Gram Parsons when the latter was briefly in The Byrds, with whom he had made the classic country rock album *Sweetheart Of The Rodeo*. The Byrds were in London and on their way to South Africa. Keith told Gram about the horrors of Apartheid and Gram decided that he had to stay in London to hang out with the top cat in the entire rock'n'roll pantheon rather than go on a tour with a band whose fortunes were declining by the month. I'm not entirely sure that political morals affected his decision to stay, but Keith appeared to think otherwise.

'Gram was an immensely charming guy – just ask the chicks,' said Keith of his late friend, who died in 1973 after drink and drugs got the better of him, as they have done for so many people who have hung out with Keith Richards and shared his appetite for a certain lifestyle but not, tragically for them, his constitution. 'When I told him that South Africa was like Mississippi all over again, he decided to leave The Byrds on the spur and stay in London. So I had to put him up. He turned me on to country music and we would get stoned, sit around with two guitars or a piano and be the happiest kids in the sandbox. He could play for twenty-four hours and not repeat a song. The strangest thing about Gram is that here we are talking about him. He's been dead over thirty years, he never had a hit record, and yet his influence is huge. I don't have any regrets about myself, but I do regret not having him around . . . just because of the loss of potential and because he was a good mate.'

I didn't manage to ask him how to write a song exactly, which was a question I was beginning to suspect might be unanswerable, at least by Keith Richards, but I did ask what the songwriting essence that linked the music he loved – blues, rock'n'roll, R&B and soul – was. 'Blues and rock'n'roll is about style,' he replied. 'It's about using the character of your voice to convey the song. You're not singing correctly, in fact you're probably breaking half your vocal chords. Buddy Holly would have hiccupped himself to death had he stuck around a bit longer.'

Keith Richards explained that he had promised to take 'the old lady' out to dinner that night, which seemed sweet some-how, and that he had to go and change so as not to incur her wrath. Before he went, he said that music and books were the only two things that interested him, and that with three months being the longest he had spent in one place in the last twenty years, his life was rather like that of a whaling captain. It hadn't taken me long to stop being starstruck, realising that one of Keith Richards' greatest skills was to make people feel at ease around him. He was unusual in that great fame, the kind that only a handful of people experience, had not taken away his dignity or his humanity.

It was the airs and graces of Mick Jagger and the buccaneering spirit of Keith Richards that made The Rolling Stones work, but it was hard to imagine the two of them getting on. I wondered how Andrew Loog Oldham had overseen the partnership in its early days. It would not be hard to ask him. A few years earlier NJ had been commissioned to do a job in Venezuela and I tagged along for the ride. I had already interviewed Andrew by telephone about his recently published memoirs, and called to ask him if he knew anywhere decent in Venezuela to hang out. He suggested his place in Bogota, Colombia, and revealed himself to be a more inspiring, generous, odd, power-crazed and downright undeniable character than pretty much anyone I had ever met – and the secret ingredient in the Jagger–Richards formula.

Andrew had presided over two of my favourite songwriting partnerships: Jagger–Richards and Steve Marriot and Ronnie Lane of The Small Faces. He would understand the dynamics and politics of the arrangement, and how I could best avoid the pitfalls that resulted in best friends never speaking to each other again except through their lawyers. So I called his flat in Colombia. His wife, Esther, answered. After various shouts and calls that went on for the next quarter of an hour, he came to the phone.

'Have you heard Neil Diamond's new album?' he said by way of greeting. The smooth singer/songwriter Diamond had just released a record that had been produced by Rick Rubin, who had made his name with rap and heavy metal bands but had also revived Johnny Cash's career a few years earlier. 'It's fucking awful. The only good thing is that he has the ability to leave you with one word and let it hang for an embarrassing amount of time. It's almost tantric. Perhaps we should call Sting about it.'

I asked him how he got Jagger and Richards to write in the first place, having in mind the apocryphal story of his locking the pair in the kitchen of their London flat in the early sixties and not letting them out until they had written a song. 'Mick and Keith were reluctant, but I operated on the belief that, if you can play an instrument, you can write a song, and Keith played guitar,' he said. 'But then I also wanted to believe that a guitar plugged straight into the wall so that nobody asked me for money for amps. As for locking them in the kitchen – we didn't have a kitchen at 33 Mapesbury Road, but I do remember leading them to writing an original. In certain moments you have the right to dictate. I told them that I was going to go to my mother's with some laundry and I wanted them to have a song for me by the time I got back. I pretended to leave the building and then listened at the door. Of course there was plenty of moaning from Mick, but they did start to get on with it, and it was not "As Tears Go By" that they came out with a few hours later. It was called "As Time Goes By" and it had five verses, three of which were awful. By the time I got into the studio with Marianne Faithfull [who had her first hit with the song], I altered the unimaginative title and edited out the silly words. It started out as a boring song and it ended up OK.'

Andrew explained that he wasn't actually in the room with them – that would have been like watching two people have sex – so it was impossible for him to tell me how the song came about. 'Listen, if I wasn't in the room, then neither were all of these people who claim to know exactly what happened,' said Andrew, sounding like an ultra-fast talk radio DJ. 'The question of who did what cannot be answered by anybody because Mick and Keith can't remember. It was forty years ago, for God's sake. But they were productive back then because relative poverty helped the process. They had pocket money, they had money to spend in clubs, but they didn't have any real money when I was working with them, and there was a period in the late sixties when they signed up with [fearsome American accountant/manager] Allen Klein when they thought that they had a lot of money but, as they only found out much later, they didn't. Allen Klein had it. So that helped, too.'

I asked Andrew how he saw that Mick and Keith were the creative forces, given that Brian Jones was the band's leader, in the early years at least.

'First of all they were being brave,' he replied. 'Can you imagine going into the studio and telling Charlie and Bill that they weren't going to be a blues band any more? Brian wasn't the problem. He would always look around the room to see which way the wind was blowing before opening his mouth. Keith claims that I told him to take three parts from his favourite songs and, voilà, he would have a hit, but I don't remember saying that unless it was backstage at some pop TV show like *Ready, Steady, Go* and we had been drinking.'

Once Andrew had established Jagger and Richards as a songwriting partnership, it seemed that the work of either would be credited to both, which I imagine could cause a lot of friction. 'I'll give you the example of Steve Marriot and Ronnie Lane,' said Andrew, when I asked him about how credit in partnerships work. 'One of them was complaining to me – I guess it was Ronnie, as Steve just told people to fuck off – about the fact that the other person hadn't made any contribution to a song that would be credited to both. So I said: "did he tell you the song was good? If he did then you both wrote the thing, because you wouldn't have known." If you're thinking about forming a partnership with somebody else you can save yourself a lot of heartache and legal fees by remembering that before you start.'

*   *   *

With Doyle out of the picture until I managed to arrange our songwriting mission to the island of inspiration, I did my best to keep on practising the guitar and carrying on with life in Peckham with NJ and the kids. It was some time in December when I concluded that my other songwriting partner, simply in terms of being a muse, was NJ. I was living with someone who, if I caught her in the right moment, was willing to sing my songs, and, without realising it, I had been writing down lyrics and imagining how they would sound if she sang them. Around this time I spoke to Patti Boyd, one of the most significant muses ever to emerge from the world of rock'n'roll. She was married to both George Harrison and Eric Clapton, and she managed to inspire their most famous songs: 'Something' by Harrison and 'Layla' by Clapton. How did she do that?

A well-brought-up girl from Hampshire, Boyd was working as a model in the mid-sixties when she was cast as a schoolgirl in a scene for Dick Lester's 1964 Beatles film *A Hard Day's Night*. She and three other girls spent a five-hour train journey with The Beatles from London to Cornwall, during which there was plenty of time to get to know this band that was already famous but not yet in the throes of Beatlemania. 'We were dressed in these wretched schoolgirl outfits,' said Patti, in a clipped, rather hesitant tone. 'The Beatles jumped on and they were charming. I thought that George, in particular, was so funny and incredibly good-looking – I had never met anyone from Liverpool before and found his way of looking at the world so humorous. We hit it off.'

Two years later they were married, but, this being the sixties and George Harrison being in the biggest pop phenomenon of all time, there wasn't much chance of his being faithful. He did, however, write 1969's 'Something' about Patti. It is the archetypal muse song, painting an image of a woman as an enchanting spirit with no explanation or definition needed about why he loves her. Frank Sinatra called it the greatest love song ever written.

'Something' is poignant because it is vague. A muse escapes definition and George doesn't pinpoint anything about Patti Boyd; as the title suggests, his fixation on her is based on nothing more focused than something. Even the depth of his feelings is uncertain. He won't commit to telling that he loves her – after all, as a good-looking member of the world's most successful band he may have had other offers – and suggests that she simply hangs around to see what happens. It seems that George wanted the best of both worlds.

I asked her about it. She was suitably vague. 'He told me that it was about me a long time after he wrote it,' she said. 'I was flattered.'

As the marriage fell apart, Harrison's best friend, Eric Clapton, stepped in, going on to write the ultimate paean to blocked love. *The Story of Layla and Majnun*, by the Sufi poet Nizami, is about a girl whose tribe prevents her from seeing the young poet who has fallen in love with her. Majnun's father takes him on pilgrimage to Mecca to seek God's help in freeing him from the bind of love, but Majnun hits the Kaaba and cries: 'None of my days shall ever be free of this pain. Let me love, oh my God, love for love's sake, and make my love a hundred times as great as it was and is!'

While Majnun, who runs away from his tribe to live in the wild among the animals, is vocal about his torments, Layla suffers in silence: 'she lived between the water of her tears and the fire of her love', goes the story. And, although they are apart, 'no tent was woven so closely as to keep out his poems. Every child from the bazaar was singing his verses; every passer-by was humming one of his love-songs, bringing Layla a message from her beloved.' Layla accepts a husband but refuses to consummate the marriage; such is her love for Majnun. Finally, Layla and Majnun meet, but stay ten paces apart from one another. Majnun recites love poetry to Layla until the dawn, when they leave one another. Driven mad and sick with heartache and grief, both die and are buried next to one another.

Clapton first fell in love with Patti Boyd in 1969; around this time a friend gave him a copy of Nizami's poem. They had a short affair, but she did not leave George for him until 1979. With some help from the percussionist and songwriter Jim Gordon, Clapton wrote 'Layla', a song that was as inspired by the Sufi love poetry as it was by his love for his friend's wife. Clapton and Jim Gordon wrote a song in which the narrator gives consolation to a woman whose man has let her down, before falling in love with the woman himself and seeing his world falling apart as a result. The parallels between Clapton and Boyd's situation and those of Layla and Majnun are clear. I asked Patti Boyd how she felt about such a famous song being based on her own, very personal situation.

'I knew about "Layla" before it came out. Eric played the song to me before it was released,' she replied, in a matter-of-fact way. 'He gave me a copy of the poem, too. I felt flattered.' Wasn't it strange when it became a hit? 'It was very strange. It's a tricky song to absorb and openly love and share with anyone because of the very nature of the subject.'

No doubt partially due to the fact that she had been asked about being a muse a thousand times before, Patti Boyd was not exactly illuminating on the subject. But another possible reason why she did not say much was pointed out to me a few days later. I was in the office, complaining about how my interview had not been particularly successful, when Timandra, an astute woman, who I share the room with, said: 'She's a muse. What did you expect?'

'How do you mean?'

'George Harrison's song is about something in the way she moves,' she explained. 'Never does he sing about "something in the way she deconstructs post-modernist theory and underlines a new approach towards moral relativism".'

I hadn't thought of that.

Chapter Four

Bad Part of Town

It must have been around one in the morning when NJ woke me up to say that she could hear noises.

'It's probably Otto shuffling about,' I mumbled, wanting to roll over and go back to sleep. But Otto was unlikely to be padding around at this time of night. A rash of fear came over me. There was someone in the house.

Peckham came with a reputation. It was a deprived area, but, so far, we had experienced no trouble at all – the main problem was the feeling that poor people get stamped into the ground. At Queen's Road rail station, which was at the end of our street, there was no ticket barrier, no inspector nor, most of the time, any person in the booth to buy a ticket from. The station was barren and neglected. The ticket machine hardly ever worked and usually had a pool of piss around it. Yet, every now and then, a small army of uniformed ticket inspectors, with up to a dozen policemen standing in a line behind them, would pounce on all of those unsuspecting commuters lulled into a false sense of security by the fact that they can't even buy a ticket if they want to most of the time. This certainly never happened in Islington, where we used to live. But that was the general establishment attitude to the people of Peckham: create an environment that fosters crime and then overreact, in a not particularly efficient way, when crime happens.

Someone had told me that the worst thing to do was to scream and shout at a burglar, as it forces them into a confrontation that they probably don't want. But he (or maybe she, but I doubt it) had come upstairs – that meant he could be going into the children's room – and I had to do something quickly.

'Is that you, Otto?' I shouted. 'Go back to bed. I'll give you one minute, then I'm coming out.'

I was wearing nothing; a source of embarrassment should the burglar decide to stick around and fight me to the death. I rooted in the cupboard. Pyjamas would look too unthreatening. In the absence of military camouflage, I put on an old T-shirt and jeans and braced myself to square up to the sight of a stranger in our home. But they had gone. The front door was open. Nothing was taken. The thief was an opportunist, searching for a few notes and passing over the passports that were sitting on the table as soon as you walked in. And only the following day did NJ admit that she had left the key in the outside lock of the front door.

The experience fired me up with a desire to write a song about it. I knew what the material demanded: raw, brutal, easy-to-grasp rock'n'roll. With a limited musical vocabulary but plenty of frustration, unpopular American teenagers in the mid-sixties wrote songs about bad women, or how terrible their lives were, or how they're such tough guys not to be messed with, unless it's their mums telling them to clean up their rooms. These songs, usually the only ones written by bands that otherwise did cover versions at their high school hops, became a genre known as garage when the guitarist and journalist Lenny Kaye compiled the album *Nuggets* in 1972. *Nuggets* featured those few garage songs that had become hits in the mid-sixties, like 'Liar, Liar' by The Castaways and 'I Had Too Much To Dream Last Night' by The Electric Prunes. Every song on *Nuggets* is a gem, despite or maybe because of their lack of sophistication.

Nuggets started the avalanche of compilation albums in the years that followed, including *Pebbles, Boulders, Rubble, Back From The Grave, Garage Punk Unknowns, Highs In The Mid-60s, Acid Dreams, Mayhem And Psychosis* and countless others featuring a seemingly endless treasure trove of ultra-obscure non-hits by forgotten losers, and the original 45s are now worth a fortune. The US and England held the richest supply, but, as collectors dug deeper, enough bands were unearthed to fill garage compilations from Mexico to Sweden. My own favourite, 'I Never Loved Her' by The Starfires, is an obscure 45 from 1965 by a tight band that otherwise did boring pop songs. I decided that 'I Never Loved Her' should be the starting point to writing a garage song of my own.

The evening after the break-in I was on the bus, almost back home, when there was some sort of argument going on between the driver and a passenger who clearly felt that he shouldn't have to buy a ticket. The driver refused to move the bus until the passenger, who was getting increasingly abusive, got off, ending up with the typical Peckham threat: 'You just made a BIG mistake, boy.'

Nobody reacted with much surprise. In my experience at least, antagonism from one of Peckham's hard-man fare-dodgers did not tend to result in the gunfire and knife retaliations they liked to suggest it would, and the only thing they generally reached for was their Oyster card, but there was always the nagging threat of the aggression exploding into real violence. Then it came to me: this was a bad part of town.

I live in a bad part of town
Watch out when the sun goes down
Better not be out on your own
Soon these streets are gonna explode
In the bad part of town

I live in a world of fear
I wish I were so far from here
Never know what you're gonna find
Living here is driving me out of my mind
In the bad part of town
In the bad part of town

Half sung and half snarled, the song would consist of three or
four basic chords. These first two verses were some way between
a cry for help and a boast, so I would need a bit more reflection
in the chorus:

The old folks say it used to be peaceful
But that was another day
When you didn't think twice about walking
Down dark alleyways
It's not like everyone's bad here
Most are just trying to get by
But when life gets this desperate
You have to ask the reason why . . .

It was all very well announcing that I lived in a bad part of
town. But where was it all leading? Not wishing to go into the
sociological explanations for an area's descent, I decided that the
next verses had to offer some sort of a solution; a hope for a
better tomorrow.

Why did it have to get so mean?
I'll start a club for disadvantaged teens
Then they'll have a place to go
For tai kwon, karate and judo
In the bad part of town

Won't you help me with my plan?
You know we can change this land
Flowers will bloom and trees will go
On streets where nobody would go
In the bad part of town
In the bad part of town
Arggghhh!

Then you could end in good garage tradition by speeding the tempo up and screaming: 'It's the bad part of town, yeah' until the required three minutes had been reached. I got off the bus, miraculously made it to the front door without being attacked by a gang of flick-knife-wielding maniacs, and knocked out a few chords that did, admittedly, bear a passing resemblance to those used in 'I Never Loved Her'. But, every time I started singing, my playing went out of time.

'Where's the melody?' said NJ.

'I'm singing it,' I told her, not a little annoyed that she had to ask me.

'You're not singing a melody,' she said casually, picking out the last crumbs from the wrapper of a bar of chocolate. 'You're talking and sometimes shouting. You have to find a melody. That's what the song is going to hang on. Without that you haven't really got anything whatsoever. I like the line about the youth club, though.'

I would even go as far as to say that 'Bad Part Of Town' was

better than 'Mystery Fox', but, unfortunately, it seemed that
those of a less artistically tuned nature failed to see its worth. NJ
was trying to read, eat chocolate and drink a cup of cinnamon
tea in peace and didn't appear to appreciate witnessing the
evolution of a masterpiece.

After about an hour, she said: 'Will, please stop.'

'What do you mean?'

'I just can't bear it any more. Do you want to sign my death
warrant? You know how supportive I've been of your learning
the guitar, but this is agony. It's torture. There is no tune. You
can't sing. You're completely out of time. There's nothing.
Nothing! Sorry, I don't mean to be rude to you and I do like it
that you're trying. But I'm really tired and I've had a hard day
and, if you keep playing that song, I think I might cry.'

'So you don't like it?'

Perhaps it did need some fine-tuning. Maybe the best thing
to do would be to listen to some good records, and talk to people
who might be able to help me find this so-called missing
melody? So I went back to the one melody-rich record by a
former garage band that had guided my musical education more
than any other: *Forever Changes* by Love.

I'm yet to find a record better than this 1967 album by the
LA folk-rock band led by Arthur Lee. It's the one record that
every girlfriend I've had likes. After the garage pop of the first
Love album and the baroque menace of the second, *Forever
Changes* is a spiritual awakening. String-laden and elegant, it
isn't rock in the traditional sense, although squealing guitars
can be heard alongside the orchestrations. It is a psychedelic
record, though: the lyrical intertwining of beautiful imagery
with fear and suffering is akin to the LSD experience. Jim
Morrison told a reporter back in 1967: 'Love and the Kinks,
they're my favourites.' That is proof that even the man with

the smelliest trousers in rock knew a good thing when he heard it.

Forever Changes was made when the band were living together in a depraved mansion up in the Hollywood Hills called The Castle, and when the main creative tension came from Lee, a teacher's son born in Memphis, who was one of the few black hippies in LA at the time; and Bryan MacLean, a wealthy, classically trained former roadie to The Byrds, who counted Liza Minnelli as a teenage sweetheart. Songs written by Bryan MacLean, like 'Alone Again Or' and 'Old Man', are the more innocent, hopeful and romantic ones. But Arthur Lee sings in a clipped mezzo tone about hummingbirds in the morning one moment and 'sitting on the hillside, watching all the people die' the next. He says on 'A House Is Not A Motel': 'more confusions, blood transfusions, the news today will be the movies for tomorrow'. He saw the reality of the hippy dream early on: these experiments in a new consciousness would bring Charles Manson to the Age of Aquarius.

The songwriting is sophisticated. On 'Maybe The People Would Be The Times Or Between Clark And Hilldale', each verse ends a word short, with the one that you are expecting to hear beginning the following verse. 'The Daily Planet' has two voices shouting out alternate conclusions. There are no choruses. The underlying darkness of *Forever Changes* was no doubt fuelled by the band's lifestyle at the time. Love's Ken Forssi and Johnny Echols celebrated its completion by holding up a string of doughnut stands.

The original Love collapsed after *Forever Changes*, with Lee using the name for a new band. Yet, it seemed that Bryan MacLean's input was more significant than Lee gave him credit for: the albums that followed are not a patch on what had come before. For much of the seventies Arthur Lee released records with ever-diminishing creative returns. By the eighties he was penniless, homeless and strung out, having managed to ostracise pretty well everyone who had supported him in the past.

For this reason I was both excited and fairly scared when the chance to meet Arthur Lee, whose music I had loved since the age of fourteen, arose. If anyone could help me understand songwriting, surely it would be him . . . but then maybe not. The first time I saw Love was about ten years earlier. He was the only original member, but he had teamed up with a young band of LA Love obsessives named, after a song by Syd Barrett, Baby Lemonade, and they could do justice to the songs in a live setting. They were playing in the back room of a pub in north London. The gig was great and it seemed like Arthur was back on track. A few months later he was at his home in LA, drinking with a friend, when a neighbour banged on the wall to complain about the noise, so Arthur went round to his neighbour's house – and shot at him. The bullets were way off, but the courts had had enough of Arthur's antics. They gave him a life sentence.

Life turned out to be five years, and, by the time of his release, enough of a cult had built up around Love and Arthur Lee to allow him a second crack of the whip. He came back to London to perform *Forever Changes* in its entirety at the Queen Elizabeth Hall in London with the help of Baby Lemonade and a mini-orchestra. The concert was wonderful. Arthur Lee's young band – the same one that he had before going to jail – was excellent, and he held it together. He was back.

Arthur Lee had not sought out London's answer to The Castle. He was staying in the altogether more dreary confines of the Holiday Inn at Heathrow Airport, about a mile down the ring road surrounding Terminal 4. The anonymity of the place was bleak – it didn't seem right to have this icon of sixties rebellion ordering a continental breakfast from the meal deal menu. I waited on an orange sofa among the walls of blue and red, where watercolours of non-committal shapes hung in a parody of artistic expression.

Arthur emerged from the lift with a scowl. He was tall and cadaverous and wore black jeans with an orange corduroy three-button jacket, Ray-Bans, and a bandana with a wide-brimmed hat over it. He was handsome in a cold way. He marched up to the front desk and started gesticulating aggressively. His manager went over and appeared to placate him. Then he came over to me. I hoped he didn't wish to shake my hand, because it was shaking uncontrollably by itself.

He moved as if he was just coming out of a trance. I asked Arthur how he was doing. 'My mind is full of cobwebs,' he said quietly, his head looking like a garlanded skull as he man-oeuvred himself into a chair. 'I stayed up to watch the Super Bowl last night and, man . . . I'm not really here yet.' A coffee appeared before him. He took it to his lips slowly.

Arthur had a calm, considered way of talking, but I had the feeling that his mood might turn at any moment. I mumbled an anodyne opening question about the music he was listening to when he formed Love. Piercing blue eyes shone over the Ray-Bans and under the black sombrero and fixed on me. His mouth did not move.

'Are you asking me who made me what I am, musically speaking?' he said, spitting out the words like shrapnel. 'I don't understand the *question*.' He raised the coffee cup once more and continued to stare at me.

I said something about primary influences. 'Listen, man,' he said, leaning forward ever so slightly. 'I was just gifted. When I was three or four years old I used to hear the marching bands in Memphis. From then on I was banging on boxes and singing in the bathroom. My mother gave me accordion lessons when I was eight and, after that, I taught myself. When I formed Love I was listening to Nat King Cole, and Elvis, who is from my hometown, and The Isley Brothers. But nobody *made* me. My purpose on this earth is to leave a mark, brother, which will never be forgotten.'

The music may well have come from within, but the career opportunities came from a less sanctified source. In 1965 the hippest band in LA were The Byrds. Arthur Lee was one of the regulars at Ciro's, the nightclub where The Byrds played five times a night, and he was smart enough to exploit the fact that the band's handsome roadie was getting more girl attention than The Byrds themselves. 'I realised that I could do something with this guy in my band, and, as it turned out, Bryan came to be an important part of my music. God works in mysterious ways, because to hook me up with Bryan MacLean was a great thing.'

Where did Arthur Lee's songs come from? They didn't conform to the hippy rock ideal. You could hear a show-tune sophistication that was presumably Bryan MacLean's influence, a rooting in R&B that made sense given Arthur's background and musical tastes, and a folk-rock style that would have come from The Byrds. I exasperated him further by asking him where the seeds of Love's songs were sown.

'To pinpoint one person or style is impossible,' he said with a sigh. 'I liked jazz and classical when I was a child, and Little Richard and James Brown were dynamic performers. Bobby Darin was great, and, of course, I've always loved Robert Johnson. But what does it all mean? I try to create my own music. That's what I think I've done.'

He did concede that there were a couple of people who matched up to his talent. Jimi Hendrix and Beethoven, for example. 'I would say that we three are on the same page, musically,' he said casually, as if talking about old friends. 'Beethoven reminds me of myself; there is a similarity of things that are on our mind and, when I heard his music, I felt that he could be my brother. Jimi Hendrix had that quality for me, too.'

I spent many hours of my adolescent life decoding Arthur Lee's lyrics. One of my favourite songs on Love's second album, *Da Capo*, was 'She Comes In Colours'. It had the chorus line 'My love, she comes in colours, you can tell her from the clothes she wears.' It was a beautiful image. It was only years later that I discovered what kind of love he was singing about: his girlfriend was having her period and he wanted to have sex with her. So when he did, she came in colours. Or rather, one colour: red.

There was another song on *Da Capo* called 'The Castle', named after the band's communal home. 'Bryan and I always had conflicts with the ladies,' said Arthur, when I asked him what the song was about. 'There is a line in that song, "A I love, B I love, so hard to choose". A is Arthur and B is Bryan and the lady is trying to choose between us. Then I say "If I was in my mind I would use". I was freaked out by the chaos caused by a lady seeing Bryan behind my back and me behind his. So the songs were about things that were going on in our lives at the time.'

I asked him how he approached writing lyrics. 'I write about things as I see them,' he replied tersely. 'I don't write about the twist or the jerk or the mashed potato but life as it is, and life isn't always bright. Listen, brother.' He leaned forward and held out one fist after another as he said in a gentle but threatening whisper: 'There has always been war and there has always been love. I capitalised on those things by putting them into *Forever*

Changes and people told me that my music was "dark". What the hell is "dark"? What's "dark" about it when there will always be people trying to make money out of war?'

Forever Changes was written under the shadow of Vietnam, with Arthur having realised that a few hippies putting flowers into the barrels of the guns of the home guard was not going to change Lyndon B. Johnson's mind about the threat of communism. When I met Arthur Lee the first Iraq War had been and gone and the terrorism that inevitably followed led to ill-defined laws on detention without trial. As Arthur Lee sang on 'The Red Telephone': 'they're locking them up today, they're throwing away the key. I wonder who it will be tomorrow, you or me?'

'*Forever Changes* took a while to sink in because we weren't flower power,' said Arthur, beginning to soften up a little. 'We weren't singing about the birds, the bees, the bangles and the bubblegum, but we were the original hippies, the real thing. The Byrds looked like hippies but then you met David Crosby and discovered what *his* reality was. Sonny and Cher were even worse. They grew their hair long and threw some beads around their necks, but, if you met Sonny Bono, you would know what I'm talking about. Love *did* have love. We had no money, and we would share everything.' Including women.

It seemed like Arthur was on top again, but the demons were to come back in force. After months of touring, Baby Lemonade rebelled against him – and, as a final last-ditch attempt to make him get his act together, chucked him out of his own band. His behaviour had been getting increasingly erratic, culminating with a series of cancelled concerts and one in Italy for which Arthur hardly bothered to open his mouth. He wasn't particularly grateful to the musicians who had saved his career: it was rumoured that he had called up members of his estranged former backing band and told them that he was going to get his prison friends from the notorious LA gang The Crips onto them. Then I heard the news that he had leukaemia.

I have often wondered why I keep going back to the sixties and early seventies. Certainly there is the romance of a past era; an idealisation of something you did not experience. An inability to adapt to the rigours of the modern age might have something to do with it, too. But there is also the sneaking suspicion that music was just better back then. It sounded great because of the quality of the equipment used (and ToeRag and its vintage gear would help our own single get that sound), the songs had a lot of energy, because people were still excited by the freshness of rock'n'roll, and there was a cultural explosion that will be recognised as a twentieth-century renaissance, with all aspects of society coming under scrutiny. But I was suffering from nostalgia for a period before I was born, and I did realise that, in understanding the song, I had to go beyond that era and talk to some people who were at least a little more current.

A couple of weeks after meeting Arthur Lee, I was in a record shop in Soho, killing time before going to the cinema. Some amazing music came on which sounded familiar. It was full of lush sweeps of sound and layers of melody over melody. It had the moody but thoroughly British touch of The Zombies, the mid-sixties beat group that had hits with 'She's Not There' and 'Time Of The Season', yet it was modern, too. It was a song called 'The Piccolo Snare' by the Welsh band Super Furry Animals.

I met up with Gruff Rhys a few days later. I had got to know Gruff, the lead singer of Super Furry Animals, about a year earlier, having met through shared friends. We got on well after

discovering a shared love of the country soul pioneer Bobbie
Gentry. I caught him at a good time: not doing much. He had a
rare week off from the recording, promoting and touring
realities of being in a band full-time, and he was spending
it with his girlfriend at her flat in Camden in north London. I
went round to find Gruff on the sofa with a guitar while Kat,
whose father was Vietnamese and whose mother was Welsh and
whose broad Cardiff accent was a surprise given her delicate
Eurasian features, fussed over the little dog she had she adopted,
made us cups of tea, and got on with the business of keeping her
tall, curly-haired boyfriend, who spends a good many hours of
the day in his own world and significantly fewer in the wider
one, in line.

'I can't really play anybody else's songs,' said Gruff. 'Because
I don't know the chords and I'm not particularly interested . . .'

'That being the major factor,' interrupted Kat.

'I can't physically play them, so I have to adapt songs I like to
the way I play and from that process comes something of my
own. It might be a case of hearing two or three songs on the
radio that I like and trying to copy them. I put my entire output
down to having a bad memory.'

'But you've got an excellent memory,' countered Kat. 'To
remember all of those songs of yours in order to play them in
concert is bloody amazing.'

'But my short-term memory isn't sharp,' he replied, falter-
ingly.

'Hmm, yes,' she said with a sigh. 'Household chores . . .
they're a short-term memory thing, aren't they?'

'Most of my songs come from going on long walks, or sitting
on a bus or being on a train,' said Gruff with an air of seriousness
that his girlfriend was failing to match up to. 'I'll start
humming a melody as I go along. Then I'll go home and I'll

try to play the melody that I had going through my head, and then I'll try and build a bed of chords to support it. Or I might see a newspaper and start singing a headline from it.'

He picked up a supplement from a newspaper that was lying on the floor. The headline ran: 'A Word In Your Ear'. After a couple of false starts, he began to sing the line like an uplifting anthem, strumming the guitar with a few chords that appeared to fit. 'You loop the phrase in your head,' he said. 'Then you give it a harmony, then you add a chord change, and then it descends into cliché and you have a predictable song. Finally, you have to imagine the drums coming in and the bass rumbling along and it's complete.'

'Can I ask your advice on something?' I said as Gruff swayed from side to side, lost in 'A Word In Your Ear'. 'I've been writing down lyrics without music, and then I've been going to the guitar and trying to strum along to the words, and then the final thing that comes is the melody, which is generally terrible. Can that approach work?'

'It probably can,' he said, hesitantly, 'but I go the other way round. When we go into the studio I'll have an ideas book of lyrics on hand. Then I will copy all the ideas down onto blank sheets of paper and stick them onto the wall. The problem with writing a complete set of lyrics, like a poem, is that you then have to squeeze them all into the song. It's better to write random lines and ideas and build up a melody from the best ones. Then you can come up with lyrics to fit the melody, which is much easier than vice versa.'

It came as a surprise to hear that Gruff wrote lyrics in this way because I felt that his words worked very well, and that they had depth, and that they were more than just random. But perhaps what remained with you from his songs were certain sentences. His song 'Hello, Sunshine' had the line: 'I'm a minger, you're a minger too. So come on minger, I want to ming with you.'

Many of my favourite songs tell stories in a very real way. 'Ode To Billie Joe' by Bobbie Gentry is the high-water mark of storytelling in song. 'It was the third of June, another hot and dusty Delta day,' sings Bobbie Gentry in her croaking, sultry, sexy Mississippi drawl. 'I was out choppin' cotton and my brother was balin' hay.' From this picture of southern rural life builds the story of how, over lunch, the narrator's mother casually announces that Billie Joe McAllister jumped off the Tallahatchie Bridge. As the father dismisses the incident coldly, stating that 'Billie Joe never had a lick of sense, pass the biscuits please,' the family remember childhood games with Billie Joe before noticing that the narrator hasn't touched a single bite of her food. The mother goes on to say that a nice young preacher came by the house, and that he mentioned in passing how he saw Billie Joe McAllister with a girl 'that looked a lot like you up on Choctaw Ridge, and she and Billie Joe were throwing something off the Tallahatchie Bridge.' By the end of the song, time has moved forward and Brother has left town to buy a farm in Tupelo, Father has died after catching a virus, and Mother doesn't seem to want to do much of anything. Meanwhile, our self-contained heroine is spending a lot of time up on Choctaw Ridge, collecting flowers and throwing them into the muddy water under Tallahatchie Bridge.

Bobbie Gentry's story of blue-collar life is set to a simple D7–G7 two-chord melody. Her powers of description are brilliant – she doesn't say that much, but, with a few place names and mentions of incidents, you get a full picture – and the way in which she clashes the family's indifference to this suicide of a local boy with the girl's heartbreak says so much about the closed nature of love, and of the effect that one human can have on another. There is a mystery at the heart of the song, too: Bobbie Gentry has always declined to say what exactly it is that the narrator and Billie Joe McAllister are throwing off the Tallahatchie Bridge.

I would have loved to speak to Bobbie Gentry, but, in the mid-seventies, she retired from showbusiness and went into real estate, never to return. She has not granted an interview since her retreat from the spotlight. Gruff suggested that, if I approached her with a view to talking about the mechanical process of songwriting rather than, say, her failed marriages, she might agree to do it. I wasn't so sure.

'She is mysterious,' Gruff conceded. 'She's very lyrical, she has an amazing voice, and she's beautiful and glamorous . . . she's got everything.'

'She's the ideal star,' I reflected.

'But unsung in her own way.'

I wondered if such great stories as 'Ode to Billie Joe' could be written under Gruff's seemingly random technique. 'I'm the wrong person to speak to about narrative in songwriting because that's my downfall,' he replied. 'I did write a story-song early on in my career. There was a guy in my class at school with bright red hair. He was going for a walk with his father through some fields one day when a farmer mistook him for a fox . . . and shot him. His father was so shocked at seeing his son get shot that he had a heart attack. They both lived, though, so I decided to build up a ballad around this story called "Foxy Music". It ended with the line: "Just because he's got red hair doesn't make him a fox".'

Of course, I happened to have a fox song of my own. Gruff appeared to be open-minded. Now I would put him to the test with 'Mystery Fox'. I hit the opening A minor to D riff before singing the words in a high falsetto. I watched his face carefully.

He was impassive. Even when I reached the line 'hefty graceful bear with your curtain of hair, you broke my arm with your gallons of charm', he did little more than jut his chin forward slightly.

When the guitar stopped resonating entirely and silence blanketed the room, Gruff said: 'That has a potentially fantastic nonsense lyric. And it's very melodic. Who said you have no sense of melody?'

'So you think there's hope?'

'Absolutely, but songwriting isn't the mysterious process you seem to think it is. Now, I'm going to set you your homework. You need to start coming up with songs as part of your everyday life. You should try to sing every lyric that you come across, especially when you're on a train or a bus or driving a car. The ideal situation is when you are doing something that doesn't particularly engage your brain, like travelling. Movement seems to help.'

It was time to ask Gruff about how he came up with my favourite Super Furry Animals song: 'The Piccolo Snare'. The most impressive thing about this is the way it keeps changing. Waves of melody come in and never repeat themselves. It sounds like a very complicated and difficult piece of music.

'I wrote that on a piano, which I can hardly play,' he announced. ' "The Piccolo Snare" is built around a very simple melody, which grows slightly and doesn't go back to the way it was. The opening line is "Have you ever seen the sun", which is a random line that happened to go well with the tune. Then came "rising up to the sound of a gun", which is a description of the Argentine flag. So it developed into a song about the Falklands War, and then it became a song about war in general. I wrote it at the time of the Iraq War. Essentially, the song wrote itself.'

'So you always start with a musical idea?'

'Yes, and then I add random lyrical ideas . . . observations, really. They're not related except for the fact that they come from the same mind, but that's not to say that they don't make sense. I'll rewrite a song ten times or more until it adds up and has cohesion. It doesn't escape from the factory until it has some sort of meaning.'

'But what about all the strings, the sweeping arrangements of your songs?' I protested. 'I haven't got a clue about how to get there and nobody is telling me. I can't imagine ever writing something like "The Piccolo Snare". I wouldn't know where to start.'

'All of that comes in the recording studio,' he said. 'Your problem is that you keep thinking that writing a song is a hugely complicated thing, which it isn't. I like to think that a song should be simple enough to sing a capella in a cave, in the event of technology coming to a sudden end in a time of crisis. And don't forget that people have been singing songs long before they have been writing down the rules of music. You should be able to do nothing more than hit rocks together and sing and the song should not be any the worse for it. Our songs are actually based on fairly conventional patterns, but we experiment within the traditional songwriting genre and we have fun with the electronic side of things when we get to the studio. While technology is still here, you may as well use it.'

'I Bet You Look Good On The Dancefloor' by The Arctic Monkeys was playing on the radio when I got back home. Made by four teenagers from Sheffield, it was an angry adolescent symphony about desire and rejection and Britain went crazy for it. It was claimed that the band's success had been down to their songs spreading like digital wildfire across the internet, but you could have buried this track underneath the Houses of Parliament and it would have got out somehow. A week after I heard it that night, it had gone to the top of the charts. Apparently the band had been given guitars the previous Christmas and, a little under a year later, they came up with this. They weren't doing anything complicated, but the music was so confident – so audacious – that it was undeniable. It sounded like the band didn't even know how well-crafted their song was.

For the next few hours we entered into the standard routine of dinner–bath–storytime–bed. Otto refused to eat mashed potatoes and I told him that he would have to sit there until he at least tried them. 'Anyway,' he said to me, 'when it gets to midnight you'll be in bed and then I'll just go to bed myself and you won't know.' I replied that I would never, ever go to bed until he ate his supper. I would poke myself with a fork every time I came close to sleep. 'Well, you have to go and live with another family then,' he said with a pout. Then he decided to eat his potatoes and peace reigned once more.

I accepted Gruff's advice about incorporating songwriting into everyday life, but lyrics about this sort of thing would come over as too saccharine. I couldn't help but wonder if I really had left it too late. I couldn't fake the youthful vigour of the Arctic Monkeys.

We stayed up late and played records that night. We listened to a British singer from the late sixties and early seventies called Bridget St John. She had a deep voice, with a narrow range, but it was resonant and affecting. There was something reassuring about the depth of her music. It invited you in.

Sadly, the world did not clasp the gentle songs of Bridget St John to its bosom, particularly after she made some bad career choices. One of her big gigs was supporting the Detroit proto-punks the MC5 at a biker festival, and perhaps unsurprisingly her gentle reflection didn't mix well with the hog roast, leather and beer on offer elsewhere. Her third album, *Thank You For*, was my favourite. It started with a song called 'Nice', which was a playful plea for simplicity, suggesting that nothing really matters in life except that 'love be nice'. She looked great, too, with her headscarf and uneven nose. I wondered what had become of her.

'I'd like to sing one of Bridget St John's songs,' said NJ, looking at the liner notes of *Ask Me No Questions*, St John's first album. 'Why don't you learn to play some?'

'It's not that easy,' I replied. 'You either have to be shown how to play a song, or you have to have the tablature, and, besides, this sounds very complicated. It's very difficult just to learn it from listening, or at least it is for me. I've got no idea what she's doing.'

'But they're perfect for my voice,' persevered NJ. 'And I like her style, too. If you want me to sing on this record for you, then all I ask is that you work out how to do one of these songs. *Ask Me No Questions* would be a good start."

It was also ageless. She wrote it when she was young, but there is a wisdom, romance and reflection to it that does not restrict it to youth. I couldn't write a song like the Arctic Monkeys, but NJ could certainly sing a song by Bridget St John, and it might just inspire me to write something similar. If I could somehow find Bridget St John, I suspected that I might get closer to achieving my goal, which still felt like a long way off despite the encouragement given by Gruff and the insight into the spooky world of Arthur Lee.

Bridget St John's gentle songs put me in the mood for English whimsy, so I put the stylus down on two of my favourite records that night: *The Madcap Laughs* and *Barrett* by Syd Barrett. The original leader of Pink Floyd, Barrett wrote songs of the most evocative nonsense before mental illness, probably latent but at least partially brought about by prodigious intake of LSD, rendered him incapable of dealing with the world beyond his garden in Cambridge. Who but Syd could have written Pink Floyd's wonderful 1967 debut single 'Arnold Layne', a twisted nursery tale about a man stealing knickers from washing lines?

Syd was to be left well alone. Knowing what NJ's brother Charles goes through in suffering from schizophrenia, it felt wrong to try to contact him and ask him how to approach writing such charmingly dark songs, which were now close to forty years old and essentially the product of another, much younger person than the one spending his time painting and gardening in Cambridge. But there were three people out there who captured a kind of Englishness in the way Syd did; songwriters who, consciously or not, wove the melancholy, romance and absurdity of the English way into their songs.

First there was Andy Partridge, the co-founder, with Colin Moulding, of the band XTC and one of the great modern British songwriters. Andy Partridge is firmly in the Syd camp, putting twists on observations of provincial Britain with humour and sadness on albums like *English Settlement* and *Apples and Pears*. He lived in Swindon.

Lodged deep among Oxfordshire's weeping willows and twisting rivers, lived Gaz Coombes. The lead singer of Supergrass had prehistoric good looks, an aversion to the trappings of stardom, and an ability to write songs that Neil Young might have come up with had he grown up in an English village and got caught by his mum smoking cigarettes on the cricket green aged fifteen. Gaz was only seventeen when, in the mid-nineties, Supergrass had their biggest hit with 'Alright', a cheery pub singalong of a song that was about nothing more than being young and keeping one's teeth nice and clean. It became the soundtrack of British youth for a year or so and it has haunted the band ever since. And Supergrass have impeccable pastoral credentials. They played their first concert to a herd of cows.

Lastly, in Muswell Hill, north London, was Ray Davies, the leader of The Kinks, who had been avatars for a very British kind of underachievement since their mid-sixties heyday. Nobody could write songs about the blank comforting misery of grey skies and broken dreams like Ray Davies. Between them, I hoped to glean enough advice to get to the heart of the English pop song.

Chapter Five

The English Song

Swindon is not a glamorous place. A couple of hours drive from London and close to the Welsh border, it is not a throbbing metropolis, a quaint market town, or a history-steeped, cathedral-dominated vista of beauty like nearby Bristol or Bath. In fact, it's hard to see what it has going for it beyond a reasonably efficient road system peppered with miniature roundabouts (microbouts) and a pleasant, if unremarkable, high street that climbs up a steep hill. The people of Swindon may well have many good reasons to love their town, but it doesn't leave a marked impression, positive or negative, on the average visitor.

That is the very reason why Andy Partridge, who was born in Malta but grew up in Swindon, has decided to stay put. He describes his hometown as 'Everywheresville', and, although he doesn't appear to have any particular affection for it, it is a perfect environment for his songwriting by being so normal and unremarkable. In the great tradition of Ray Davies and Syd Barrett, XTC's songs find beauty in the mundane and things worthy of comment in the provincial.

Andy lives in a cosy but, on my December visit at least, extremely cold terraced house in the Old Town, the closest Swindon has to a picturesque neighbourhood. 'You look like a man who could do with a cup of tea,' he said, and brought me into his low-ceilinged kitchen, where wooden work surfaces, a clutter of old tins on inexpertly constructed shelves and a large, gnarled wooden table gave the impression of a homely, slightly sentimental room that had clearly been used by the same person for quite a while. Andy had perfectly round glasses to match his perfectly round head, and he wore a large paisley shirt. He made a pot of almond tea that, he told me, he had been enjoying for years, but he was distraught that the only company that made it had changed the formula and not for the better. I could tell that he wasn't like the kind of person who adapted well to change.

'So,' he said, as he pushed the inferior almond teabags around the pot, 'perhaps the first thing you should do is to play me one of your songs.'

I hadn't been prepared for this. I was thinking that we would spend a good hour or so going through his top-secret songwriting tricks before I subjected this total stranger to my own woeful musical efforts. But he told me to go to the tiny living room at the front of the house, which was womb-like in its excess of furnishings – books lining an entire wall from floor to ceiling; the kind of armchairs that, once sunken into, offer no escape routes; trinket-like ephemera everywhere – and I took out the guitar and launched straight into 'Until Daylight'.

My playing wasn't too bad, but the singing was atrocious. I could hear myself going out of time, and I would speed up to try and catch the guitar parts. What melody there was to begin with disappeared entirely. It was agonising and I wished that I had made the song shorter so that my torment would come to a quicker end.

'Right,' said Andy, leaning forward with tutor-like author-ity. 'Can you take this? Put your guitar down, which is horribly out of tune, by the way. It doesn't matter if you're Segovia;

playing an out-of-tune guitar is like trying to throw a ball using your foot. It will always go wrong.'

I did what he said and waited for the verdict, but it wasn't to come yet. 'Now, I want you to sing me the song again.' I made a Pavlovian lurch for the guitar. 'Leave the guitar alone,' he commanded. 'I want you to sing me the song without accompaniment.'

I had never done this before. So far, on the few occasions that I had sung, I generaly hid behind both the sounds and the physical presence of the guitar. This was distressingly exposing, rather like those dreams where you find yourself standing on stage in front of an audience with no idea about what you are doing there, possibly naked. But I did as he told me.

'OK. That was much, much better. What you are doing now is a melody. What you were doing before went like this: "Urrrrgghhaahhhhhoooooo . . ." It was like the siren of a toy police car when the batteries are about to die – you should have bought Duracell. A song is made of the juxtaposition of the melody dancing with the chords. Your chords were doing some dancing – pretty good, I was impressed for someone who has only played for a year – but your melody wasn't so much dancing as being dragged around like a piece of dog shit on a bottom of the shoe of the guitar.'

I looked at the bottom of my shoe and, finding nothing odorous there, frowned.

'A good song will be good no matter how it's arranged, no matter how many instruments are playing it, or whether no instruments are playing and somebody is simply standing up and singing it,' he explained. 'You can sing all of your favourite songs without an instrument. Why is that? Because they have a definitive melody that moves quite a lot. A good melody is the musical equivalent of the New York skyline. The melody you just sang me without an instrument was semi-defined, but the one with the guitar had no definition at all. It was a totally different beast. Why is that?'

'I think because I'm finding it difficult to sing and play guitar at the same time.'

'In that case, you're thinking about playing the guitar too much,' he announced. 'Your job now is to define your song. Do you know what the notes on a keyboard would be?'

'No, I haven't got a clue. I can't play piano and wouldn't even know what the notes were if I heard them.'

'In that case, we have our first exercise. We need to isolate the notes you're singing and pick them out on a keyboard.' There was an old stand-up piano in the corner of the room that Andy led me to. 'I can't play piano either; it doesn't matter. What's your first note in this song?'

He played a few notes on the piano that he thought it might be. 'Maybe it's higher than that one?' I said. 'No, lower . . . or maybe it's higher after all . . . actually, I don't know.'

'Here we have a classic beginner songwriter's dilemma,' he said, folding his arms. 'You never sing your song the same way twice because you don't really know how it goes. Right now you're saying, "I've done a sculpture, here it is," and you're showing me a drawing of your sculpture followed by a completely different drawing that bears no relation to the first. Then you show me a third picture and now I'm *really* confused. Sing me the song again.'

I tried once more. When I finished, he said: 'Can you hear those notes in your mind?'

'I think so, but I don't know what they are. For example, the first chord is in G. Does that mean that the first melody note should be in G as well?'

'Not necessarily,' he replied. 'The chord sequence and the

melody complement one another, but that doesn't mean they do the same thing.' Andy banged out three notes on the piano that roughly matched the rising pattern for 'close the door', the first three words in 'Until Daylight'. 'Are those the opening notes of the song?'

'I think they are,' I said, nervously. 'I mean, yes.'

'That wasn't what you were singing. You're saying the words, not singing them.'

I kept trying to sing the notes that he was playing on the piano. 'No!' he shouted. 'Feel the stairs beneath your feet! Your foot is your singing voice and the correct steps are the correct notes on the piano. You're jumping around on the stairs when you should have your feet firmly planted on them, and sooner or later you're going to fall over. You don't have to be a great singer – Bob Dylan isn't – but you have to *know* your song, and you have to *define* it. Sing those notes!'

'Close the door . . . close the door . . . close the door . . .'

I thought that he might start hopping about like Rumpelstiltskin, spinning so fast that he disappeared through the floor, never to be seen again. Yet his agitation was also his elation as his teaching methods began to take effect. My singing was getting better. 'Good!' he snapped. 'And again. And again.'

'Close the door . . . close the door . . .'

'You think you know what you're doing right now,' he said, leaning his head against the piano and gasping for breath, 'but it's like a chimp with a pencil. The chimp is making some great marks on the paper, but he thinks he's drawing a picture of Admiral Nelson. It may look like Admiral Nelson in your mind' – I think he might have actually seen a chimp wearing a beret and a painter's smock when he looked at me now – 'but, if you want to make other people think it looks like Admiral Nelson, you have to actually make it LOOK LIKE HIM.'

'Close the door . . . close the door . . .'

'What I'm trying to make you do is understand what defines a song,' he puffed, pounding his fist on the top of the piano. 'You appear to have got to grips with chord changes, but I don't think you really understand yet that you have to have the same, defined melody over those chord changes, otherwise the whole acrobatic balancing act falls apart.'

He took a deep breath, sat back in his armchair, and told me about the first song he ever wrote, when he was fifteen. It was called 'Please Help Me', and it was a cry for help to nobody in particular, asking for aid in escaping from his parents and the diabolical relationship he had with them. He resurrected the song for my benefit, with its caterwaul-like refrain 'Pleeeease help meeeee', with the extended 'e' of the 'me' reaching ever-higher notes until Andy's voice collapsed entirely. So this was the same man who had crafted such classics as 'Dear God' (a letter written by a child to his creator) and 'Senses Working Overtime' (about what it is to be alive). 'Please Help Me' sounded rather like the sounds a cat might make if you shoved it into a Kenwood blender and pressed the 'chop finely' button.

'Interesting change in the time signature on "Until Daylight",' said Andy, talking about the chorus that everyone hated. 'That's very Syd Barrett. But, if I were your producer, I would say that this song is too long to sustain human interest. Songs have a natural lifespan of around two to three minutes. The classical composers knew that. They would have a melody, work it to death for a couple of minutes, and then move on. Now, what else do you have?'

'Bad Part Of Town' was still only half-formed, leaving one other. 'There is this song called "Mystery Fox", but it's a bit embarrassing.'

'What's embarrassing about it?'

'Well, I do think it has something, but it's fairly ridiculous.'

'Then you're not embarrassed by it. You just haven't realised its potential.' He closed his eyes and clasped his hands together and raised them to his mouth, like an emperor being presented with a new courtly minstrel troupe and considering their worth before deciding to employ them or put them in the stocks. 'Continue.'

I performed it for him. To my surprise, he took it reasonably seriously.

'Four rounds of the same thing can get a bit monotonous,' he said. 'You need some changes to break up that melody and pattern. Perhaps a chorus wouldn't go amiss. I've written worse songs than that, though. At least it's a good title. It's so much more than a conventional, everyday fox.'

'How did you learn?' I asked.

'By asking: How does Ray Davies do it?' he replied. 'How does Burt Bacharach have so many hits and why do people like his songs? You've got to get anatomical. You've got to get the scalpel out, carve up the body and pull out the guts and say: "the knee bone's connected to the thighbone. And I never knew that pipe was in there, what's that connected to? It's the heart, wow! And why are there two of these? It's the lungs! And there I was thinking that the lungs were down in the legs." If you want to be as good a painter as Rembrandt, get close to his paintings and study the brush strokes. You won't find out how a car engine works by watching it drive by. You need to pull it to pieces.'

Andy had never had any lessons. His father showed him a few chords after he had learned to play skiffle on a navy ship, but that was as far as his education went. In wanting to learn to play guitar like Jimi Hendrix, he discovered that Hendrix would tune all the strings down so that they were loose and could drag notes out for longer and be bent further. To work out the magic of the songs by Burt Bacharach and Hal David, he sat down in the room we were currently in over a weekend, played their songs again and again, and worked out their formulae by drawing graphs. He drew a circle for an instrumental, a square for a chorus and a triangle for a verse, and realised, through the overlaps of the symbols, that they created a hybrid of verse and chorus that he named the vorus. The title of the song was also the first thing you heard – 'The Look Of Love', for example, or 'Do You Know The Way To San José?' And the structure went: title line, reply, title line repeated, rhyme to reply. It turned out that many famous songs were based around the vorus structure. Having learned that there was a fairly well-defined formula to many of the best pop songs, Andy used it himself as a starting point from which to jump off where necessary.

I hadn't come up with a formula for my songs yet because I didn't know of one. This approach to making art of any kind is often criticised, but being able to use the formula in the first place suggests a certain degree of sophistication that I didn't yet possess. But what I didn't understand was this: if all these songwriters were following age-old traditions, why did they end up sounding unique?

'I'm a human mincing machine,' he said, when I asked him this. 'I shove in The Kinks at one end, and, by the time it's come out of the mincer, it's all mangled up with my personality. And warning: this Kinks tune may contain elements of Beatle once it's been through my mincing machine. And now that I'm poking around a bit, what are those orange bits I see? Oh crikey, it's The Beach Boys!'

Something strange had been happening since I picked up the guitar a year previously. Ever since the age of twelve I've been buying records and ritualistically playing them while studying

the liner notes and pretending that the outside world does not
exist, but my record consumption had been taking a steady
decline. The children were a contributing factor – while they
were awake they did not generally allow you to listen to records
in peace – but it wasn't just that. I had become more interested
in learning how music worked, and trying to formulate my own
musical ideas, than I had in just hearing what other people had
done. There was still the thrill of discovering something new;
that never went away. But I did have the feeling that my
formative years were over; that being a musical consumer was no
longer enough. I asked Andy if, decades into his own creative
output, he was still interested in hearing new music.

'Less and less so, because there is still a hell of a lot of other
people's crap that has gone into me that I have to get rid of,' he
said. 'It's human nature that you get most of your input up until a
certain age, and then you spend the rest of your life trying to vomit
it out. There are all my own experiences, the books I've read, the
paintings I've seen and the records I've listened to – even the food
I've eaten. I have to empty all of this stuff out of me until there's
nothing left. How can people not be creative? Perhaps you just
become bad-tempered, like Mick Jagger, who, after an incredible
run, has been repeating himself for the last thirty years. The
problem is, creativity is like coal. There's only a finite amount
inside you. And I'm not sure how much longer I can keep going.'

'Why do you write songs in the first place?' I asked him.

After a pause, he replied: 'I think it's perversely, weirdly
oedipal. I want to climb up higher than my heroic father
figures. I want to kill them and wear their skins, because they
will look better on me than they do on them. I will defeat Ray
Davies, Lennon and McCartney, and Bacharach and David with
their own weapons; I shall exorcise their ghosts from my head
by doing something better than they did. I'm going to pile up

their corpses and climb to the top of them, just like Brian Wilson wanted to do with Phil Spector when he played "Be My Baby" again and again until he went mad. But then I also have to pay the rent. Because I'm crap at bricklaying.'

Like Lawrence – although significantly more successful – Andy Partridge was a great songwriter and a terrible business-man. Deals had gone wrong, partnerships turned sour, money-making possibilities lost. And I caught him at some sort of crossroads. He told me of his terrible fear of dying alone as a poverty-stricken and probably quite hungry old age pensioner, and, after making a few attempts at being a songwriting gun for hire, in which he collaborated with the hugely successful pop hitmaker Cathy Dennis, he was back at the house in Swindon, with its shed at the bottom of the garden filled with recording equipment, worrying about money.

Part of his current problem was that his now near-total knowledge of how pop was made was killing his love for it. He talked about the first time he heard The Beatles' 'Strawberry Fields Forever', and how he could not imagine how such a sound was created. Now he knew exactly where the backwards tape sounds or the mellotron or the slowed-down drum patterns came in and the mystery had gone entirely. This knowledge was having a bad effect on his own output, because his profession-alism was rejecting every bit of creative splurge that he emitted. He even had less respect for his masters now. He had discovered that they were just mangling their influences too.

'The "editor of your mind" is the bastard,' he said, with a trace of bitterness as he slumped into his chair. 'You spew out all this creative stuff and then the editor in your head comes along and says: "I don't like that bit, I don't like that bit, yes, I like that bit, so I want three more of those." You have the creative and then the editor, but now with me the editor is creeping up and becoming the first in the chain and he's stopping the creativity from coming out at all. I have to get him back in the queue, in his place.' He stared blankly into space, shivering slightly in the sterilising cold of the room. 'Sorry, have I gone off the beetle track?'

'I'm beginning to realise,' I said, thinking of all the advice I had had over the last few weeks and the fact that 'Bad Part Of Town' was all I had to show for my efforts, 'that writing a song is difficult.'

'Oh, I don't know about that. I think you could improvise a song right now. Go on, pick up that guitar and give me a song. Think about "the drone". That's what a lot of folk songs are based on. It can be very inspirational, the drone – just play a single chord and create a melody over the top of it.'

I picked out the chord of D and just kept it going, until some words began to form in my head. 'I was walking through the fields one day, the sukebind was in bud and it was the month . . . of May . . .'

'Where your melody?' he shouted. 'That's just more rubbery nonsense!'

'And I did see a maiden, dancing in the wood . . . she was naked, and that was . . . good . . .'

'Better, much better, keep going . . .'

'The maiden was a beauty, so pure and so wild, and then I noticed . . . that she was with child . . .'

'More melodic movement please . . . you're losing me . . .'

'I said to her "Where is the man that did this to thee?" and she replied "T'was no man, it was . . . in fact . . . a tree . . ."'

'You're talking. I want to hear singing. Feel the stairs underneath your feet. Sing!'

'For in these woods lies magic, a fertile one indeed, and for the lusty trees here, they need girls for to . . . breed . . .'

'There you go, you see?' said Andy. 'It's not so difficult after all. Now, if you had that on tape you might find some ideas in there that would be worth using. Turn the editor off and just vomit, and then go back and pick through the lumps. You might find something in your story of – what was it? – a girl that was dancing with a sexually voracious tree? And, once you get a melody going, you will have a song. In the nature of everything that gets done, maybe 5 per cent is worth holding onto.'

'Do you think there is any secret in songwriting?'

'Well, how do you write a song?' he said, sinking into his armchair. 'You start with an idea that you wish to express, and it would help if you have a chord basis underneath. Your melody should make an interesting skyline against the earth of the chords, although you can get away with a boring melody if the chords are doing really interesting things, like in the "One Note Samba" by Tom Jobim – the melody literally stays on a single note throughout the entire song but the chords are doing such interesting shape shifting underneath that it works. Although I wouldn't attempt to try and write a bossa nova song. That's far too difficult.'

Andy Partridge had taught me a lot in the space of a few hours. He had shown me how to define a melody, and how to create a song out of nothing by improvising to a drone and building up from there, but I had also got a little bit of a glimpse into the reality of the songwriter's life. Andy was middle-aged, quite well known, with a string of hits behind him and a high critical standing, but he was faced with money and career worries. At least XTC were back in fashion. A new wave of bands had discovered the old new wave of the early eighties and XTC were standing the test of time as its most literate members.

'I've only had to wait twenty-five years for us to become fashionable, but I suppose it's good,' said Andy, as I prepared to negotiate Swindon's labyrinthine one-way system and get on the road back to London. 'I suppose I'm pleased. But it's not going to make me rich. For every five pounds that a song of mine makes the record company, I might get a few pennies. Perhaps your next project should be looking into the evils of the music industry – but then, maybe that's not such a good idea? People have been killed for revealing too much.'

A few days before Christmas, I drove to the Oxford village where Gaz Coombes and the three other members of Supergrass grew up. I walked into a low-ceilinged pub with the kind of wide brick chimney and log fire that looked like it had been kept alive for the last 500 years. A rather doleful Labrador rubbed against my leg before collapsing in front of the fire, and the two old men by the bar, who looked like they had been taking their regular spots and ordering pints of bitter for about as long as the fire had been burning, asked me about the weather outside. I ordered a coffee, which seemed to confuse the barman, took a table in the corner, and waited for Gaz, from whom I had already received a series of increasingly apologetic messages: he had driven to Nottingham that morning to pick up a piece of recording equipment and was running late.

Gaz was twenty years younger and significantly hairier than Andy Partridge. He walked in with a big smile, sideburns emphasising his simian features, said hello to the men at the bar, ordered a pint of bitter and sat down. He reminded me of a younger version of me: a little too polite for his own good. He was also unsure of himself, despite the fact that he was reasonably famous, good-looking and personable. Apparently the Japanese girls go crazy for him. When I told a Japanese friend that I was meeting up with him, she got very excited. 'Can I come?' she asked, the answer to which was no. Then she said in her thick Tokyo/London accent: 'I fancy him something rotten. He's just so . . . apelike.' Apparently in Japan there are few higher compliments that you can pay a man.

'I really don't know what the answer is to the question of how to write a song,' said Gaz, when I told him about what I was doing. 'So maybe the best thing I can do is take you through "Low C".'

This was a song that Supergrass had released as a single a few weeks previously. It sounded like John Lennon at his best, with a simple riff and words that, as far as I could tell, were lamentations on a teenage love affair. 'I went with my girlfriend to see Neil Young do an acoustic show and I noticed that he used a lot of weird tunings, in particular taking the bottom E string down as low as it could go,' said Gaz enthusiastically. 'So I started playing around with tunings and that song came about through that. It sounded nice; I tuned the bottom E down to a C and structured the song on a C to A minor chord change. Everything else – the melody, the lyrics – was based around the feeling I got from that sound.'

He explained how he had already thought of a few lines, including 'I wonder if I care if I saw you again' before writing the song, and that this was a common way of doing things: to have some thoughts to hang the bulk of the song on, with the rest of the words coming later. Once the tune of the song had emerged, Gaz sang nonsense lyrics until something emerged. He then tested them out on the other band members. I felt a little envious of Gaz. I really wanted to test out song ideas on Doyle, but he had made it clear that, until we got to Eigg, his creative juices were remaining cryogenically frozen.

'If I'm writing songs at home, my girlfriend tends to be a

good person to bounce words and melodies off,' he said. 'If she's humming one around the house a few days after I've written it, then I know I'm onto a winner. But it's simple, really. The entire career of Supergrass has been an attempt to copy Neil Young and David Bowie. Having failed to do that, we came up with our own sound.'

It seems that the history of creativity is the history of mistakes. We try to copy our heroes and it comes out differently as we apply, consciously or not, or own imagination and personality to what we are doing.

This was all very well, but he wasn't actually telling me how to come up with a melody myself. And, although I had the guitar in the boot of the car, I was feeling too embarrassed to get it out and whack him over the head with 'Bad Part Of Town' in front of an audience of the pub's aged locals. So I asked him to give me a clue as to where to locate the key to the melody treasure chest that lay locked up in the subconscious of every man, woman and child on the planet.

'All you need to do is simply try and copy the melody of the songs you love,' he replied. 'You'll get it wrong, so something new will emerge. Don't you ever think of your favourite bands and say: "What would they do with these words?" Don't you want to have the tambourine and the shakers coming in, and then have a big booming drum sound, and then have the kind of guitar riff that Jimi Hendrix would use? Don't you?'

I had been thinking along those lines over the past few days. We had been at a Thanksgiving dinner thrown by some American friends a few weeks previously when a ladybird had landed on my arm; a rare sight in November. It didn't seem like it could be bothered to go anywhere. I tried to make it fly away but, even when I nudged it with the tip of my finger, it just made a bad-tempered shuffle further up my arm. 'What a lazybird!' I said to my friends. 'It can't be bothered to fly.'

A couple of days later I was on a bus, crawling along the Old Kent Road and wishing I was at home, when my thoughts returned to that ladybird. I started to write words about a lazy ladybird that lands on the arm of an equally lazy man, who is sitting in the woods trying to escape from the troubles of his city life for an hour or so. I kept thinking about the songs of Ray Davies and The Kinks, which caught moods so well through describing quite specific things through a little narrative, and the playful charm of Syd Barrett and those early Pink Floyd singles, and the Englishness of it all, and did my best to emulate them. Unfortunately, my tune was exactly the same, note for note, as 'Sunny Afternoon' by The Kinks. That was taking the idea of homage too far.

I told Gaz about my attempts with 'Lazybird'. 'That's a key point,' he said, waving a cigarette at me. 'If we ever managed to do what was going on in our heads, we would be accused of plagiarism and very quickly get sued. But we get it wrong because we keep on playing things until they change. You stopped at the point where you thought of using somebody else's tune for your words, when, in fact, that should be the starting point. If you kept singing that "Sunny Afternoon" tune with your "Lazybird" lyrics for long enough, it would end up as its own song with its own melody.'

I felt that Supergrass were a product of their environment as much as their influences. However much they might want to sound like Neil Young, they would always reveal themselves as the nice, funny boys from the shires that they were. This was confirmed for me when Supergrass's bassist Mick Quinn, who met Gaz when the latter was working in the local Harvester restaurant, shuffled into the pub. I told him about the Kinks/ Barrett-inspired 'Lazybird'.

'There's always a directness and a logic to Syd Barrett's music, and the best songs by The Kinks,' said Mick, who was personable, with a slightly mournful air, a little like the Labrador currently feeling sorry for itself over by the fireside. 'He knows what he's doing. You have to make sure that your song sounds like you *mean* it to sound the way it does.'

'But there's nothing wrong with trying to think like your heroes,' added Gaz. 'When I'm stuck, I ask myself: "Does this chorus sound cool enough to be on the *Ziggy Stardust* album?" But of course you're trying to express yourself, too, so you're pulling away from your heroes at the same time as using them to guide you. That's where originality lies.'

It was time for the Supergrass boys to leave. They asked me what I was hoping to achieve through all of this.

'To write a good song,' I replied.

'The one that you think is good won't necessarily be the one that other people like,' said Gaz with a smile. 'We still don't know why all the schoolchildren and grandmas liked "Alright" so much, because we didn't think it was anything special. We haven't performed it in years. It was about nothing more than being thirteen and discovering girls, and it's hard to sing "we are young, we vote green" when you're settled down with a kid and you've got five albums under your belt. Well, we'd better go. Good luck with it all.'

So Ray Davies was Andy Partridge's songwriting hero. And Lawrence had mentioned him quite a bit, too. I was with Lawrence once when he produced, from his alphabetically ordered and dust-protected record collection in his flat that he had never cleaned in the seven years he had been there, a run of albums by The Kinks from 1973 to 1978. 'This,' he announced in his quietly dramatic way, 'is considered by anyone who likes The Kinks to be the most hideous collection of music ever known to humanity.' One of the albums in the series, *Schoolboys In Disgrace*, featured a disturbing cartoon of a cheeky boy sticking his bottom out of his shorts for an aroused master to whack with his cane. The run began with Ray Davies's concept albums about a South American dictator, *Preservation Act 1* and *Preservation Act 2*, and went on to include *Muswell Hillbillies* and *Soap Opera*. Lawrence had two copies of these Kinks albums 'just in case'. 'I'm not into these records to be perverse,' he claimed. 'Ray Davies moved from singing about reality on his sixties hits to a kind of plastic reality on these. It's a shame that everyone hates them so much.'

The album that did it for me – and which showed Ray Davies's songwriting abilities at their most elegant and natural – is 1968's *The Kinks Are The Village Green Preservation Society*. I'm not going out on a limb here: it's one of those albums that everyone should discover sooner or later. At the height of hippydom, Ray Davies announced himself as a curmudgeon of the highest order by praising conservative England in the title song, listing all the old-fashioned things he likes (Donald Duck, music hall, variety) and condemning the things he doesn't (skyscrapers and anything else associated with modernity). The album includes the songs 'Animal Farm', a Londoner's dream of the simple life among sheep and goats, and 'Walter', a lament for a childhood friend who has grown up and grown dull. The meanings of the songs are direct, which was not in tune with the Dylan-influenced trend of the times. They belong more to the tradition of music hall – they're not a million miles away from the descriptive charm of the songs of Lionel Bart's *Oliver* – than they do to rock'n'roll, despite the fact that, a few years earlier, The Kinks made the most raw rock'n'roll songs ever to come out of Britain.

The Kinks are great romantics. At our wedding NJ and I had three songs: 'Alone Again Or' by Love, simply because we both loved it so much; 'Lady Jane' by The Rolling Stones, because it always makes me think of NJ, whose actual name is Nichola Jane and is known simply as Jane to her family, who follow a bizarre tradition of having first names that they don't use; and 'Waterloo Sunset' – it felt fitting, since we got married on a boat about fifty feet away from Waterloo Bridge. The meaning of this last song has been analysed endlessly, so I'll be brief, but there is something so poignant about Terry and Julie, who always sound to me like a couple of office workers, meeting at their special place every Friday night as the crowds surge past and the narrator watches them in solitude. These songs would have been perfect together, but, unfortunately, the wedding DJ got confused as NJ made her entrance. It wasn't 'Lady Jane' that she made her bridal walk to but 'Under My Thumb'.

A request to meet Ray Davies was met with a yes and I was, inevitably, excited. Here was a man who could tell me how to write the perfect pop song. And he would provide all the answers to my questions in handy, easy-to-digest bullet-point form, perhaps with a flow chart to help illustrate a mathematical formula that, once known, provides one with a fruit tree of future hits ripe for plundering by the stars of the day.

It was a January afternoon when I went to Konk Studios in Muswell Hill in North London, which Ray Davies set up two decades ago in order to give himself a degree of autonomy from the music industry and to have a way of earning money should the records stop selling (which they did). I was ostensibly meeting him to interview him about his first-ever solo album, *Other People's Lives*. As is so often the case with the new albums of great sixties and seventies bands and singers I love, my heart sank within the first ten seconds of the first song. Why does Ray

Davies, whose band had such a fantastic sound in the sixties, have to do what every other modern ageing rocker does and have booming drums, a horribly clean guitar and a production that sounds like it has been chosen by a board of directors? I didn't like the title, either. It's obvious that Ray Davies writes about other people's lives, as 'Waterloo Sunset' illustrates. But the lyrical observations were still good. Only he could write a song about fat Australian barmaids and get away with it.

I rang the doorbell and was met by a pleasant woman called Julie, who was suffering from a nasty bout of the flu. She took me into the studio control room, sniffing all the way. Five minutes later, Ray Davies came in, wearing an expression that belonged to someone who was expecting bad news and was already resigned to it. He looked good for his age. He must have been around sixty, but he had an unfussy hairstyle (and all his hair) and he looked natural in a pair of old jeans and a T-shirt. His mouth had, however, taken a permanent downward turn.

It didn't seem like too much corporate hospitality and room service had blunted his awareness of the world, but perhaps depression had? In 1973, the same year that his brother, Dave, made a rare foray into songwriting with 'Death Of A Clown', Ray ran into a hospital claiming that an evil clown was chasing him. He was treated for severe depression. (The strange coincidence is that, on their first tour of the US in 1966, The Kinks almost spent a night in the house of a local promoter called John Wayne Gacy, the serial killer who dressed up as a clown, killed a handful of boys, and kept their remains in his basement.) You can hear a very British character in The Kinks' music: hopeful while expecting disappointment. And, although he was polite, Ray gave the impression of wanting to be anywhere but talking to me.

'It's actually impossible to tell someone how to write a song,' he said, when I told him about my goal. 'Because every time I sit down and write one, it's like I'm doing it for the first time. You will end with a question mark, because nobody's got the rules.'

This quick deflection of my probing was counteracted by the fact that I happened to know he was teaching a course in songwriting. And I found it hard to believe that he always wrote a song like it was the first time ever, because songwriters, like anyone else dealing with creative endeavours, develop their own patterns and fall back on them.

I put it to him that, given his extra-curricular activities in the field of education, he might have more to offer on the subject than he claimed. 'There is a huge amount of people who have written books about songwriting who want to get my ideas and get on the course. I always tell them that I have no ideas,' he replied, with the satisfaction of someone who had just executed a tricky chess move. 'Journalists are forbidden. TV companies have tried to do things and they never succeed because it's an experience that you cannot teach. As Duke Ellington said, "If you have to ask me what jazz is, you ain't got it." Doing it is the key. We all pick up our own methods along the way.'

If Ray Davies wasn't going to divulge any of the secrets of his craft, I could at least ask him how he got started. 'One of the most important moments of my life was when I first heard "Tupelo, Mississippi" by John Lee Hooker on the radio,' he said. 'What I loved about the track was that he was singing live, and you can hear a car horn in the background. It broke down the mystery of recording because the records I was exposed to previously, through the collections of my sisters, who were a generation older than me, were all well crafted pop songs by matinee idols. John Lee Hooker played well, but he was loose; he hit a riff and did some semi-speaking over the top. It turned me against perfection, because listening to it was like a documentary. It captured a chance encounter and made doing something similar seem possible.'

I asked him about that run of records by The Kinks in the mid-seventies that Lawrence had championed. 'A wonderful time,' he replied, just about smiling. 'There are some good songs on those albums, especially *Schoolboys In Disgrace*. The band were tight because there was such a short turnaround: *Preservation* came out in '74, *Soap Opera* in '75 and *Schoolboys In Disgrace* in '76, with major tours with big productions in between. It was a good period. Of course, people didn't understand it at all. I remember that at that time it was the thing to take drugs at a Kinks gig because we were so straight, with such a cartoon approach to good and evil, that we were considered quite psychedelic. I think the audiences from that time loved the concerts. At least the ones who didn't fall asleep loved them. We knew that those albums would be great pieces of art . . . one day.'

All of this was useful in a broad sense, but I needed practical information. He did, at least, give me hope in suggesting that you didn't need to be able to sing to be a singer. 'I'm not a great fan of Woody Guthrie,' he said, 'but he's important because he had a non-singing voice, so, without him, we wouldn't have had Bob Dylan or Ray Davies, because we wouldn't have been allowed near a recording studio in the fifties and the early sixties. We can't sing, but we've got something to say.'

I felt like I was starting to get somewhere, like his initial distrust was eroding. But I guessed, partially because he kept glancing at his watch, that he didn't really want to be here with me that much longer. I had an idea.

'You've been a massive help, Ray,' I said, 'but I still I think I've got a long way to go in terms of knowing how to write a good song myself. I really am an absolute beginner at this. Do you think that we might meet up again for half an hour or so, so that I could bring my guitar along and we could bash out some ideas?'

Something not too far from an amused smile coursed the width of his face. He rubbed his chin. After a pause, he said: 'Yeah, why not. Speak to Julie about it. We'll meet up for a cup of tea. It's good that you're a beginner. That's a refreshing state to be in.'

I couldn't have been more ecstatic if he had invited me to be a new member of The Kinks. Here was one of the great song-writers of the modern age, and he was really going to show me how it's done. Who cares if his new album was no classic? He had earned his stripes. I shook his hand vigorously, as he explained that he really had to go now before rushing out of the room. I went to see Julie, his assistant, and told her the good news. She said that I should call or email her over the next few days and she would arrange something.

I did indeed call, and email, Julie more than a few times over the next few days. But I never spoke to her, or to Ray Davies, ever again.

Chapter Six

Up, Up and Away

'You've done it.'

I was with Lawrence in his little flat. It was early in the New Year and the cold outside was harsh. I couldn't imagine how Lawrence, with his skeletal frame, holes in his shoes and flimsy clothing, could cope with it. I had just played him my garage song 'Bad Part Of Town'.

'You're not just saying that?' I asked him. 'Bad Part Of Town' was far from complete, after all.

We were sitting on the carpet of his room, in the absence of anything else to sit on. 'That is a proper song,' he continued. 'Or at least it will be one day. I said to you: do you want to do Incredible String Band-style nonsense, or "Up, Up And Away"? And you said "Up, Up And Away". "Bad Part Of Town" – that's your "Up, Up And Away". It's even got a middle eight.'

What he was calling the middle eight was what I thought was the chorus. The section in the song that begins with the line 'the old folks say it used to be peaceful' needed a change of mood. Realising that just copying The Starfires wasn't enough, I copied 'Itchycoo Park' by The Small Faces as well. That song has a nice chord change from G to B minor that I decided to nab.

'No, no, that's your middle eight. Why did you think it was a chorus? I'm great at middle eights. People generally do them for

too long and have too many of them in a song, but that's a good
one you've got there. Try and sing the third line in the same way
as the first two, though. For some reason you're making it
different. It doesn't have to be. You need to simplify your song.
You've got a lovely melody there. Honestly, it's lovely.'

This was the same melody that had made NJ accuse me of
signing her death warrant, but things had been bad for
Lawrence since the last time I saw him and that might have
explained his lack of judgement. To be honest, I think he was
just hugely relieved to see someone – anyone – and he probably
thought that, if he told me the truth about 'Bad Part Of Town',
I might leave. He'd had a horrible Christmas and New Year
stuck in the flat. 'It was the worst ever,' he said. 'I had no
money, nobody to talk to. Normally people phone me up and
invite me to a party on New Year's Eve, but this year nobody
did. I've never been so bored in all my life.'

He was also being faced with eviction. One afternoon over
Christmas while he was out, the building's agents had come in
to his flat and snooped around, ostensibly to fix the heater, even
though it wasn't broken. The next day he was served with an
eviction notice. To make matters worse, some junkie friends of
his had come round to the flat and broken the needle of the
record player. 'I can't even play records now,' he said, glumly.
'All I've got left is television and celebrity magazines.' He
pointed to one that was lying on his bed. On its cover was a
photograph of the American socialite (and adopted daughter of
pop-star Lionel) Nicole Richie looking emaciated over the
headline: 'Nicole's shocking weight loss!'

'I can't believe they're saying that she looks awful,' said
Lawrence lightly. 'She looks great. She's about as thin as it's
possible to be, which is ideal.'

I explained to Lawrence my current problem: trying to sing

and play guitar while keeping in time. 'That's weird,' he said. 'I thought that came naturally to everyone. Let's say you're starting out and you've got a Beatles songbook. You learn the chords and the words at the same time, don't you? As soon as I learned one chord, I wrote a song, and I don't think I even had any idea about what being out of time was. You're thinking about it too much when you shouldn't be thinking about it at all. You shouldn't even know what it means to be in or out of time. Did someone tell you that you were out of time?'

'No, but I can tell,' I told him.

'But it sounds fine to me. I like the way you only say "Bad Part Of Town" once in the first two verses, but twice later on. That's good – that's called holding back. You don't want to bombard the audience in the first chorus and let it all go at once, because that would be premature. At the end you can repeat the first verse, but faster.'

'Bad part of town, yeah . . . bad part of town . . .' As he had commanded me to do before, I was sticking to a simple strumming pattern that was controlled though damping the strings and only playing a few chords.

'Jesus, Will, you've done it!' he said in high-pitched surprise. 'But you're really attacking the guitar. Can't you learn to play a bit softer? The harder you play it, the less control you have.'

'Flowers will bloom and trees will grow,' I sang, 'on the streets where nobody would go, in the bad part of town, bad part of town, yeah . . .'

'That's lovely, that bit,' said Lawrence, nodding reflectively. 'This bad part of town of yours could be anywhere, couldn't it? It transcends boundaries.'

'So would you say I've made progress?'

'Totally! You've always had something going on with words, and you've always loved music, and you've got something creative within you – that's obvious by the way you've picked this up. Now you need to fine-tune this song, because you've got material that is worth working on.' He paused for a moment to pick up a cigarette stub from the ashtray and light it, laying waste to its last few millimetres of tobacco. Then he stubbed it out again with a loud exhalation. 'And there are no restrictions on age. Someone who is seventy can still write a beautiful song. You'll never be able to stop it now, because writing songs is like a little therapy session for you.'

Lawrence was prolific. From 1980 to 1990 his band, Felt, had released an album a year, and now he was finding that he had to stop himself from doing any more because he had three albums' worth of material for his current band, Go-Kart Mozart, which he was in danger of forgetting if he added any more to it.

'When I was in Birmingham, I suffered from boredom so badly,' he began. 'It was terrible. I had nowhere to go, no friends, and I used to think, "God, it's two hours until my next favourite programme. What will I do? I know, I'll run through the songs on the new album." So I would play every song off the album in order, and then do it all over again. It's a great way of filling time. If I pick the guitar up, I'm always writing. That's my pleasure. I can't stop.'

Lawrence had so much material that he had to work out new ways of foisting it onto the public. His latest idea was to have a Go-Kart Mozart Mini-Mart; a collection of songs that he didn't really care about. 'It's a low-quality supermarket value range version of Go-Kart Mozart,' he said. 'It's a cheap album with cut-price songs to go alongside the real album.'

Lawrence's best songs were a mixture of fantasy and auto-biography. He had a song called 'At the DDU', which had the line 'a massive shot of meth won't help you at the DDU'.

'That's based on recent experiences, that one,' he said. 'A shot of methadone won't help you at the Drugs Dependency Unit, because it won't.'

Lawrence helped me some more with the structure, suggesting that I mark the end of each verse with a definite major chord, or perhaps a suspended chord if I wanted to give a sense of mystery. I asked him which chord would be right to finish the song with and he told me that I just had to find it through trial and error. 'I don't go for what some academic says in a book about chord sequences,' he boasted. 'I used to make chords up by sticking my fingers down on various places on the guitar at random, but, when I played them to the guitarist in Felt, he would say, "That's F Major Seventh Diminished". I would get angry and say "No, I just made it up, it's mine!" and he would tell me that every time you put more than one finger down on the guitar, you're playing a chord. I just happened to find them by accident.'

Lawrence was forty-three and his songs were getting better and better. The average pop or rock musician seemed to make great albums in their youth and then go downhill as the money in the bank piled up. Perhaps it was Lawrence's ongoing financial struggle that kept him fresh?

'I'm still hungry,' he said, by way of explanation. 'Obviously I want to be a millionaire, and be rich and famous, and never go on a bus, or the underground, or mix with normal people ever again, but I still think I will write good songs when I get all of that. It's a state of mind.'

Ray Davies and The Rolling Stones appeared to have lost their muse. It seems to be about money and a comfortable lifestyle, but that's too simple an explanation. Lou Reed's still got it and Neil Young has too. Gram Parsons came from a wealthy family and he wrote great songs. But the vast majority of people who don't achieve that kind of success give up writing songs once their youth has gone. I didn't see why it couldn't be a form of self-expression that went on throughout one's life, whatever fruits it yields.

'Why do these people lose it?' I asked Lawrence.

'Hey, let's hope we never find out,' he replied. 'People say, how do you write a song? Who knows? Let's leave it like that, floating in the ether, because it's best not to question artistry sometimes. People say that it's god-given, but that's rubbish. There is no god.'

I called up Andrew Loog Oldham to find out why great bands lose it, as his former wards had. 'What is their new album called – *A Smaller Bang*?' he said of The Rolling Stones' *A Bigger Bang*. 'I saw an old friend recently and we were talking about how awful the new Rolling Stones album was. My friend said, "but Andrew, these people don't even have to press the buttons on elevators." And not being able to pay some chick child support is a whole different thing from not *wanting* to pay some chick child support. How can a person catching the tube to get to a nine-to-five job relate to that? With The Rolling Stones it's a case of: can the public relate to the people up there on that stage? Because everyone imagines being up there themselves, and that can only happen if you are still writing for the public, which they stopped doing a long time ago. Paul McCartney is the same. How can he write a good song when he's worrying about whether the fleet of jeeps he has just bought has leather seats or not?'

NJ was in a reasonably amenable mood that evening. She even suggested that we practise 'Until Daylight' using the advice given by Andy Partridge. The only problem was that we had borrowed a friend's cat to deal with the small problem of a mouse running around the kitchen and crapping in the food cupboards, and the cat, rather like our children, appeared to object to my guitar-playing. Every time I started it would push its head against the neck of the guitar. 'Widget!' I snapped. 'I'm not going to stop just because you're trying to irritate me, so you may as well not bother.'

'She's not Otto, Will,' said NJ casually, breaking off a square of chocolate. A few minutes later she ran through the song. I thought she sounded pretty good – a little too dramatic at moments, perhaps, but otherwise, not bad.

'You know, the problem is that I just don't particularly like singing this,' she concluded. 'You have to move on and write something new, or at least learn how to play "Ask Me No Questions" so that I can do that. Bridget St John's songs are easy to sing – they have a natural, easy flow and she seems to have the same range as me – so, if you want me to come to ToeRag Studios with you, I suggest you learn how to play one.'

One evening I was looking through a month-old copy of *Time Out New York* that had been lying around the house and I spotted a preview of a concert with Bridget St John on the bill. It only had one line about her, describing her as a pure-voiced folkie from late-sixties London or something, but it also mentioned that the concert had been organised by an English DJ called Andy Votel. I knew a little about this guy: he was based in Manchester, he ran a small record label, and he appeared to like a lot of the same kind of music as me. I decided to contact him, to see if he could lead me to Bridget St John. He gave me her email and she replied quickly. It turned out that she lived in Greenwich Village, Manhattan, and said that I was welcome to come and talk to her any time that I liked – all I needed to do was get over to New York. I gave her a call and asked her how that gig had gone. 'It was all right,' she said in an American accent, which I wasn't expecting, 'but it was really cold. There aren't many places that are warm in New York in December, and this was a draughty hall. You can't even think, let alone sing, when you're freezing. I was glad when it was over.'

She sounded friendly enough, and the more I thought about it, the more I realised that making that trip to New York was a necessity. Here was an almost-forgotten singer of great talent, whom NJ had connected with, who was accepting the idea of educating me in the art of her craft. But I couldn't justify spending a lot of money to go to New York just to speak to Bridget St John. I had to look into other song-related reasons to make it out there.

New York had a rich songwriting pedigree. It was here that the sons of Jewish eastern European immigrants created the urbane and glitzy but sassy Broadway musical – Stephen Sondheim with *West Side Story*, Kander and Ebb with *Cabaret* – and it was here that a young generation of songwriters put quality into production-line pop in the early sixties. Neil Sedaka, Carole King and Gerry Goffin, who had met at Queens College in Brooklyn, were all employed by the music publisher Don Kirshner to write R&B songs for the white teenage market. The Goffins – Gerry and Carole were married in 1960 – were given a tiny office in the Brill Building on Broadway that had, according to King, 'just enough room for a piano, a bench and maybe a chair for the lyricist – if you were lucky. You'd sit there and write and you could hear someone in the next cubby hole composing some song exactly like yours. The pressure was really terrific.' When their daughter was born, they set up a playpen in the corner of the office and asked a secretary to keep an eye on her.

I first came across the music of the Brill Building era through watching a film called *The Wanderers* when I was fourteen.

Based on a novel by Richard Price, this is the story of an Italian gang in New York that are fighting to survive against their arch rivals, The Baldies; shaven-headed hoodlums with a series of inventive torture routines. A rite of passage portrait of growing up and trying to get laid, the film features that innocent, non-self-conscious teenage music that was wiped away by the sophistication of Dylan and The Beatles. At the end of the film, the lead character comes across a Dylan figure playing in a coffee house that his girlfriend goes to. This coincides with the death of Kennedy, and you know that the old adolescent time of hairspray, milkshakes and going all the way to fourth base has died forever.

It is the songs in the film that symbolise the working-class, Italian/Jewish/Black culture of New York in the very early sixties: 'My Boyfriend's Back' by The Angels, 'Walk Like A Man' by The Four Seasons and 'Stand By Me' by Ben E. King. Phil Spector had a large part to play in the sound of the girl groups of the era, and Goffin and King supplied many with their most sophisticated pop moments.

It was a strange idea that one could write songs to order, but perhaps that helped give Goffin and King's finest songs their unpretentious charm. The songs had to work well and hit the required length, with verses and a chorus and words that people could understand, and, because King had a gift for melody and Goffin could capture real emotions in simple lyrics, the songs became commercial pocket masterpieces.

Over in Detroit a production-line team from the other side of America's racial divide were taking a similar approach. Lamont Dozier and his friends, Eddie and Brian Holland, had been employed by Berry Gordy, the founder of Motown records, to turn up to work on time, clock in, and supply any number of hits for Motown's in-house roster of stars, including The

Supremes, The Four Tops, The Temptations and Marvin Gaye, before it was time for tea. They did what they were told – on $25 a week in 1962, with lunch thrown in for good measure – and gave the American Songbook some of its most joyous and everlasting contributions.

Just before I picked up the guitar for the first time, I met Lamont Dozier in London. He was in town to pick up an Ivor Novello award for his contribution to songwriting. 'The wages were more like a car fare to and from the studio,' said Dozier, an easy-going man with a benign manner, an aversion to exercise, and a fondness for steaks. 'When we got there, we were just pleased to be given a chance to make music, and it's a long way from that to being at the awards last night, where there were over 1,200 people cheering. I'm not so deluded to think that they were cheering me: it was the songs. When we wrote those songs we struck upon a divine intervention and we rode with it. So thank you, Holy Father, for letting me put my name on your music.'

It sounded like the kind of thing American rappers would say at awards ceremonies. But the difference was that Lamont came across as genuinely humble; just another well-meaning, slightly bumbling middle-aged man worrying about his weight who had just happened to have written a bunch of songs that half of the world could sing at least a few lines from, 'Stop! In The Name Of Love', 'I Hear a Symphony', 'Baby Love' and 'You Just Keep Me Hanging On' among them. Who was he to take credit for them?

It turned out that Lamont Dozier had wanted to be a singer himself, but Berry Gordy convinced him to put his own career on hold as he provided material for others to become famous with. Alongside God, he credited his English teacher and his music teacher from downtown Detroit, Mrs Burke and Miss

Smitting, with inspiring his songwriting in the first place. 'When I was eleven years old I started writing poems, and my first was called "A Song", which was about what a song does to a human spirit,' he explained, still looking rather like a little boy. 'Mrs Burke was a very erudite teacher. You had to sit up straight in her class and do what you were told. On the blackboard she kept that poem of mine up for six weeks, and, by making me feel like I had struck upon something so powerful, she gave me the confidence to pursue my goal. Miss Smitting was a German lady who showed me that I could make people feel good one day. So these two elderly white women, who were working in the black housing projects because they cared about people, set me on a quest that continues to this day.'

Talking to Lamont Dozier made me realise how often the great songs happen by accident. 'Heatwave', the biggest hit for Martha Reeves and The Vandellas, was based on a piano exercise that Dozier did as soon as he had punched the clock at the Motown offices. 'This Old Heart of Mine' was written as a warm-up song for Dozier and the Holland brothers to get into synchronicity with; they would play it first thing each morning before getting down to something more serious. Berry Gordy heard it by chance once and asked which band it was for. 'This Old Heart of Mine' was a hit for the Isley Brothers and Rod Stewart went into the Top Ten with it twice.

Then there was 'Where Did Our Love Go?'. Lamont Dozier had written it for the husky voice of Gladys Horton, lead singer of the Marvelettes, but her reaction on hearing the song was to call it 'garbage'. Berry Gordy usually forced his acts to perform the songs he wanted them to do, just as he would force them to attend charm school under the fearsome tutelage of Motown's elocution and comportment teacher Maxine Powell, but The Marvelettes had just had big hits with 'Please Mr Postman' and

'Playboy' and they weren't in the mood for being pushed around. Dozier had already cut the track and company policy decreed that any studio time that did not yield a product had to be paid for. But the song was in the wrong key for everyone but Gladys Horton. Lamont Dozier had no choice but to go to the very bottom of the Motown heap: The Supremes.

The all-girl Supremes had had a series of flops. 'They couldn't give us any lip because they needed a song,' remembered Dozier. 'So they listened to it, and they all started crying because they hated "Where Did Our Love Go?" so much, probably because Gladys Horton had already expressed her feelings about it.'

Reluctantly, The Supremes went into the studio to record the track, grumbling constantly about only ever getting the hand-me-downs that nobody else wanted. At the time Lamont Dozier and the Hollands were furious at their attitude, but only after the track was finished did anyone realise that this bad feeling is exactly what gives the song its magic. 'Diana Ross's bitter delivery was perfect,' said Dozier. 'She was singing in the wrong key and she was pissed off because she hated it, and that gave it a sultry, sad and moving feel. The backing singers hated it, too. That was the first of thirteen consecutive number ones for The Supremes. I knew that there was something there, although I didn't know if it was going to be a hit or not, but something was urging me on to do this song. I certainly wasn't ready to shelve it. Then it went straight to number one and stayed there for a month and a half. Isn't that something? The Supremes went from the bottom to the top.'

At the time of talking to Lamont Dozier, I didn't know that I would soon be trying to write songs myself, but I did ask him where the spark of a great song came from. 'The music speaks to you and it tells you if it's worthy of being finished or not,' he said. 'In a sense the songs write themselves; we're just antennas. A divine situation is taking place when you write songs that touch people and that's why they have lasted for so long and crossed so many boundaries: they're from a spiritual place.'

He paused for a moment to wipe his brow. 'A bigger hand than ours is at work here,' he continued. 'We struck upon a divine intervention and we rode with it, listening to the muses every day until we got into the moment of the song. We would look at each other and all feel the same, and, once you felt something, the key was not to fight with it but say, "Let's see if it likes going this way?". The songs tell you where you should go.'

If I could meet up with a professional New York songwriter as well as Bridget St John, someone who had written at least one of the classics of the American Songbook as a gun for hire, then I could make a trip out there worthwhile. The chance to do so came from an unlikely situation. One night I was at a place called Heavy Load, a rock disco in the basement of a London pub that plays hairy, guitar-based music from the late sixties to the early seventies and attracts the kind of crowd who believe you can never have too much denim in one lifetime. 'Immigrant Song' by Led Zeppelin, 'Crosstown Traffic' by Jimi Hendrix and 'LA Woman' by The Doors sound good when you drink a lot of beer – and if you add a few whiskies to the mix and wait until 3.00 a.m., even 'Freebird' by Lynyrd Skynyrd. I was sitting in a corner of the bar, doing not much more than raising a glass of whisky, when I was introduced to a French woman called Florence. She was having a rare night out, away from the daughter she brought up by herself in south London. She talked about how she had been living in New York ten years earlier, and had been in a bar, pregnant, when she met a charismatic songwriter and they embarked on a love affair.

It turned out to be Chip Taylor, the man who wrote such rock'n'roll staples as 'Wild Thing', 'Angel Of The Morning', 'Any Way That You Want Me' and 'Try (Just A Little Bit Harder)' while employed as a professional songwriter in New York. Florence was no longer romantically involved with Chip, but they remained close, and she promised that she would put me in touch with him. A few days later I got a message from Florence that Chip was still living in New York, and still writing and performing songs all the time, and that, as long as we could go to the diner on the ground floor of his apartment block, he would be happy to meet up for a coffee some time. A new adventure presented itself.

Chapter Seven

New York

When I told Lawrence about my forthcoming trip to New York, he told me to look up a guy called Jake Holmes. Jake Holmes had made two strange albums in the late sixties: *The Above Ground Sound* and *A Letter To Katherine December*. The first consists of songs played on bass and two electric guitars with no drummer, and the second is symphonic, orchestral pop. Both of them bombed. *The Above Ground Sound*, however, had a cover of 'Dazed And Confused' by Led Zeppelin. The only thing was, Jake Holmes's album came out in 1967, two years before Led Zeppelin made their debut.

It turned out that Jake Holmes did indeed write a song called 'Dazed And Confused', and that Jimmy Page took the title, came up with a new set of lyrics, and changed enough of the melody and the arrangement to escape a plagiarism lawsuit. I tracked down Jake Holmes and told him about my plans. He said that he would be pleased to meet me and talk about songwriting, and that I should come to his office on Fifth Avenue. Even if those Led Zeppelin royalty cheques had never arrived, it sounded like things had turned out OK for Jake.

Otto and Pearl came into our room even earlier than usual on the morning I was due to leave, so we sent them downstairs to watch the cartoons on television. My flight wasn't until midday and I calculated that it was safe to stay in bed until nine.

Otto marched into the bedroom twenty minutes later, Pearl dutifully following in his wake. 'The cartoons are over and now the television is boring,' said Otto. 'It's just the news.'

I pressed my face into the pillow, hoping that, if I ignored them for long enough, they might let me sleep for a few minutes more. 'The news said your aeroplane can't fly, Daddy,' Otto added. 'There's too much snow on the wings of your aeroplane in New York.'

I chuckled at my son's endearing flight of the imagination, got dressed and kissed goodbye to the family. It was only on the train to Heathrow that I picked up a newspaper to discover that Otto was right: New York had been hit with the highest snowfall since 1947 and had ground to a halt. The day before there had been no planes coming in or out of JFK airport and flights were in turmoil.

Fate, however, was smiling that day. After twenty-four hours of cancellations, my Air India flight was the first to come through to JFK. It arrived in New York mid-afternoon, and I looked out of the tiny aeroplane windows to see flat slabs of white punctuated by the occasional figure, dressed with pneumatic cold-busting efficiency, padding through the emptiness. I took the subway train that passes through the city's drab suburbs and arrived with guitar and suitcase at the Hotel 17 in Manhattan.

It was a good place for a nascent songwriter to be. Cheap, quiet and in the heart of the downtown Gramercy district, the 17 is a cavernous warren of tiny rooms, all with haphazard decor and layouts. The bathrooms are at the end of the hall and the water pipes clank, wheeze and talk to each other in their own special language. Once fashionable, it was now filled with budget-minded middle-aged German tourists and run by lackadaisical Latin dudes who didn't take chances: you paid in advance for everything, even the telephone. I threw the guitar case down onto the bed and watched it bounce a couple of times. Outside the window the narrow, high-walled garden was thick with snow.

The following afternoon I met Jake Holmes. I padded through the snow, past the cleaners, housewives and business-men who were out on the streets of Gramercy shovelling the sidewalk and cars with public spirit-fuelled efficiency, and made my way up midtown to his office. But it wasn't just an office: it was an entire recording studio complete with ultra-friendly receptionist, gold discs on the walls and an air of smart efficiency. I was reasonably sure that royalties from *The Above Ground Sound* didn't pay for all of this.

'Hey Will, sorry I'm late!' said a cheerful thin man with silver hair and multi-coloured stripy jumper as he marched towards the huge black leather sofa I had sunken into. He seemed like the kind of laid-back middle-aged dude every kid wanted as his or her dad. 'Let's go into my studio so we can get a bit of peace and quiet.' He took me into a room where the Indian rugs on the walls contrasted with the digital sleekness of the recording consoles that filled most of the space, and began his story.

Jake Holmes was tutored in the Greenwich Village folk club scene of the early sixties, where the folk-blues pioneer Dave Van Ronk, the songwriter Tim Hardin and a young Bob Dylan played acoustic guitars at places like the Café Bizarre and the Café Wha?, where the terrible coffee was overpriced and the hat was passed round at the end of the sets.

'I was always a songwriter, even though I knew next to nothing about music,' said Jake, in his loud, fast Manhattan patter. 'The first thing I wrote was a hate song about the kid next door who was always causing trouble. My first gig was with a parody folk group that would sing songs about teenage single mothers in an Elizabethan style. Pete Seeger called us the most tasteless folk act that he had ever seen. Then I played The Night Owl, where Cass Elliot of The Mamas and The Papas was hostess and The Lovin' Spoonful were in the corner. We were all hanging out in this tiny scene, trying to become stars in some way.'

Here was someone who didn't have much of an education in songwriting, but who somehow came up with original material that sold – well, about eight copies. 'When I formed the trio which made *The Above Ground Sound*, everything we did was a case of "let's try it",' said Jake, excitedly. 'I don't know if it was arrogance or an inability to do what others did, but we really didn't follow the usual rules. If you give me instructions, I'm a mess but, if you let me pretend that I'm creating everything myself, I'll be fine. I couldn't walk in a straight line back then.'

'Dazed And Confused' came out of this experimental period. 'A lot of people thought that it was about drugs. It was actually about a girlfriend who was messing with my head,' he said. 'Like most of the songs we did, it came out of us jamming, but with me wanting to have some lyrics that were considered and not just thrown over the top.'

Jimmy Page got to hear 'Dazed And Confused' when Jake did a concert at The Village Theater in New York with The Yardbirds, who Page briefly played guitar for. 'The Yardbirds began to include it in their sets but, at that stage, they gave me credit for it. I guess at some stage Jimmy Page decided he would revamp it and make it his own.'

I asked Jake when he first heard Led Zeppelin's version. 'I don't know, maybe a year after it happened,' he said with a shrug. 'And it was weird, but I honestly didn't care because I was off doing other stuff by then. Besides, Jimmy Page could get away with it because of a Tin Pan Alley law that stated you could have two bars of the exact same melody before you got done for plagiarism. What Jimmy Page took was part of the arrangement and not the top melody. You can copy the bass line because that is just part of the arrangement, but my song was based on the bass line and the guitar line, so, in essence, he could take the *bulk of the song* and not fall foul of the plagiarism rule. But you know what? It was just a blues riff that made up the melody anyway, and I think I got more mileage out of being ripped off in the long run. All the kids in my son's school think I'm a genius because of Led Zeppelin's song.'

I had met musicians who were eaten up with envy because they believed that Paul Simon, or David Bowie, or some such major star had ripped them off, but it's not as if their lives would have turned out markedly different if those people *hadn't* ripped them off. There is a certain amount of destiny to these things and someone like David Bowie was always going to be a star because of the sheer force of his personality, so where he gets his material is, to an extent, unimportant. Nothing comes from nothing. Many of the sixties acoustics copied their melodies from ancient folk songs that were in the public domain. Martin Carthy is still peeved at Paul Simon for taking his arrangement of the English air 'Scarborough Fair', but it's an old tune, without a known author. As Gaz Coombes and Andy Partridge hold told me, everyone copies everyone.

Amazingly, given the fact that neither of Jake Holmes' albums sold much at all, his next gig was to write an album for Frank Sinatra. Jake proudly supplied the blue-eyed one with the biggest flop of his career. Frank Sinatra wasn't built for psychedelia – love beads don't go well with Martinis – but

Sergeant Pepper had changed the world and the old guard didn't want to get left behind. 'It sold maybe fifteen copies,' said Jake. 'Frank's singing had fallen by then, but he was still very respectful of songwriters and great to work with. He would ask me permission to change a lyric that was actually a misprint. He would study the way cabaret singers delivered their material. He wouldn't smile through a sad song, because he understood that at the heart of singing is storytelling.'

That got me thinking about how, given that I couldn't sing myself, I should really be thinking more carefully about the person I was writing songs for. NJ and Mara Carlyle, my singer friend, for example, are very different people. It was an idea not only to consider the voice of the person singing your song, but also their character.

'I certainly wrote specifically for Frank,' said Jake, when I brought this up. 'I had an image of him being an older guy with a younger wife who takes off his wig and faces up to the reality of his situation. I kept thinking: wouldn't it be interesting if he played to his real character and played to his age? I imagined him leaving his family for a much younger woman, and then, when that doesn't work out, he goes back to them . . .' Jake pondered upon his great dream for Sinatra in silence for a few seconds, before shouting: 'What the hell was I thinking? Frank Sinatra's not going to take off his wig! It would have fucked his career forever!'

Jake Holmes' career took an interesting turn after the Sinatra debacle. Having made his stab at pop success and proved that he didn't fit in, and knowing he wasn't going to be the next Bob Dylan or even the next Billy Joel, he became a jingle writer. And about five seconds of music, which became known throughout the world and played on advertisements for the better part of a decade, made him very rich indeed. Anyone who was around in the eighties and nineties will know how the slightly hysterical, punching-the-air tune to 'Gillette: the best a man can get' goes. Those seven words and handful of notes helped pay for the studio on Fifth Avenue we were currently sitting in.

'I did very well out of that one,' he confirmed.

For whatever reason, Jake Holmes has an inability to write hit singles and an uncanny knack for coming up with jingles that are unforgettable. 'It's fun,' he said. 'You have a problem to solve. You get a line, a demographic of the people the advertisement is going out to and maybe a certain style the advertising company wants you to write in. Then you have to write a careful, concise lyric and the whole thing is a puzzle. You get to work with the best musicians in the city, and, if I write something that is too far out, an arranger will make it palatable, but it will still have that twist that makes it memorable. I can do all these jingles because I have an innate sense of melody.'

I asked Jake where his melodies came from. 'You get a groove going, you flux, and something comes out of that. I'm not one of those people who walk down the street and have a song pop into their heads in its entirety; I have to sit down and do it. Even talking about it makes me nervous, and I'm afraid I couldn't teach you how to do it because I don't really know myself. A French intellectual interviewed Fellini once. He said, "You know the scene in your film where the girl comes down the stairs in a black dress? It's a symbol of your mother." And Fellini said, "It is? How interesting." That's how I feel with music. People analyse it and tell you why it works and then you say to yourself, "I did that? So how do I do it again?" '

He suggested I try an approach that Paul Simon uses. 'It's real deep. He will sing dummy words over a track until some

kind of musical sense emerges, and this way the words themselves are as musical as they can be. He's cutting up a fuzzy
thing and he puts it more and more into focus. Alternatively,
why not try and write with computers?'

'I'm hopeless with technology,' I replied. 'I've only just got
the hang of text messaging.'

'Then you might want to collaborate,' he said. 'Find someone
who sings and who you get along with. I did 80 per cent of a
musical but the guy who sang it, who did that remaining 20 per
cent, was invaluable. Play the song on guitar and get someone
to sing the melody as best they can, because they act as the
instrument you play the song on and they help you discover if
the phrasing and the pitching works. It's like the woman who
says, "Why should that bastard get any credit for the baby? He
fucked me and left me and I had to carry it around and do all the
work for the last nine months." True, but try taking the guy out
of the equation.'

Talking to Jake Holmes was a massive education, through his
example as much as what he said. He was a cool guy, living in a
cool city, enjoying his life and his work. And, despite churning
out product that many serious singer-songwriters would turn
up their noses at, his commercial approach freed him up to write
for his own sake. Alongside making huge amounts of money
through commercials, he did poetry slams at the Nuyorican
Poets Society, a black and Hispanic urban phenomenon that
gave young men and women a chance to find an audience for
their lyrical dexterity. He was determined to win one of the
slams, although he had been told time and again that there was
absolutely no way an old white guy in a multi-coloured jumper
was ever going to get anywhere. I asked him why he kept on
writing songs at all.

'Yeah, that's a good question,' he said, leaning back in his chair. 'I write to experiment, I write to fool around, I write to entertain my kids, I do silly things off the cuff and then think, "Shit, that was good. I should have written that down." I've got enough money to not work another day in my life. So what am I in it for? Do I want to be rich? Not really. I definitely don't want to be famous. And, man, I'm just as fallible as anyone else. I wrote "boredom creeps in on vanilla feet" for my song "The Elusive Butterfly Of Love" – I got raked over the coals for that one and with good reason. I guess I just enjoy it.'

It was late afternoon and the snow had turned to dirty wells of slush at every street corner. I had a bit of time to soak in the city before meeting Bridget St John that evening. When I was growing up, New York was painted as a place of glamour and danger, where teenage gangs with denim jackets and flick-knives circled you on the subway and arty types lived among the winos of the Lower East Side. There was the fabulous wealth of the Upper East Side too, of course, but what stuck in your mind was the image of Travis Bickle walking the melting streets in *Taxi Driver* to the sound of Bernard Hermann's orchestrations; or Fred Neil's 'Everybody's Talkin' ', sung by Harry Nilsson, as Jon Voight (Chip Taylor's brother, incidentally) struts through the city with increasing desperation in *Midnight Cowboy*; or The Velvet Underground living in filthy warehouses, being rude to everyone and making records that nobody would hear for another twenty years. Then there were The Ramones, surly and silent, leaning against a wall in the Bowery and playing to 100 people at CBGB, the tiny, graffiti-covered club that became the home of punk.

Manhattan wasn't like that any more. Now you can walk around Avenue D at four in the morning – a no-go area ten years previously – and get a decent cappuccino while you're at it. The smoking ban, theoretically a good thing, had made the bars, clubs and music venues seem like film sets. I walked over to the Bowery to see what was left of the old New York. CBGB was soon to close after thirty-three years, allegedly because the derelicts staying in the flophouse upstairs were complaining about the noise. A nearby side street had been renamed Joey Ramone Place, which was nice, but now that all of The Ramones, bar drummer Tommy, were dead, the street name seemed like a memorial not only to a lead singer but to an era.

The best songs of The Ramones are like the finest Tom and Jerry cartoons: brilliant in their dumb inventiveness and with a wit that is entirely natural. I first heard The Ramones through my brother, who bought their double album *It's Alive* when he was fourteen and I was twelve. It transfixed me. They looked great: like skeletons with bowl cuts. The songs were typically only a minute long and all that separated them was a frantic '1234' from bassist Dee Dee, but they were deceptively clever. In 'We're A Happy Family', Joey Ramone paints a comically grim picture of his dysfunctional family life in Queens: 'We're friends with the president, we're friends with the pope, we're all getting rich, selling Daddy's dope'. Joey goes on to list his grievances before concluding with his ultimate horror: 'Daddy likes men'.

The Ramones were a product of a reality that had gone, but there were other New York songwriters who reflected wider experiences. At the top of the heap is Carole King. Her 1971 album *Tapestry* is one of those albums we always saw in friends' parents' record collections, with the front cover of the hippyish woman sat next to a cat on a wooden bench by a window – a reassuring image. It was years later that I discovered she was the author of the classics from the golden age of girl groups. Pop music in 1960 was still pretty innocent in terms of sexual awakening, so the visceral honesty and uncertain sexuality of

Carole King and Gerry Goffin's 'Will You Still Love Me Tomorrow', as sung by The Shirelles, was heady for its time:

> Tonight you're mine completely
> You give your love so sweetly
> Tonight the light of love is in your eyes
> But will you love me tomorrow?

After a pilgrimage to the soon-to-be defunct CBGB and a stroll up and down Broadway in homage to the Brill Building songwriting greats, it was time to meet Bridget St John. Bridget may well be one of the last remaining links to the old Greenwich Village singer-songwriter scene. She lived on Bleecker Street, next to MacDougal; once the very heart of the folkie beatnik coffee-house world that Dylan emerged from. Now the average Greenwich Village dwellers are wealthy, famous people, like Gwyneth Paltrow and her right-on boyfriend Chris Martin of Coldplay, but Bridget was still paying the same rent for her tiny fifth-floor apartment that she had paid when she first moved there thirty years earlier. She had a job working with elderly people, did the occasional gig, and wrote songs on her guitar when she had the time.

I walked up the many flights of stairs to meet a well-preserved, curly-haired woman in her late fifties. The flat had a chaotic, ramshackle charm: the kitchen turned into the living room, the windows didn't look like they had been opened since Bridget paid her first rent cheque, and there were all kinds of rusting tins and chipped pots filling the rough wood shelves above the small formica table. Everything was slightly wonky, just as a bohemian Village apartment should be. Bridget put the kettle on – proper English tea, not the discoloured water that Americans drink – and promised to do what she could to help me with my goal. When she spoke, she had a habit of looking at you then downwards. It was almost coquettish.

I caught her at a strange moment in her career. The four charming albums that she had made in the late sixties and early seventies sold little, and she had given up music as a full-time job when she moved to New York. But a new generation was discovering her, just as a generation of white kids in the sixties had discovered the country blues musicians of the thirties and forties, who, by then, were working as farmers or cooks. She was pleased for the attention if a little bemused. 'It's nice that people are interested, yet you cannot help but think: that was then and this is now and why would anyone want to hear what I did thirty years ago?'

Bridget St John grew up in East Sheen, a London suburb a short bicycle ride away from Richmond, the place of my own childhood. She was a quiet child of middle-class parents and had no idea about rock'n'roll or the Swinging Sixties, but she did know that the piano and violin lessons weren't doing it for her.

'My violin teacher was sympathetic to my situation,' said Bridget, with a slightly embarrassed smile. 'I was holding the violin like a guitar and she said to me: "you're not really cut out for this, are you?" '

Being shy and never keeping a diary, she expressed herself in childhood by writing poetry. It made sense to put these poems to music once she did get a guitar, aged eighteen. 'Soon I was following the process of writing songs that I still keep to now, which is to hear something in a chord that suggests certain words. I can't read music for the guitar and I don't know what notes I'm playing, because I don't play chords in the usual way. All I need to know is: if you put *this* shape on the guitar then *this* is the sound it makes.'

Bridget St John's songs really don't sound like anyone else's, but, in forging her own style, the key was meeting the Scottish guitarist and singer John Martyn, who introduced her to the world of unusual tunings. As part of her French degree at Sheffield University, she was meant to study for a year in France, yet, being too nervous to actually turn up to register, it ended up being three months in Aix en Provence in the south of France, where she met two American girls and hung out with them. One knew John Martyn and, when they hitched back to London together, they introduced Bridget to him. John taught her that, with guitar tunings like DADGAD – invented by the pioneering acoustic player Davy Graham as a way of transposing the sounds of the oud onto the guitar – you could make an interesting sound simply by strumming the thing. Bridget invented her own finger-picking patterns and chords and a new style was born.

Bridget would most probably have been happy writing and singing her songs for her friends – or maybe just for the walls of her bedroom – had it not been for John Peel. In the late sixties the British DJ was looking for new acts for his *Night Ride* BBC radio programme, and a friend played him a tape of songs that Bridget had recorded at the singer Al Stewart's house. Peel played the songs, introduced Bridget to his listeners as his favourite female singer-songwriter, and suggested to her that she collect them together for an album. He was planning to start a new record label with a new agenda: to not rip off the artist. (It had another, unexpected agenda: to not sell any records.) So Bridget's debut album, 1969's *Ask Me No Questions*, was the historic first release on Dandelion. Peel took Bridget out on a national tour of student discos, and her only live performances before then had been in the 'quiet room' of the student halls of her university – the place where everyone went to get stoned. 'It was a good way of dealing with anything; you know, if people aren't listening don't expect any feedback,' she said. 'But it certainly wasn't anything professional. The only way I could get up the confidence to do the discos tour is because I trusted John.'

I asked her if she was ever part of a scene. 'I should say I definitely was not,' she replied firmly, although I imagined that, with her flowing dresses and gap-toothed smile, she was the kind of girl that people wanted on their scene. 'The only reason I played Cousins [a legendary sixties Soho folk club] was because John Martyn took me there, although I do remember Davy Graham, who I shared a bill with once. It was really sad. He was completely messed up and seemed to be calling out from the stage for his girlfriend, who he had long since split up with.'

Perhaps because she never really established a strong identity or following, Bridget got a trial by fire from the bands she ended up sharing a stage with. She was booked as the support to the heavy blues-rock trio The Groundhogs, who had recently had a hit single and had built up a following with the heavier side of the hippy movement. 'That was terrible,' she recalled. 'From the moment I walked on stage it was bedlam and everyone was screaming and shouting for The Groundhogs. At the time I took it personally, but I've since learned that it had nothing to do with me; those people had paid money to see someone else and they were impatient. I'm thin-skinned, though. I can still remember when Nick Drake and I supported Fairport Convention and a reviewer wrote: "I don't know why the promoter even bothered to book the opening acts." We were devastated, but since you have no control over what anyone writes about you, I would suggest that it's best not to even read reviews, positive or negative. It's all just gravy on top of what you do and it doesn't help creatively.'

We moved on to my songwriting lesson. She told me not to

worry about too much theory; in his later life Beethoven never heard a single note that he wrote. Then she said that one's technique or playing style really didn't matter as long as you could convey the feeling that you wanted to express.

'I'm sure I play my own songs differently all the time,' she said. 'Making mistakes is fine, because out of that evolves something, so a good way to write your own material is to fiddle around with the guitar and try to play a song that you like from ear, because it will come out differently.'

Her second piece of advice was to find a strong melody. 'You might find it easier, in the early stages at least, to create a melody on the guitar that the singer can then follow,' she said. 'All of my songs are based on a melody and I find it grating when I hear songs that are based on a few chords but without any clearly defined tune. One way to do it is to play a set of chords again and again until something suggests itself to you.'

I wasn't leaving until Bridget taught me to play 'Ask Me No Questions', the starkly beautiful song in which the singer offers a fleeting, secret romance with no strings attached – and as the title suggests, no questions asked. I had listened to this song dozens of times at home and never got any closer to working out what she was doing. It turned out that it is in a strange tuning – D, A, D, F#, A, D – and it is played with a capo on the second fret.

It took me ages to work it out. She was patient. The first five seconds of music took me about half an hour to get right because the finger-picking pattern was so unusual . . . unusual but actually simple, making 'Ask Me No Questions' an easy song to play – once you know how.

What I had mostly been doing so far was writing fragments of songs. I would come up with a little idea, or a set of lyrics, but the songs were never really completed – 'Bad Part Of Town' was

still lacking a definite arrangement. 'Ask Me No Questions'
created an atmosphere and the gentle, seductive music suited
the words perfectly, and, as such, it was a complete entity.

'But I think *entirely* in fragments,' she claimed. 'An awful lot
of things come to you in a fragmentary way unless you can
maintain that stream. What usually happens is that an idea will
come to me on the subway and, by the time I've reached the
turnstile, I've forgotten half of it. The songwriting process is a
way of disciplining those fragmentary thoughts and making
them whole. I can't remember the circumstances of writing
"Ask Me No Questions", but I can guess: I would have been
fiddling around with chords in the tuning, putting my fingers
on different places to find out which sounds worked and which
didn't. I have no idea what the chords or the patterns of notes
are; I just know when the sounds have the right spirit.'

After two solid hours of practising 'Ask Me No Questions', I
still didn't really have it, but I could see where my fingers were
meant to go now, so it wouldn't be hard to practise along to the
record when I got home until I nailed it. NJ would be pleased,
which would help maintain peace upon my return. Under no
illusions about the quality of my own singing, I needed NJ on
my side if I were to make the dream of recording a single a
reality.

'The most important thing for you to do, if you really want to
write a song, is to give yourself *time* with the guitar,' said
Bridget. 'That's how everything comes about: by experimenting
and being free. If you're always trying to learn something new,
or if you only pick up the guitar every now and then so you have
to re-learn what went before, you won't be able to do it.'

Bridget's output had been minimal since the golden years of
the early seventies. This was explained by the same reason that
everyone stops playing guitar or singing all the time: adult life

takes over. When she had her daughter, Christie, and raised her as a single mother, she knew that she didn't want to be touring all the time and only seeing her occasionally. So she opted for the more stable situation of pulling in a wage.

'I am still interested in writing songs,' she said. 'When I was in England, making music was all I did. That's not possible now, but I'll always make music for the sake of it because it takes the anaesthetic element out of life. And, if you really concentrate, who knows what might come out of you? Listen, nobody made you learn to play guitar, but you did and you took to it. Nobody is making you write songs, but you're doing it anyway.'

By the end of the evening – and if I outstayed my welcome, Bridget was too polite to say so – I understood how Bridget St John's clever songs were made, and it didn't seem so hard after all. I also admired the way she had carved out a good life for herself, and showed few regrets that her remarkable talent was known by so few.

'All I can say is: you have to think about the work and not the outcome,' she said before I left to go back to the hotel. 'Nick Drake was struggling to make ends meet and that lack of recognition was painful for him, so you have to remember that it's about the work, otherwise it might destroy you.'

She smiled and opened the door. 'Maybe you don't always get the recognition that you hoped for,' she said, as I stood on the landing outside her apartment. 'But, unless you're completely bound up in your public image, you're always moving forward, and you don't repeat yourself, and you let the past go. It's different if you're part of a big publicity machine that is controlling every part of your image, but I don't have that problem and I'm far too private a person to want that kind of life. And whatever your level of success, you will have written

songs that mean something to someone. That should be enough.'

My third New York person was a very different kettle of fish.
Chip Taylor was twenty-one when he wrote 'Wild Thing' in
five minutes in 1965. 'Wild thing, you make my heart sing,
you make everything . . . groovy . . . Wild Thing . . .' and
then, after all of this chest-beating, there's a funny little solo
in the middle in which the troglodyte skips daintily around
his cave for a bit before going back to his Neanderthal stomp.
It has been the standard for every neophyte rock'n'roll band
ever since.

Chip Taylor was blessed with finding a group that seemed
proud of the fact that they could barely play. The Troggs had
the right name, the right look, and the right accents (West
Country British). They revelled in their lack of musical graces
and brought an earthy leer, like the village stud wiping the
sweat from his brow before he sends another milk maiden up
the family way in the cowshed, to an already suggestive song.

There were plenty of late fifties and early sixties rock'n'roll
songs that celebrated youth and rebellion, but it was the
American garage bands of mid-sixties America that got being
an outcast down to a T. Downtrodden but defiant, self-pitying
but boastful, the average garage track was like the class nerd:
smugly superior in the fact that everyone hates them and they're
bad at football. 'You're Gonna Miss Me' by The Thirteenth
Floor Elevators is a case in point: the girl has left singer Roky
Erickson, and he's the one supposedly suffering, but, according
to him, it's her loss. It's also damn hard to write a great garage
track like, say, 'Yeah' by The Alarm Clocks. It may sound
sloppy, amateurish and dumb – OK, it *is* sloppy, amateurish
and dumb – but try recreating that sound and that feeling.

'Wild Thing' is the ultimate garage song, even if its most famous version is by an English band.

I had a few hours to kill before I met Chip Taylor, so I decided to check out Tin Pan Alley, the home of music publishing before rock'n'roll changed the rules. Back then you really did have to know what you were doing. Starting off around 27th Street in the early twentieth century and moving up to the 40s and low 50s of Manhattan by the 1930s, Tin Pan Alley was nothing to see even in its heyday; just a collection of offices that were located near the theatres they sold sheet music to. Now there was little of note on 27th Street beyond a few Chelsea coffee bars and delis, but I looked up at the little windows above the shops and restaurants and tried to imagine Cole Porter, Hoagy Carmichael and George Gershwin in their white shirts and braces, cigarette in hand, dotting the notes onto sheet music paper, and thought of how democratised the whole process of songwriting had become in the years since.

In those days the songwriter had a job that was protected economically, through the American Society of Composers, Authors and Publishers (ASCAP), and professionally, through the fact that it required a lot of training, education, and hard graft. Cole Porter did not write by feeling, as Bridget St John did, or by exercising his eccentricities, as Jake Holmes did, but through the kind of reworking and adherence to structure that is now associated with scriptwriting or scoring classical music. Vocalists of the forties, like Bing Crosby, Perry Como, Billie Holiday and Frank Sinatra, rarely wrote their own material: that was somebody else's job. Songwriting was as much of a profession as dentistry and law.

Rock'n'roll changed all that, effectively killing off Tin Pan Alley and bringing about the most significant event in the history of twentieth-century music: the introduction of blues, or at least blues-influenced music, to a white audience. At a time when the Tin Pan Alley singers were writing from a highly trained perspective, itinerant black guitarists and singers in the South were taking the gospel and folk songs they had grown up with and turning them into the blues, getting a point across with repeated lyrics and simple melodies. The result was a style of music that was direct and innate – everything that the ballads and show tunes of Tin Pan Alley were not.

A case in point is the Reverend Gary Davis, a wonderful blues and ragtime guitarist who left his native South Carolina in 1940 to make a living as street-corner preacher and guitarist in Harlem. He was the author of the classic 'Cocaine Blues', and, in the sixties, a New York publishing company wanted to buy the rights for the song, which would make the Reverend a lot of money. He was duly called into the offices of the publishing company, whose employees were congratulating themselves on tracking down the man who wrote this much-covered classic. The New York protest singer Dave Van Ronk, who had brought the Reverend to the publishing company, asked him to confirm that he did indeed write it.

'I did not write that song!' said the Reverend, dramatically. And then, after gasps from everyone else in the room, he announced: 'It came to me in a dream.'

A direct style of white music was coming from the South during the forties, too: hillbilly music, later known as country and western. The combination of blues with country gave birth to rock'n'roll, and rock'n'roll began the process that meant anyone with a couple of chords and a handful of words could write a song. That is where Chip Taylor comes in. 'Wild Thing' would always be so much more of a songwriting inspiration for me than 'Lady, Be Good' or 'I've Got You Under My Skin' because, as wonderful as those songs by George Gershwin and Cole Porter are, I couldn't ever possibly hope to emulate them. 'Wild Thing', on the other hand, only has three chords. Even I could cope with that.

I arrived at the large, brightly lit and busy corner café below Chip Taylor's flat, ordered a coffee, and sat down at a formica table for about five minutes before a grey-haired man with glasses and a resigned manner appeared and introduced himself as Chip Taylor. He sat down opposite and ordered a large breakfast with specific instructions – I remember him impressing upon the waitress the importance of his bacon being cooked not merely well done, but burned to a crisp. Then he leaned over the table, looked me in the eye, and told me the story of his life at a slow, steady pace.

Chip, who was born and raised in New York, knew early on that he wanted to make his career in one of two things: as a musician or, failing that, as a professional golfer. He had record deals with the labels Kim and Warner Brothers in his late teens, but he didn't have a hit with either. Then Chet Atkins, the country guitarist and the head of RCA Victor in Nashville in the early sixties, got to hear some of his songs. That led to a staff job with a New York-based company called Blackwood Publishing – Chip originally wanted to be a star, but being a backroom boy penning songs still meant that he would make a living from his first choice of career.

A record executive asked Chip to come up with material for a new rock'n'roll band called Jordan Christopher and The Wild Ones. 'The morning after I got the call, I started fooling around with a little strum in my own limited way of playing,' he said. '"Wild Thing" came out in a matter of minutes. I had to do a country session that afternoon and we didn't have portable tape recorders to save our ideas back then, so I went over it again and again until it was imprinted on my memory.'

Chip returned to the studio after recording the country session and laid down a take of 'Wild Thing'. 'I decided to just go into the studio and record whatever came naturally without thinking about it,' he continued. 'And I think that is the magic of "Wild Thing". The pauses and the hesitations, which were all a result of not knowing what I was doing to do next and trying to hedge my time, are what give the song its character.'

I told Chip that the music matches the message of what the guy singing the song wants, which is primitive. 'And his playing is primitive, too,' he said. 'Because that's the way I play.'

'Wild Thing' must have driven the surviving Tin Pan Alley songwriters crazy. With all their wit and sophistication and musical knowledge and erudition, a three-chord song comes along and dates everything that has gone before through its sheer thuggish audacity. 'I loved songs that followed the classic lines, and I wasn't trying to break any rules,' he said. 'But I have also never cared about making things fit into past formulas. If I wanted a silence in a place that you wouldn't expect it, I would put it in.' The demo that Chip Taylor recorded that morning in the studio is the same song as the finished version by The Troggs that became a hit all over the world.

The following year Chip Taylor wrote 'Angel Of The Morning', which was a hit for Merrilee Rush and P.P. Arnold. It's a tender-hearted ballad from the perspective of a woman walking away from a one-night stand or an affair to tell her lover that she won't cause any trouble for him now that he's had his way. It could be construed as the kind of self-effacing submission feminism was designed to battle against, or as a proto-liberationist message about a woman being able to make her own choices, but its prettiness and sweet charm is undeniable. It sounds sophisticated.

'It's just "Wild Thing" slowed down,' said Chip, crunching into his burnt bacon. 'With a few interludes added.'

'I can't believe it,' I replied. 'What about all those strings?'

'The producer does all that shit,' he said with a sigh. 'Believe it or not, that's what it is. The magic comes when the brain is not engaged. So, after twenty minutes of playing that sloweddown "Wild Thing" riff, I added a little note that sounded real nice to me – I took a finger away from the E chord and thereby created a suspension. Then the first line came out: "There'll be no strings to bind your hands, not if my love can't bind your heart", and I didn't know what that meant; all I knew was that I had a monster chill. "There's no need to take a stand because it was I that chose to start." Those words were just blown out. All of a sudden I was this woman. That song didn't take more than fifteen minutes to write.'

I said to Chip that 'Louie Louie' by The Kingsmen and 'Wild Thing' by The Troggs were the singles that kick-started the garage band revolution. 'Yeah, it seems that way,' he said with a nod. 'I'm pleased about that, because I like things that are inspired, not crafted, and "Wild Thing" was certainly inspired: simple, organic, and with a certain dumbness and unpretentiousness.' In Chip's original version, the recording engineer made a whistling sound through his hands for the instrumental in the middle of the song. When Reg Presley of The Troggs heard it, he thought an ocarina, an oval-bodied children's wind instrument, made that sound. 'He's been carrying that damn ocarina around with him ever since,' said Chip, and drank his coffee.

The song changed Chip's life. It was blasting out of radio stations and garages all over America. It made him rich. He was free to pursue his interest in writing southern-flavoured, R&B-based songs, but, as the years passed, so the battles with rigid-minded record companies increased. By the mid-seventies, he was back to being a country singer-songwriter with a deal with Capitol records, which operated out of Nashville, but the company wanted him to record in their studios and use their session musicians and he preferred living in New York. So, in 1980, he decided to spend the advance for a new album on gambling. That was the end of his music career for the next fifteen years.

'I worked really hard at being a horse-race handicapper,' he said, a shine in his eyes revealing a love for the bet that hadn't died. 'I had an analytical approach to upcoming races and I never picked up a racing form and looked at it without knowing exactly what was behind the stats. I had four or five data books by me all the time. I teamed up with a legendary horse-race player called Ernie Dahlman. We became very good friends and worked hard at what we did, and, from the mid-eighties to 1996, I did that every day and made a lot of money. I was also a card counter at blackjack, but the casinos in Atlantic City banned me. Then, when the courts said that they couldn't ban the card counters any more, they would make my life very difficult. They would sit a pretty girl next to me and find out what I liked to drink. They would give me glasses full of Rémy Martin, one after the other. Then they would follow me around and, as soon as they saw me make the big bet, they would shuffle the cards. It got to be pretty disarming, so I thought, nah, I'll stay with horses.'

Chip had a change of heart in the mid-nineties that turned him into what he is today: a singer-songwriter in the alternative country tradition. His mother was seriously ill, he had been listening to music again, and the calluses on his fingers had long softened up. So he told Ernie Dahlman that he wasn't going to gamble any more, and resolved to do what he had set out to do as a kid but had never achieved: be a performer of his own material. A record deal was promised and it fell through at the last minute. Depressed and despondent, he hit the cognacs at a New York nightclub called Pravda. That's where he met Florence.

'I walked in and I was so depressed, and Florence was really nice, and I had a strong feeling for her, even though we could hardly communicate because she didn't speak English. So she asked me what I did for a living and I said: "I'm a songwriter." I didn't want to lie to her, so I thought: "OK, I'm back. That's what I'm going to do." Pretty soon after I had a record deal.'

Women, from the sound of it, have been the guiding light for Chip's life and his songs. He recalled being twelve and seeing a girl near a swimming pool about fifty feet away. He told the friend he was with that he was going to marry that girl and he did. 'We're divorced now, but I don't know how that happened,' he said, shaking his head. 'She's my heart and will always be the most important person in my world.' In 1999 Chip was performing at the Austin, Texas, music festival South By Southwest when a fiddle-playing young local woman called Carrie Rodriguez came to see his show. 'I had instant feelings for her,' said Chip. 'Pretty much when I got up on stage she was the focus of who I was singing to. So, the next day I asked her to sing for me, even though she had never been on a stage before. That's the story of my life: something from nothing. It's always been that way, from meeting my wife to writing "Wild Thing" to doing what I do now.'

'So all of this is leading, I'm afraid, to my writing a song of my own,' I told him. 'What advice would you give me?'

He shook his head a little. 'That's a hard one. I'll give you an example. A friend of mine made me listen to his song and give a critique of it. It was a song about a flower, and every little part of the flower related to the girl he loves. It was real clever and thought-out. At the end he said, "what do you think?" I said: "you know, I don't like to think that hard. If I wrote a song about a flower and a girl, it would be a lot simpler because I don't want to prepare my brain as a listener or a writer." The next day I wrote a song called "Red, Red Rose". It went: "I'd like to buy you a red, red rose, a red rose, a pretty red rose. I'd like to buy you underwear, underwear for under there" and so on. I guess my advice is: don't worry too much about being clever. Just do what comes naturally.'

Chip stopped his story to eat his extremely burned bacon and flick through a newspaper – and I couldn't help but notice that the page was turned to the racing results. So here was a guy who had an eye for the women, and hung out in bars, and liked to throw down a few notes on the horses, and followed his heart, not his intellect. He was cool-headed and quick-witted – useful skills, I would imagine, for both gambling and songwriting. Although I wouldn't necessarily want it for myself, the life that Chip Taylor lived was as inspiring as the life he sang about in his songs. It was hard to tell where one stopped and the other began.

Chapter Eight

Finding Your Voice

By a twist of fate I found myself going back to New York two weeks after I returned to London. I was commissioned to go out there to interview Chan Marshall, the Atlanta-born singer who performed under the name of Cat Power. And, as it happened, Marshall was inadvertently to teach me a lot about the importance of finding one's own voice – an important lesson if I was to get anywhere with Doyle on our proposed songwriting trip to Eigg – and would illustrate how vital the song, as an outlet for expression, can be.

I had met Chan Marshall a couple of years earlier. She had impressed me with her charisma, her beautiful songs, and the fact that she appeared to know almost nothing whatsoever about playing guitar, piano or singing, all of which she somehow did very well indeed. At that meeting she stayed under the covers of the bed in her London hotel, chain-smoking Marlboros and reeling off a litany of disasters that had befallen her through her short life.

Then, in late 2005, she recorded an album called *The Greatest* with a group of top Memphis session musicians. *The Greatest* had the rich musicality of southern soul but the understated delicacy of Chan's previous records. On the title track she sings, 'Once I wanted to be the greatest' before concluding that with age comes the acceptance of not having to be so great after all. 'Willie', my favourite song, appeared to be some kind of celebration of a good and honest romance. It was songwriting in which the singer was sharing through her voice, her words and the music that accompanied them, her very being with the world.

The great thing about these commissions is that they give you a rare glimpse into a side of life not normally available. I stayed in The Rivington, an expensive hotel in the Lower East Side – surely the ultimate sign of the gentrification of this former slum neighbourhood – that was so new, modern and fashionable that you just had to look at your room door in a meaningful way and it would glide open. In my minimalist room, two walls were made entirely of glass and gave a panorama of Manhattan. The black-clad bellboy proudly showed me all the high-tech gadgets the hotel had to offer, including a bathroom where water poured out from a hole in the ceiling and a variety of taps that controlled warm jets shooting out from all four corners of the bathroom. Unfortunately, this system was too sophisticated even for him – he got sprayed on the leg by a rude wall-jet as he tried to turn on the overhead shower.

Chan Marshall was staying at another expensive hotel about ten minutes' walk away: The Mercer, a favourite of the international rich and stylish. The slightly scary German fashion designer Karl Lagerfeld, who for some reason is never seen without sunglasses and a shirt that looks like a surgical neck brace, had come up to her the day before and told Chan how much he loved her music, and she had told him how much she loved his clothes, and they both loved everything, and hoped to get something for free out of all this loving – concert tickets for him, clothes for her. I arrived on time and waited for about an hour for her to come down from her room. Finally she arrived, in dark glasses – perhaps Karl had given them to her – looking very thin indeed. 'I'm sober,' she announced by way of introduction, and I told her that I should think so too at 10.30 on a Tuesday morning. She meant that she had stopped drinking entirely. It transpired her record company had cancelled an entire world tour because she had become close to suicide with despair and exhaustion. Now the new tour *had* to be a success. Her career – her life – was depending on it.

She was edgy and highly-strung. She fussed over the tea that was brought to her (Was the water freshly boiled? What kind of tea was it?), before breaking into an imitation of my accent when I ordered a coffee. 'Oh Gawsh, black coffay? Bloody hell and bollocks.' There was something unnerving about her nervous energy and I could think of no witty response to her ribbing.

A lot of musicians boast about how little they know to boost their credentials as a primitive, untaught genius, but Chan Marshall really did have such limited understanding of how music is structured that it was a feat on her part to *not* know more than she did after well over a decade in the business. 'I only found out last week that what I thought was E minor on the guitar is actually an A chord,' she said. 'It took me eighteen years to discover that.' But she had gone into the studio with this handful of ultra-tight session musicians, and they had followed her lead and worked out how to play her songs. 'I don't know chords, I don't know notes, I don't know anything,' she claimed. 'So it was a little intimidating to go and play my songs in front of these guys – I mean, I get nervous playing in front of my grandmother. But I forced myself to do it, and they sat around with their pencils and paper and jotted down what I played in their own language.'

I asked Chan what her song 'Willie' was about. 'Oh, "Willie"
is a piece of cake,' she said, shaking her pot of tea and making a
little rattle with the dainty silver spoon that stuck out of the top
of it. 'I was in Florida visiting my grandmother. I had just
played a show and I was getting a cab to my grandmother's
house. The cab driver is a black guy, about sixty-five, and he has
his sunglasses on. I try and make conversation, but he won't talk
to me so I back down. Finally he says, "I've got to take five
dollars to my friend." He pulls down this gravel road and this
white lady walks around, really cute, aged about forty-six. She is
barefooted and so pretty, older but really pretty, and that's the
first time I see him smile. He gives her a hug and five dollars,
and she says "Call me when you get back". He's smiling when
he's back in the cab and I know he's thinking about her. I keep
my mouth shut. Then I say, "Are you married?" "No Ma'am."
"How come?" "I guess I never found anybody I want to spend
my life with." "That's a good reason." "Yes Ma'am." Then I say
to him, "Maybe you should ask that lady." And he turns round
to look at me for the first time. Then he says, "I just bought the
ring. I'm going to ask her next week."'

'Why do you write songs at all?'

'There is an inevitability that I would have been dead a long
time ago if I hadn't done something, whether it was playing
guitar or painting a picture or writing a sentence on the
typewriter over and over. I needed to make some sense of life
and push reality away – or learn how to engage with it.'

Obsessions with Keith Richards and Bob Dylan meant that
becoming a songwriter was the best option. 'It's a hunger that
has been fed,' she continued, stirring her tea with tick-like
precision.

'What's the reward?'

She put her hand on my knee and looked at me with mascara-clad eyes filled with need and a strange kind of pride. 'Self-respect. It gives you a bearing. And the key is to keep doing whatever gives you your bearing, whether that's folding Victorian napkins and putting them in a drawer or jogging every day or writing songs. I have a feeling and a memory and the song comes from that. It's like a closed bud, or an embryo of a wish, and hope and forgiveness enter into it, too. Whatever all those words make up, that's what it is.'

My problem was that the songs I loved were so much better than anything I was coming up with. Chan Marshall's 'Willie' was impossible to emulate because she had found a way of throwing her personality and her experiences into a beautifully crafted moment. Bobbie Gentry's 'Ode To Billie Joe' captures an entire melodrama, complete with suspense and mystery, indifference and tragedy, within its lilting two-chord frame. How did The Beatles express such simple sentiments with ease and sophistication, and why did the Motown songs of Holland–Dozier–Holland cut to the core of what it is to be human? What was it about the songs of Burt Bacharach and Hal David that had universal appeal, when Hal David's lyrics were often so specific in describing mundane, daily events and in naming places like Tulsa, Phoenix and San José?

I was getting caught up in this web of songwriting angst, a few days after returning from the Cat Power trip, when the way forward was pointed out by, of all people, my daughter Pearl. At the age of three, Pearl loved music. She sang to herself all the time, in particular 'Twinkle, Twinkle, Little Star', possibly the most ubiquitous piece of music ever written by a classical composer (Mozart, and the English lyrics were written in 1806 by a woman from Colchester called Jane Taylor). It was interesting to see the songs that she latched onto. Alongside

Mozart's pop smash nursery rhyme, she also loved songs by Lawrence. He had a song called 'Building Site'. The lyrics went: 'Building site, building site, building site, building site, building site, building site, we're on a building site.' Pearl had successfully memorised all of them.

Another song Pearl had taken to singing was Bacharach and David's 'Do You Know The Way To San José?' It was easy to understand why – the melody pulled you in through its cheerful simplicity. But the songs of Bacharach and David also have a character that is often lacking in mainstream pop. There is an elusive quality about their songs, from 'What's New Pussycat?' to 'The Look Of Love', which could only have come from their shared minds. That was the key. Alongside professionalism and craft, they had something of their own voice in those songs. It was what Pearl was responding to: the simple character or melody inside the structure.

Bacharach was around in England for a few television performances and interviews to promote a frankly terrible new album on which he made unwise collaborations with rappers, but it was like trying to have an audience with the pope. I couldn't get to meet him. Hal David, meanwhile, appeared to have become the half of the partnership that quietly slipped out of sight. I wasn't sure why. The lyrics to 'Twenty-Four Hours From Tulsa' and 'What The World Needs Now' are as original and as deep as the music, and universally poignant. Hal David's words are never bland. It was Lawrence who had originally suggested I try talking to him. 'Nobody bothers with Hal,' said Lawrence in high-pitched Birmingham indignation. 'He's 50 per cent of the equation! I don't understand it. I bet you he'd be happy to talk, as he never gets any of the attention.'

As it happened, Lawrence was right. It took a long time to track him down, but eventually I managed to write a request for an interview to Hal David's wife, Eunice. They were living in Los Angeles but travelled constantly. As Eunice later pointed out, one of the great things about Hal's job is that he can do it anywhere, at any time; all that is needed is a pen and a piece of paper. She wrote back to say that I could call to arrange a time to talk to Hal on the telephone, which resulted in about a month's worth of increasingly pleading messages from me on their answering machine. Finally, they came back – they had been in South Africa and then Europe – and Hal was ready to talk.

Hal David, born in Brooklyn in 1921, became a songwriter following a childhood grounding in music (he learned to play the trumpet), a stint as a journalist and a wartime posting in the Special Services division in Hawaii, where he wrote his first songs for army productions. Following the advice of his song-writer brother Mack, he tried to make money from songs after demobilisation, although it wasn't instant – for the first few years he and his then-wife, Anne, living in an attic in Long Island, survived on her wages as a schoolteacher. In 1947 his career began when he sold 'Isn't This Better Than Walking In The Rain?' to the bandleader Sammy Kaye. This led to a regular gig: writing songs for Guy Lombardo at $50 a week.

In 1958 Hal David met Burt Bacharach. Four years later they had their first hit, 'The Man Who Shot Liberty Valance', inspired by a John Wayne movie and sung by Gene Pitney. So began the most prolific and successful songwriting partner-ship in post-war, popular music history. Everyone knows a Bacharach and David song, and quite a lot of people have had a hit with one. Their golden age commenced in 1962, when they met Dionne Warwick, then a young singer studying at Hartt College of Music and singing in a vocal group called The Gospelaires. Bacharach got her into the studio to record 'Don't

Make Me Over' – the title and content came from a terse
response from Warwick at one of Bacharach's criticisms – and
the three worked together, almost exclusively, until 1975. They
had hits with now-standards like 'Walk On By', 'Trains And
Boats And Planes', 'Do You Know The Way To San José?' and
'The Look Of Love', which were all written for her voice and
temperament but evidently not confined by it.

Keeping in mind the unlikely goal of achieving a harmo-
nious working relationship with Doyle on our Eigg sojourn, I
found out how Bacharach and David managed to come to some
sort of agreement in their creative partnership. They did most of
their work over the telephone: Hal David stayed in New York,
while Burt Bacharach lived in California. They would then meet
for three or four weeks for intensive sessions in either place to
crystallise ideas they had been working on. 'The separation
keeps our outlooks fresh,' claimed Bacharach. They had little to
do with each other socially. Dionne Warwick sued the pair for
an alleged violation of an agreement to produce her album in
1975, and the partnership ended soon after that – but not before
providing the world with songs that have saved friendships,
marriages, lives and sanities.

I asked Hal David where the genesis of a song came from.
'There are different ways for everyone – some – some start with a
melody, and for others the lyrics come first,' he replied in a
polite but hesitant voice that was broken by age. 'With Burt
and I it changed from song to song. For "Alfie", I wrote the
lyrics first – I remember the first line took me hours to write and
then the rest of the words came quickly – and I had no idea how
it would end up sounding. But, for some songs, the music was
finished before I came in with the first line.'

'How can you give a musical sense to the words when there
was no music to put them to?' I asked.

'I always knew that lyrics are not poetry, that they are meant to be sung,' he replied. 'It's good to have a title to start you off or maybe a line that comes into your head, and to keep some sort of rhythm pattern as you write the words, even though nine times out of ten it isn't one that ends up being used.'

He groaned a little, and then continued. 'Musicality and the meaning of words follow parallel tracks. You learn little tricks; you find out that certain words just don't sound right and that you should give emphasis to the words that fall on the down-beat. But you get to that through experience. All that's really needed is an instinctive feeling for music and an imagination.'

I asked Hal David if one needed a grounding in music theory before you could write lyrics that worked. 'You can be a good lyricist without too much knowledge of all that, but music has to be natural to you,' he said. 'You can be . . . maybe not completely blank, but without any great musical education. The key is to hear the music *in* the words. During all those years with Dionne Warwick, I could hear her singing the words as I was writing them. We did have the luxury of having a singer who could do everything, and also we had no choice but to write songs for her – we were producing her records and had to provide her with material.'

Songwriting was Hal David's profession and he treated it as such. For most of the sixties and seventies he would spend Monday to Friday working from nine until five and breaking for lunch. He wrote from an armchair with a pen and paper. The process could be instantaneous or it might take years, as did 'What The World Needs Now', one of the most romantic of all the Bacharach and David classics.

'That song is an example of the fact that whatever you have in your head comes out differently on the page,' he said. 'Often you write a few lines before coming to an impasse that takes you down a different road. I came up with the chorus for "What The World Needs Now" in the time it took to put the words down onto paper, but I couldn't find a verse for them. I had "Lord, we don't need another" . . . what?'

Hal thought of all the things we didn't need to contrast the love that we did need, such as aeroplanes that go faster and cars that can do more things, and the words seemed pertinent and yet all wrong. 'I kept fooling around with it until I eventually came up with "Lord, we don't need another mountain". The song was transformed: now I was dealing with nature and spiritual forces as opposed to material, man-made ones. It took me two years to get there, but I'm glad I stuck with it.'

Most of us have never been to the places named in Bacharach and David's songs, but they give a sense of identity, belonging and yearning. 'It's not really a conscious thing,' he said, when I asked him if this was a stylistic trick. 'Tulsa, Phoenix, San José, LA . . .' he rolled over the sounds of the names. 'Certain places sound good in certain songs. I had never been to Tulsa when I wrote that song. Had I been to San José? As a matter of fact, I had. I probably used these names because I have always liked travelling, so there's a longing to go somewhere while you're stuck in the same place. I had a minor hit with a song called "99 Miles From LA". Some guy asked me: "Where in California is the person who is singing that song?" and it completely stumped me. I had never thought of where he was: it's the destination that matters. LA.'

Hal David developed his own voice by being influenced by the New York songwriting greats who came in the decades before him, in particular Irving Berlin and Johnny Mercer. Hal learned from Berlin's ability to write songs that struck a universal chord – this Siberian émigré wrote 'God Bless America', the country's unofficial national anthem. From the

Savannah, Georgia-born Mercer, he learned the value of using colloquial speech in lyrics: 'Jeepers Creepers' and 'I Wanna Be Around' are two Mercer hits. 'Those guys had the ability to say something important with beauty and simplicity, but what's most important for a composer or lyricist is to have your own voice,' he explained. 'The fact that I revere Johnny Mercer doesn't mean that I'm going to write like him; I couldn't if I wanted to, as he's from the South and we write from the perspective of our own history and our own imagination. I found my voice by writing lyrics that are conversational and casual, like "This Guy's In Love With You". Another thing that separates one lyricist from the other is what they hear in the music. Ten different guys will hear ten different meanings.'

He told me of how songs are triggered by overheard conversations. 'One time I was in London at a dinner party, in a mews house in Belgravia,' he said. 'Someone announced that someone else wasn't going to turn up and the hostess said: "that's one less bell for me to answer". I went home that evening and wrote: "One Less Bell To Answer" – "one less spells the answer. One less egg to fry".'

I could hear Hal's wife, Eunice, in the background, telling him to get off the phone. So I quickly asked him how he came to write my favourite Bacharach/David song of them all: 'Raindrops Keep Falling On My Head', the signature tune to *Butch Cassidy And The Sundance Kid*, a good film that is made great by the music that accompanies it.

'Burt came up with the music first, but it was in the movie that I saw the words to that song,' he replied. 'Paul Newman's Butch and his girlfriend, played by Katherine Ross, are riding along on a bicycle with her on the handlebars, and it's sunny, and they're so carefree, but he's creating a fantasy for himself. That scene comes at a time when everything is going wrong in

Butch's life and he knows that he's doomed. The song was about
a fantasy of happiness.'

Before Eunice grabbed her husband and yanked him away for
– I imagine – his breakfast (it was early morning over in
California), I asked for straight advice on writing lyrics from the
man who has written some of the most poignant songs of the
twentieth century. 'Try starting with a title that you like – that
often works for me. Don't fall in love with your own lines, and
be prepared to discard a good one if it isn't consistent with the
idea behind the song. Create an emotion that others respond to
and keep it simple. And most of all, find your own voice. Just
write naturally and it will emerge.'

That evening I took a bus from my house in Peckham
through the south-east London neighbourhoods of Camberwell
and Elephant & Castle before crossing the river Thames and
ending up at Holborn, in the heart of the city. The bus passes
the Beyoncé Nail Parlour on Queen's Road, a row of African
butcher shops on Rye Lane, where it's not unusual to see a large
man in white overalls lugging a carcass on his back, and the
Miracle Pot restaurant on Walworth Road. That day a crowd of
excitable schoolgirls scrambled on and, after having sung an
American R&B tune a capella very loudly, started screaming 'oh
my DAYS' as they huddled around a girl who appeared to be
having an argument with a boy over the other end of a mobile
phone conversation.

'I'm not the one who's wrong,' she kept shouting at the boy.
'I'm not the one who's a liar . . .' then, after a while, she said, in
a much quieter but still petulant voice: 'I know I'm wrong. But
that doesn't mean you're right.'

I wrote down a few phrases, like 'Miracle Pot', 'oh my days'
and 'I know I'm wrong'. Something might come from any one
of them, and, thinking about Hal David's advice, I decided that

reflecting this world that I saw every day might be the way forward. These overheard words would help start something new, and, for the first time in ages, I began to feel optimistic that I might actually be capable of writing a decent song.

I thought about the planned trip to Eigg and how it would pan out. It was likely that Doyle would come up with more music than me – he was the better guitarist – while I would be writing the words. (Doyle's wit rarely translated onto the page.) My plan was to come up with four or five songs that we would, with any luck, record at ToeRag, and then make a single from the ones that worked best. Out of the songs I had written so far, only 'Bad Part Of Town' was worth pursuing, and that was a rip-off of 'I Never Loved Her' by The Starfires. But, with the overheard bus conversation, and with the inspiration of Chan Marshall and Hal David, I was getting excited all over again. Now I needed Doyle to move it forward, to turn the fragments of musical and lyrical ideas into something concrete. I decided to give my inspirational songwriting partner, the man who would help me craft a three-minute pop masterpiece, a call.

'What do you want?' said Doyle through a mouthful of sausage. 'I'm about to watch *Terminator 2*.'

'Where's Yukiko?'

'She's gone to Japan, hasn't she?' he replied, grumpily. 'The funny thing is, she's been driving me crazy recently, especially after she tried to feed salmon to the DVD player. But, now that she's gone, I kind of miss her. The little flat seems a bit big without her.'

'Well, she *is* your wife. Anyway, the point is we have to get ready for our trip to Eigg. I've found a stone house that we can stay in for £150 a week. It's got running water – cold, obviously – and the toilet is in a separate stone hut. It's perfect.'

'Yeah, but you forgot one thing,' said Doyle.

'What's that?'

'Neither of us can write songs.'

'You're not going to back out on me, are you?'

'I'm up for a bit of the old roughing it up on Eigg,' he said with a sigh. 'Getting drunk and lighting fires is the closest I'm ever going to get to a spiritual awakening. And maybe it will inspire us to write something half-decent, but I doubt it. What you have to remember about us is this – we're not very talented. Now leave me alone. *Terminator 2* is about to start.'

The optimism felt only minutes before the phone call had been unceremoniously squashed like a ripe orange under a hob-nailed boot.

When life is looking bleak, there's a place to go to down the end of my street where the atmosphere has the ability to confirm my pessimism in a reassuring if mildly depressing way. It's an old-fashioned workingman's club called the Hatcham Social. The club ran out of money in the late seventies and its decor is an authentic period piece as a result: orange globe lights, chipped tables with curved edges, a deep Axminster carpet capable of absorbing any amount of spilled beer, mirrors and shields on the walls with gold plastic frames, and even posters for the kind of seventies-style entertainers for whom the Hatcham must have been be the high-water mark: portly, beaten-looking men with names like Ricky Champ, Ace Valentine and Lover Boy Lucky. The Hatcham may be downtrodden, but it's friendly and it wasn't too hard to become a member. I went before a stony-faced jury of three middle-aged men holding jugs of ale. After asking a variety of questions in a monotone voice about my age, profession and marital status, I was asked who my nominee was.

'I don't have one.'

'I will be your nominee. Who is your second?'

'Ditto.'

'He will be your second.' The jury pointed to a man slumped in a corner, just about managing to hold a pint of beer upright. The man let out a belch and started sobbing uncontrollably. 'Welcome to the Hatcham.'

A few days before Doyle and I were due to leave for Eigg, my friend Tim Siddall and I went to the Hatcham. We were the only people in there, apart from one regular whom I had never seen leave his stool by the bar – his beer belly appeared to have wedged him in, making movement impossible. All he could do was utilise his right arm for leaning towards his pint of bitter and raising it to his mouth and his left arm for flicking the ash of his Lambert & Butler cigarette into the gigantic ashtray perched in front of him.

Tim is tall, angular and handsome. I don't know of a single one of our female friends who hasn't harboured a crush on him at some time or another. Perhaps it's his taciturn northern manner, or the way his upper lip refuses to move when he speaks. He has the kind of mind that is only capable of focusing on one or two things at any given time, and he was currently focused on the end of the world. He told me that peak oil was about to run out. The USA had invaded Iraq because of the oil shortages, and they would soon be invading another oil-rich country, like Iran or Venezuela, and the cars would stop running and the machines would stop turning and we would be plunged back into a feudal existence. If I were thinking about growing my own vegetables, he added, now would be a good time to start.

'It does sound like cause for concern,' I replied dispiritedly, taking a swig of beer, 'but, to be honest with you, all I can think about right now is that I set myself this goal to write songs and I'm failing miserably. I've spoken to all these great people and got all this advice from them, and it's going nowhere. To make matters worse, Doyle has concluded that we're doomed to failure before we even start.'

He gave an almost imperceptible nod, then said: 'I have the answer to both the end of the world *and* your lack of inspiration. Fixed-wheel bicycles.'

I should have known that coming to the Hatcham with Tim was a bad idea. I sighed and asked him to explain himself.

'It's a bicycle without any gears,' he replied. It was interesting to watch the way he could make these sounds come out of his mouth without actually moving it. 'The pedals are fixed to the back wheel, so you can't freewheel and you can't stop pedalling. You're going to love it.'

'That sounds like some kind of torture,' I said. 'What happens when you go down a steep hill?'

After a worryingly extended pause, he replied: 'You just have to pedal really fast.'

And how would this instrument of suffering help us when apocalypse struck? 'There won't be any cars, and you won't be able to get the gears fixed on your bike any more, because the world's distribution networks will have come to a halt,' he said, in a tone that suggested I was being deliberately obtuse. 'Besides, riding it will turn you into a super-human capable of surviving anything.'

He hunched over his pint like a handsome eagle of doom, took a gulp, and put it down. 'I forgot to tell you – your bicycle wouldn't have any brakes. You have to try and pedal backwards if you want to stop, which takes some practice. But then, when you get the hang of it, it's like the machine becomes a part of you, which is perfect for the end of the world. You've seen *Mad Max*, haven't you? The ones who survive are the ones that accept the synthesis of man and machine. It's hard to know where one ends and the other begins.'

'Why are you telling me all this?'

'This is the material you need for your songwriting,' he said, looking almost animated. 'You're trying to write the perfect song based on a conventional idea of what that is, and you've got it all wrong. You've got to go down more unusual paths. Once you get a fixed-wheel bike, you'll be so inspired that you won't ever be able to stop writing songs about it. It's going to help you find your own voice.'

He went on to tell me that the great songwriters, in his opinion Mark E. Smith of The Fall and Bob Dylan, were not really interested in music but in a communication of their worldview. That's what I needed, he said: a strong worldview, ideally one that included fixed-wheel bikes. 'You're worrying about all the wrong things, like whether you can sing or not and whether your songs are going to work as pieces of music. Did Mark E. Smith ever worry about his singing voice? Did he, fuck! He can present his words with conviction, and that's why he's a genius. You need to portray your world with confidence and forget all this nonsense about writing a cliché of a pop song.'

The man whose belly had wedged him into the bar turned slowly to look at us. He just about managed to put down his cigarette for a moment to give me the thumbs up and a flicker of a smile. They were right. I was never going to write the perfect song, but Doyle and I could still write *some* sort of song. Whether you are Cat Power or Hal David or the Hatcham Social Club's own Ricky Champ, you still have the right to express yourself. Finally, I felt ready to face my demons — and Doyle — on the island of Eigg.

Chapter Nine

Eigg

'Have you called him recently?' asked NJ, as I packed my all-weather cagoule into the sad-looking holdall that had been used for the children's clothes on every family trip we had ever taken since the birth of Otto. 'You'd better make sure he's going to turn up.'

I had called Doyle twice a day, every day, for the last two weeks. Sometimes I even managed to get through to him, and he would invariably either be semi-conscious, pulled out of sleep by my call, or working on the railway tracks, concentrating on fixing a fault and mindful of not letting 200 tonnes of speeding iron catch hold of his trouser leg. And it always appeared that I was presenting him with the details of our trip for the first time. 'We're coming back on Wednesday? I thought you said Tuesday. The sleeper tickets cost £175 each? Does that include a hooker or something?'

At 10.30 p.m. on a Tuesday evening in May, I sat on the floor of Euston station, leaning against the quick-assembly wall of Tie Rack, when a hobbit-like figure with a mass of curly hair and wild staring eyes bounced towards me. 'Dude!' he croaked. 'We'd better get a couple of pints in before this train arrives. I've got to smoke about ten cigarettes to make sure there's no bloodshed on the sleeper. My nicotine levels need to be high enough to go through ten hours of withdrawal.'

'But you'll be asleep for most of that time,' I pointed out. 'Surely you don't need to smoke when you're sleeping?'

'You haven't shared a room with me before, have you?' He took out his secret weapon: a box of snuff. 'This,' he said, taking a pinch, 'is my only hope.'

After downing a couple of pints that I didn't really want at the station bar, we found our sleeper. There was just enough space to stick one guitar case on the rack and one on the floor, and I took the top bunk. Doyle stared at a sign on the door that said 'No smoking in the toilet'. 'See, that's just designed to piss you off,' he said, taking another pinch of snuff. Some music was piped through our efficiently compact quarters that sounded familiar.

'It's that song you're always playing,' said Doyle with a sniff. 'The instrumental one.'

Just audible through the tiny speakers was 'Anji' by Davy Graham, the song that I had attempted to master as a rite of passage to learning the guitar for the first time the year before. 'It's a sign,' I said. 'The gods have plans for us.'

'So have I,' said Doyle. 'It's called getting drunk.'

We went to the first-class buffet carriage, which the waiter, not unreasonably, wanted to expel us from but couldn't, due to the fact that booking a sleeper to Scotland turns you into a first-class kind of person whatever your appearance and hygiene standards. He brought us a menu that listed about six types of single malt whisky, variously described as distinctly peaty, fragrant on the nose, and tinged with brine. I made my way through the list, a finger dancing over the floral descriptions of these sophisticated creations, before deciding on a Macallan. 'And for you, sir?' said the man, turning to Doyle.

'I'll have a lager.'

Having never been north of Watford Gap before, Doyle was worried about the Scottish. 'When the train pulls into Glasgow and we go into the station,' he said, leaning towards me conspiratorially, 'throw a 50p on the ground and walk away fast. That should keep them off. If that doesn't work and they still keep coming for us, make a shape like a bear.'

As the train rumbled past Milton Keynes, Manchester and Liverpool, Doyle turned his attentions to the goal of the trip. 'We can't write songs. It's not going to work. What's the point of it anyway?'

I told him my plan of having a handful of songs that we could take to ToeRag Studios and turn into actual recordings, or at least have our debut single – the first release by our band, Double Fantasy – by the end of it. I explained that we wouldn't have to get into the murky world of proper distribution or record promotion: all we had to do was press up, say, 300 copies of the single, which we could then try to flog down the pub or get into an independent record shop like Rough Trade. We could also put the songs up on the internet so that anyone with a computer could have the songs for free. The point is that the songs would really exist. What happened after that would be in the hands of fate.

'The end goal,' I told him, 'is to record a single. Imagine how great that would be, to have a piece of vinyl of our own, with songs that we have written and played ourselves.'

'I'm not interested,' he said, clutching onto his can of McEwan's as if it was about to be snatched away from him.

'What do you mean, "not interested"? You're already coming to Eigg to write songs with me, aren't you?'

'See, Will, what you have to understand is that I'm a very pessimistic fellow,' he said, looking suitably pessimistic. 'I don't want to write a song or do any of that stuff because it's all vanity. If you want to be famous as well as rich, you go for something that makes you believe that you're an artist, like making music. I'm the opposite. I don't want any kind of attention. I hate my job – it's soul-destroying and anyone with any sense would do something else – but the point is that it's hard work that I get paid for, and that means a lot to me. Do you understand what I'm saying? I do my job because it means I can get a house and buy a camera for Yukiko.'

'What's this got to do with recording a single?'

'See, because you're a bit of a bleeding dolly bird, you want a life of fame and flashy cars and beautiful women. I don't blame you. Who wouldn't? It's a much easier way to make a few quid than working on the railways. It's like Yukiko says to me: why don't you ever wear nice clothes any more? Because, unlike you, I'm not trying to be a man about town. I just want to work, be with my wife, watch *Terminator 2* every now and then, and smoke a BLOODY cigarette.' He slammed his fist against the wall then stared tragically at his crumpled hand.

'Doyle,' I said, feeling that I wanted to take his can of McEwan's lager and bounce it on his head but knowing that this would not be a good start to our professional partnership, 'I'm thirty-five years old. I only started playing the guitar a year and a half ago. I'm married with two children, I can't sing, and I'm paying for the single myself. I'm not about to become a pop star. Can't you see that the whole point of this is to write songs for their own sake, just like you can learn to play the guitar for its own sake? I'm trying to see if it's possible to be creative, and to produce this popular art form that has always existed, if you don't have any special artistic powers and if you live a normal kind of life. And I want to have a single in my hands at the end of it. Is that too much to ask?'

He stared at me in silence for a bit, and said, 'So you don't want us to become the next Jagger–Richards?'

'I think we left it a bit late.'

He looked relieved and, less obviously, disappointed. Then he raised his can. 'I'll drink to that.' He stared hopelessly at the table for a few minutes before saying, 'But, if we were going to be the next Jagger–Richards, it's obvious which one of the two *you'd* be . . . bleeding dolly bird.'

After another whisky – it was two in the morning – I told Doyle that I wanted to go to bed. 'What's the matter with you?' he said. 'We're on a songwriting mission and you want to go to bed after a couple of drinks? You're paying £175 for this. Make the most of it!'

He began to lecture me about all kinds of subjects that he had a shallow knowledge of, gleaned from watching daytime television on the weeks he was working night shifts, including survival techniques in the wilderness that he appeared to believe we were going to have to utilise. 'I'm going to get by on primitive skills,' he said, looking as if he wouldn't survive the eight hours to Glasgow. 'I'll light a fire by rubbing two sticks together. I know all about it. I've seen Ray Mears do it on TV.'

Even if we weren't going to have to spear a passing sheep for our breakfast and skin its hide to make our clothes, Eigg would at least afford us a dream that we had both harboured for years: to get it together in the country and make rock'n'roll. Ever since I had first heard Bob Dylan and The Band's *The Basement Tapes*, and read about how Dylan's former backing band rented a house called Big Pink in Woodstock, New York State, with a view of Overlook Mountain and wrote the songs for their first two albums there, I had imagined being in an old stone house with guitars on the inside and the wilderness beyond. Eigg would be our own Big Pink. We would have no distractions beyond the sea and the mountains, and, as outsiders to Scottish island life, we would be inspired by it. After all, The Band's Robbie Robertson wasn't a Southern farmer losing everything he had after the dissolution of the Union following the Civil War, but that takes nothing away from the passion in the words to 'The Night They Drove Old Dixie Down'.

We climbed into our bunks, the train rattled and shook its way towards Glasgow, and Doyle began to snore.

After a night and a day of travelling by train and ferry, we arrived on Eigg. Many of the houses there have fallen into decay, and ploughs rust in the middle of long-dormant fields. Colouring the beauty of the place is an undertow of despair. Eigg's charm is that still feels wild, as if anything could happen here. In 1577 the MacLeods of Dunvegan invaded Eigg and the inhabitants hid in a cave on the southern shore of the island. The MacLeods discovered the cave by following the tracks of a scout in freshly fallen snow, lit a fire at the cave's mouth, and smothered the entire population of 395 people to death. It didn't feel impossible that, in 2006, two skeletons, with a few curly locks clinging to their fractured skulls and still clutching broken guitars, might be discovered in an old stone bothy, with ripped pieces of paper with angrily crossed-out lyrics lying on the floor.

In the eighties, a millionaire playboy and former racing driver called Keith Schellenberg owned the island, but his weekend parties of guests helicoptered in from London proved unpopular with the locals. Schellenberg's vintage Roll's Royce, airlifted onto Eigg, was mysteriously torched one night. He ended up by announcing, 'Something is rotten in Eigg', and calling its inhabitants a bunch of 'barking mad revolutionaries'. He sold the island to an elusive German artist, who promised to make all kinds of improvements on the island and never did.

Then, in 1996, Eigg's population made history by buying their own island with the help of lottery money, a huge fund-raising effort and money from the Scottish government. Now Eigg is run as a trust. A harbour has been built and there is a shop and a tearoom. But, however respectable it seems, there will always be something uncontrollable about the place.

A red-haired man in a battered red car with a red-faced child in the back picked us up from the harbour and drove us to the Sandavore bothy, a 400-year-old single-room cottage with walls close to a metre thick that sits sunken into a secluded hillside in the middle of the island. The Sandavore has a large fireplace in the middle of the room, two beds, tiny windows that are like little eyes watching the windswept inactivity outside, a cooker with a cylinder of gas, a large white sink with a single tap, and an outside toilet so small that gymnastic manoeuvres have to be executed to use it with any degree of accuracy. I claimed the double bed and Doyle threw his filthy blue rucksack onto the rusting metal fold-up next to the door. 'What do you have to do to get a cup of tea round here?' he said, and went outside to chop some logs in the drizzle.

'What the hell does "ibid." mean?' asked Doyle, a cup of tea by his side, five minutes later, sitting cross-legged by the fire and peeling off strips of wood with his pocketknife. 'You always see it in the indexes of books . . . ibid.'

'I don't know. I've seen it too. Ibid . . . it sounds like a mythical bird. Something that was once worshipped but now only exists as a barely remembered ghost of a myth. Ibid, reveal yourself to us.'

'That could be our psychedelic number,' said Doyle. ' "The Search For The Ibid." '

We stared at a candle in a moment of psychedelic reflection before realising that we had not eaten for the last twelve hours.

Nor did we have any food. Doyle, as he tended to do in moments of crisis, lit a cigarette.

We walked down the one road that runs through Eigg as the drizzle turned to rain, and kept going until we came to the teashop by the harbour twenty minutes later. We shuffled into to the clean wood-panelled room, where sliding glass doors opened out onto rocks above the sea, and the five men and two women gathered around the bar turned to face us. They stared, not in an unfriendly way, but with unbridled curiosity.

'Are you the musicians in the Sandavore?' asked the cheerful-looking woman behind the counter. 'The ones who have come here to write songs?'

News travelled fast on this island. We had only told the red devil about our endeavour and that was not more than two hours ago. 'We're not musicians, we're just doing it for fun,' I told her.

A woman sitting behind a glass of red wine and a table stared at us in an out-of-focus way. 'That one looks like Donovan,' she said, waving a finger at Doyle, 'and that one looks like David Essex.' There was something about her appearance – the amount of make-up she had on, her just-stepped-out-of-a-salon hairstyle – that suggested hostility or least defiance to this rural life.

She came up and stood next to me, staring in a slightly maniacal way. 'Are we good?' she said in a little-girl voice. 'Are we good?' None of the other people in the teashop showed any reaction. She announced that she was in the process of getting divorced. Her daughter, who must have been around eight or nine, was pulling at her to go home. 'Byronic,' she said, grabbing my face. 'Has anyone said that before?'

'No, not really,' I said through squeezed cheeks.

'Is that annoying for you? Byronic? Are we good?' Her

daughter was tugging at her shirt. It was like a drunken parody of a daytime television presenter. She was pressing herself up against me. I thought that somebody might come to my aid, but no: Doyle was hiding in the corner and the locals didn't appear to notice. Finally I said to her, 'I'm going out for a cigarette.' It was meant to be a way of escaping, but she took it otherwise. The rocks around the harbour and the sea beyond them were still illuminated by the late northern light. It might be mistaken as romantic.

'Are we good,' she purred, as I did my best to look completely transfixed by the task of rolling a cigarette. 'Are we gooood.' I could feel my cheek making an involuntary twitch. Finally she sloped inside, saying with a wink, 'See you in a minute.'

Doyle appeared. 'I think you're in there.'

'A fat lot of good you were. I thought you might have come to my rescue.'

'I wouldn't worry,' said a large man in fishing overalls, who was leaning against a wall with a can of McEwan's and had been watching the whole sorry seduction. 'She's got cabin fever, her husband had enough and left the island, and you're fresh blood. If it weren't you, it would be some other poor soul.'

I protected myself by talking to a man who had turned up with a guitar. His name was Iain and he was sleeping in a tent by some woods about half a mile from our bothy. He came every year to Eigg, he said, and saw how long he could stay until his money ran out, which was when he returned to his hometown of Dumfries, where he worked in a bookshop. He said that he might drop by on us one night. The woman appeared again, the light of near-insanity shining in her eyes, and she just had time to launch into her tale of how she used to be a singer in London when Doyle finally proved to be of some use and said that we had better get back before it got dark. She offered us a lift. We declined.

There was just enough light left for us to follow the barely-there tracks that led to our bothy. There was now a fully developed storm on its way, and we took in a few logs to dry out. Doyle tried to cook a sausage in the fire by piercing it onto the end of the stick, but the stick caught fire and the sausage dropped into the embers. 'Charcoal is good for you,' he said, as he crunched into the blackened lump.

I poured us whiskies and played 'Angie' by The Rolling Stones, singing along as best I could.

'You've got it all wrong,' said Doyle, as I tried to remember the words. 'It's not "Angie". It's "Ayyyyengeee".'

'You don't have to try and sound like Mick Jagger just to sing the bloody song,' I retorted. 'That's your problem – you're too literal.'

'It's not about singing like Mick Jagger,' he said from his default position: cross-legged, by the fire, head down, chopping wood and looking like he had a vendetta against his fingers. 'It's about feeling it.'

I sighed. Doyle was always going on about 'feeling' it, because he felt that he had to assert how much deeper he was than me.

'Your singing is actually quite fascinating, because it's *so* bad. It's like you've got no soul at all. There's nothing there. You sing "you can't say we're satisfied" like you're announcing that the 5.15 from Brighton is subject to delays owing to the wrong type of leaves on the track.' Then he sang in his best croak, eyes closed, gurning horribly: 'Yow cayn't sayyy weee're sat-is-fy-yi-yied . . .'

'Just because you can sing doesn't mean that you have soul and I don't,' I retorted. 'All you care about in life is food, money and cigarettes. How can that be soulful?'

'You have to imagine that you're really in love with Angie and that your heart is breaking. Where's the emotion? You're clearly musical. You picked up the guitar really quickly. But I've never heard such atrocious singing in my entire life. Even Ned the Electrician from work can sing better than you. He's only got one tooth. And he's deaf.'

The rain had grown into a storm. Blankets of lightning blasted the hills with flashes that shone through the tiny square window. Our bothy was so smoky that my eyes were watering; the resin of the wood was blocking the chimney. We kept a steady flow of logs over the old fuel burner to dry out, so, with the steam they created and the smoke from Doyle's cigarettes, you could hardly see a thing. There was water coming down from the side of the stone chimney. There was nothing to do but play our guitars.

Doyle ran through a Neil Young-like chord sequence that he had come up with. It would sound good with a hangover and a feeling of regret. I thought of the kind of words that would fit: a hesitant apology from someone, a woman probably, after an argument. And, for some reason, I kept thinking about Peckham: of walking past its bleak tower blocks on a Sunday before coming to Peckham Rye park, which, interspersed with duck ponds and playgrounds, softens this dejected but somehow compelling area of London. I thought of walking through the park with NJ, of having rice and fish at the wonderfully named Miracle Pot, and of that bus ride a few weeks earlier when I had decided, on Hal David's suggestion, to take inspiration from overheard sentences and shop names. It was the universal feeling of Sunday. Churches were invented for the purpose of dealing with it.

The first words that I wrote down had little to do with what was going through my head, though.

It was deep in midwinter
When I did you wrong
But now the roses bloom
The swallow is in song

I showed it to Doyle. 'You're trying to make it too perfect,' he said, with a dismissive shake of his head. 'It don't work. You've got to have lines about the green-eyed toad or the lizard of wrath.'

'If you're so clever, why don't you write it?'

'No, man, I'm the musical genius. It's your job to interpret my music into language. You have to think freely. Use your imagination.'

Maybe I was too tired. With the late drinking followed by Doyle's cacophony of snores from the night before, I had hardly slept. Now the wind and the rain were howling and the bed was tempting. I knew the words were too precious, and pretentious, but still it was annoying to have Doyle pointing that out. He climbed into bed and lit a cigarette.

'You have to get away from normal writing,' he said. 'You're not writing poetry but songs. Remember, literature is pointless.'

This was a new one. 'Would you like to explain to me,' I said slowly, 'your reasoning behind that statement?'

'Literature is just about trying to show how clever you are, and using words and language when you should be telling a story. I think of it in the same way as I think of wine tasting. What good does it do? People say that great books change lives, but I can't see how. Why read a book that's difficult and has no story? It's like that Thomas Mann, or James Joyce.'

'Have you read them?'

'No, I don't have to.'

A little bit of information was a dangerous thing in Doyle's hands. It allowed him to reduce the history of literature to a middle-class folly.

'Literature covers a lot,' I said. 'You like *The Lord of the Rings*, don't you?'

'Of course,' he said. He had often talked about how he had found escape as a teenager in *The Lord of the Rings*. He spent so many afternoons at The Fantasy Centre, a bookshop on Holloway Road in north London, that the socially challenged men who ran the place refused to answer his barrage of questions about the books in anything but Elvish. 'But that has a story,' he said. 'It has a function.'

'I don't see why that couldn't be defined as literature. And you like Charles Bukowski, don't you? His books are literature because they engage you in what it means to be alive; they reflect his way of seeing the world. In fact, your argument is so monumentally stupid that there isn't even any reason to talk about it.'

'Wine tasting,' he concluded, and started off on the first of many snores. The equivalent of 'Mull Of Kintyre', Paul McCartney's sentimental ode to his favourite place in Scotland and one of the longest-running number one hits in the history of the British charts, was unlikely to emerge from our little bothy any time soon.

'The Singing Sands,' said Doyle from his bed, as he lit the first cigarette of the day the following morning. 'That's where we have to go to write "Ibid". The Singing Sands can inspire us.'

The Singing Sands was a beach in the opposite direction from the harbour, on the far side of the island. We made sandwiches from bread and cheese given to us by the woman who ran the harbour tearoom, and carried our guitars. We took the one road that ran the length of the island and walked for an hour and a half, on a day that was remarkably hot and dry for north-west Scotland in early May, before we realised that we had come out without any water.

'We're going to have to ask at one of these houses,' I said to Doyle. 'You can do that in the countryside and nobody minds.'

A woman came out of the house we were passing. The feeling of a rock dropping into my stomach hit as I realised who she was: the sexually frustrated television-presenter-imitating divorcée from the harbour. This time she gave a terse hello and disappeared back into her house.

'Go and ask your bit of fluff,' said Doyle. 'You might get more than just a glass of water.'

'Shut up. What about this house here? You go and ask.'

On the other side of the road was a run-down-looking white house, set a long way back from the road by a gate and a muddy expanse of land beyond it. There were some chickens marching about in that uptight way of theirs and two horses looking passively inquisitive from a stable to the side of the house. There was also an overweight Labrador and a sleepy Old English Sheepdog lazily staring at us.

'I'm not going,' said Doyle. 'Those dogs will attack me. Look at the bloodlust in their eyes. They smell fear. And whoever is in that house will take one look at me and say: "They're round the back. The ones with the green lids are for recycling and the ones with the black lids are for the dump".'

'It looks like I have to do everything around here,' I muttered, and opened the gate and walked up to the house. The dogs barked a bit. Before I got to the door an ethereal woman, white hair in bunches held up by what looked like wild flowers, appeared. She was in her pyjamas.

'Sorry to bother you,' I said, 'but my friend and I have come out without water and we're thirsty. Could I trouble you for a glass?'

'Yes, of course you can,' said the woman, staring at me with intense interest, a look of apprehension turning to one of excitement. She must have been in her early seventies and had fine features, a great beauty once. She went into the house and reappeared with two glasses on a small wicker tray, which had a cloth on it. 'Tell your husband to come up to the house. He doesn't have to stand all the way down there,' she said. 'Why don't you come in? There's no reason for a nice young lady like you to have to stay outside.'

I told her that I was, in fact, a man, and that even my most psychologically warped nightmares had never involved marriage to Doyle. She nodded and smiled and told me that she was open-minded.

The door opened out onto a very bright room that smelled of animals and was filled with boxes, papers, half-finished paintings, books and magazines, some of which were arranged in piles and others which were strewn across tables and the floor. There was a green and red stained-glass cross hanging over a window that looked out to the sea and some antlers next to it. There was a horse's skull and a painting of a horse's skull beside it on another wall. Pieces of paper filled with childish writing were stuck to the walls. Mounted on an easel was a canvas with a painting-in-progress of an amaryllis, a guitar and a jug of water.

'It is very fortuitous that you should have arrived now. So fortuitous, in fact, that I believe the amaryllis brought you here,' she said, waving a hand in the air. 'And you are musicians too! I was a concert pianist before I became a painter. But this was before a series of cataclysmic events in my life that resulted in my losing everything. The power of the amaryllis dreamed you up! I have been working on this painting for the last six months and I never seem to have the time to complete it' – I could not help but wonder what this woman, clearly living on her own, did on this remote island that took up so much of her time – 'but, now that you have arrived, I can see a way forward. You see the guitar? I bought it in a junk shop. When I took it home I noticed that somebody had painted a pentagram on it. I was so horrified that I spent hours and hours scrubbing it off. Since my conversion to Roman Catholicism twenty-three years ago, there is no way that I could have the sign of the devil in my house. It wouldn't go with everything else here.'

A budgerigar in a cage in the far corner of the room made a squawk that sounded rather like a warning. 'That's the Imperial Budgie,' she said, flapping her hand in its direction. 'In 1996 I decided that I would live again and get budgies. This was after my husband had stolen everything I ever owned, leaving me poverty-stricken in a tenement block in Glasgow, where the children would throw stones at me and I was terrified to walk out of my front door. I kept parakeets – they're illegal birds, actually – that I smuggled here. But they chewed up all the furniture.'

What had we walked into?

'You look rather interesting,' she said to us, in an accent that was hard to place: it was close to upper-class English but with inflections from Scotland and something else, too. 'Wait a minute . . . I've seen you before!' she said to me. 'You are a singer on television, aren't you?'

'Ah, now I think you are mistaking me for someone else,' I said, failing to suppress a little smile.

'Here we go,' said Doyle, shaking his head as he pulled a cigarette out of its packet and rolled it over his fingers. 'Syd Barrett, Marc Bolan, David bleedin' Essex . . . who is it this time?'

She pressed a finger to her mouth and looked up to the sky before her face popped with conclusion: 'Diana Ross.'

'That's more like it,' said Doyle.

'Oh, for Christ's sake.'

'I would like to paint you. Especially you,' said the woman, turning to Doyle. 'You have such a sweet face that I think you would go rather well with the amaryllis. You share its healthful qualities.'

I looked at Doyle's plant counterpart. Sure enough, it was wilting too.

Given that she had been working on the painting of the amaryllis and guitar for the last six months, I wondered if agreeing to this proposed sitting was such a good idea. I saw an image of Doyle, six months on, remaining much the same but with a huge beard and long hair, grey and hopeless, as this woman tried to capture the exact state of decay of his teeth.

She told us that her name was Jenny Johnson, and she appeared to have a lot of grievances with other islanders. She talked of an English couple who were out to destroy her. She told us a complicated story of a Roman Catholic church that was supposedly on the island, but we weren't sure where; it had contained an extremely valuable painting by Artemisia Gentileschi that had been taken to Sotheby's to be auctioned, except at some point, it had been swapped for a fake and the real one was returned to Eigg, or was consigned to the sea, or both. She became enraged as she told us about wild horses on the island: introduced decades previously, the islanders decided that they should be shot and that their hides should be turned into sofa covers or something. She came to Eigg because she was 'tricked by fate, even though I swore I would never come here'. I think a millionaire was paying for her survival, giving her an allowance of £12,000 a year.

She said, 'One must fight for one's place on the spiritual

plane just as on the material plane', as she brought us coffee. I saw a framed photograph of Jenny as a young woman, a sepia print in profile, and she was indeed stunning; the kind of looks that, once gone, must have felt like a curse. She claimed that someone on the island had come into the house and smashed a number of the windows, but I never found out why.

Every now and then I told her that we had to go to the Singing Sands, but she ignored me. She asked us what kind of music we were making.

'Diana here is hoping to make a disco classic,' said Doyle.

If I had had one of Diana Ross's stilettos at that moment I would have eye-butted him with it. 'We've come here to write songs,' I told Jenny. 'We're going to the Singing Sands for inspiration.'

'Then you must hear my latest composition,' she said, moving towards the piano with the slightest of smiles. 'It is in D sharp minor, which I always feel is the key of the Holy Spirit, and to me it sounds like Verdi.' She started playing – superbly, powerfully – but she never stopped talking. 'So this represents my return to Eigg and the troubles I knew I must face here,' she said, as the piano plunged into the darkest notes, 'and then followed a time of great uncertainty. What should I do? Should I stay or should I go?' The composition ended on a suspended chord. There was a pause. 'But I knew I had to stay here, I had to face my demons! I had to go to A flat!' she screamed, pounding the piano as the music raised to a glorious crescendo. Then it became calmer and so did she. She closed her eyes. 'But I ultimately accept my duties as a Catholic. And so we end on D sharp.'

Not for the first time I told her that, interesting as it had been to meet her (and it really had), we must leave now. Doyle said that he needed to go outside for a cigarette. 'How sweet of you to think of my welfare,' she said to him, 'but you can smoke in here because I smoke too.' After Doyle's cigarette, I tried once again to leave. This time she said that we should indeed go to the Singing Sands, but that we should take her dog, Mia. 'It is quite hard to find,' she said, 'and Mia will show you the way. Fortune brought you here. Mia will take you there.'

'Did you understand any of that?' I asked Doyle as Mia, a charismatic long-haired sheepdog, did indeed make sure that we were on the right path, always running ahead but looking back to check on us.

'She was some kind of a visionary,' he replied. 'She saw the black diva trapped inside you. And she's an artistic bohemian. That's why she's got all these grievances – because people here aren't going to be able to understand her. It's like the men at my work. They don't have the ability to understand anything artistic; they'd rather go and pick a fight with a paving stone. So you end up getting eccentric as a result of that isolation.'

Mia led us down a rocky path and across a swampy bog, but she knew the way to keep feet dry, taking us to raised areas in the bog and stones that could be leapfrogged across. We arrived at the Singing Sands, a wide expanse of white beach marked out on either side by rocks sculpted into surrealist artworks by the beating of the sea. It looked like a Dali landscape.

We climbed over the rocks to find a waterfall crashing down through a narrow crevice: you could walk along a tiny ledge ten feet up from the ground, balancing by leaning against the other side of the rock face, and reach the sheets of water that came over the cliff's edge thirty or forty feet above us. We padded through the dry sand, which did indeed sing in a squeaking sort of way, if not exactly harmonised with the sun and the earth, and found a plateau on which to bring out the guitars.

'D minor is the most psychedelic key,' I said. 'We should use that.'

'D sharp minor is the key of the Holy Spirit,' Doyle added. 'The way towards the Ibid has already been pointed out for us.'

I started an arpeggio in D sharp minor. Doyle built on it with a resolution from C to B to A, which was unusual and had that carousel quality of one of the early songs by Love. I moved it into the most basic chorus of all – G, D, A – and he added some notes to that. As Doyle played, I thought about what we had seen already on Eigg and what an Ibid might be, and of the strange old lady whose dog had just taken us down to this quiet place.

> Grey-haired lady, can you tell us
> If the ibid walks among us
> We will follow your good dog
> Down rocky paths to swamps and bogs
>
> Fearful bird or wrathful creature
> Saint of glory, holy sinner
> Shall we praise you and exalt you
> Or defy you and destroy you
>
> *Chorus (twice):*
> Ibid bless us with your grace
> What I'd give to see your face
> Ibid take us to the sky
> Open up your wings and fly
>
> Climb through caves of bloody history
> Mountains rich with ancient mystery
> Are ibids in earth's great hollow?
> Or in skies beyond the swallow

Chorus

Rest awhile on singing sands
Give yourself to ibid's hands
Rich man's castle, poor man's gate
The ibid decides your fate

Chorus to end

As I wrote the words I kept in mind the kind of imagery used by Syd Barrett, and thought of those three English songwriters who had given me advice of a kind early on: Andy Partridge, Gaz Coombes and Ray Davies. 'Ibid' sounded nothing like any of them, but it was at least fairly British and a little bit mystical. 'What do you think?' I asked Doyle, half an hour or so later.

'They'll do,' he replied with a sigh.

Beyond the crashes of the waves, it was quiet at the Singing Sands. We could make as much noise as we wanted, but the peace engulfed you and you responded to it. It made me think of how art is shaped by restrictions and circumstances. Robbie Robertson wrote 'The Night They Drove Old Dixie Down' with his one-year-old daughter sleeping in the room next door, hence it is quiet – he didn't want to wake her up by playing it.

We dropped Mia at Jenny's house on the way back and Jenny wanted us to come in. She gave us a batch of eggs laid that day by her hens, showed us round the junk-filled rooms upstairs and told us that we had to come back one day to stay with her. She insisted on taking a series of photographs, almost all identical, of the two of us standing in the middle of her living room with the budgerigars and the painting of the amaryllis behind us. 'It really is some kind of a miracle that you should have arrived today,' she said happily. We promised that we would see her again.

Back at the bothy we ran through 'Bad Part Of Town'. Doyle pointed out that, in trying to do a garage song, I had lifted an established song ('I Never Loved Her' by The Starfires) and given it a new lick of paint, but only one coat.

'We've got to do something about that,' he said, shaking his head. 'If we go into ToeRag and play that to Liam he'll blow his nut.'

Doyle quickly saw what was needed, which confirmed my suspicions that, given a bit of encouragement, he could be an excellent songwriter. After noodling around for a quarter of an hour, he had a new main riff for the song. It had the same rhythm and was still in the key of E, but now it had a run of notes and a more dynamic opening chord sequence. Every other part of the song remained the same. Unfortunately, despite its simplicity, it was difficult to play the new riff because it required quick jumps to very different finger positions. I tried to cheat at first by playing an open-string version of C, but Doyle spotted it.

'You have to play the bar chord,' he admonished. 'Otherwise it loses its depth. You're just going to have to do some bleedin' practice.'

'Ibid' was pretty tough too. Why couldn't Doyle just come up with something simple? 'Because I'm a genius,' he replied, looking lupine with his four days of growth and overhanging monobrow.

We played guitars for an hour before Doyle went into his usual evening frenzy of wood-chopping and pocket-knife-whittling. After a while, he made a ring of wood chippings, in the centre of which he sat, cross-legged, staring with wild intensity at the log victims of his axe's fall, like a druid spilling sacrificial blood to appease a wrathful god. The occasional cries of 'ouch' were all that broke the monotony of the sounds of the axe, the knife and the fire. In the peace of the room, I thought again about Peckham, and that

girl on the bus who had been shouting down her mobile at her
boyfriend. I also thought about NJ and the kind of things that we
argued about, and realised where I had been going wrong in the
lyrics to Doyle's seventies Neil Young-style chord sequence. I had
started with too much of an idea and then tried too hard to make
the lyrics fit to it. The words, finally, started to flow.

Because I'm wrong
Doesn't mean you're right
It looked like that
On a Friday night

Rice and fish
At the miracle pot
It took a miracle
To see what you've got

Chorus:
Don't be surprised that I tried to hide
From the look of hurt in your dark brown eyes
Because the things I say and the things I do
Is the long way round of coming back to you

Afternoons
Down on Peckham Rye
We got soaking wet
Now my feet won't dry

You said 'I'll hang around
Because I like the view'
And then I replied
'No-one's asking you'

Chorus

Stay with me
While I comb my hair
And decide upon
What I'm going to wear

Please don't think
You don't have a use
Because I need someone
To wax my leather boots

Chorus to fade

I tried the lyrics out on Doyle, expecting sarcasm. 'They're good, man,' he croaked, momentarily leaving the wood and the fire to test them out on the guitar. We worked out a very basic verse–chorus–instrumental structure. For better or for worse, the song was written.

'If NJ can work out a way to sing it,' croaked Doyle, 'that one might just be half-decent. It should be called "Coming Back To You".'

Just as the dented aluminium kettle that was sitting over the leaky gas stove came to the boil, there was a knock on the door.

'It's probably your bit of fluff,' said Doyle, casually. 'She's come back to get you in a half-Nelson and finish off what she started.'

'You answer the door!' I whispered. 'Tell her I'm not here!' I jumped up and looked for somewhere to hide.

The old wooden door creaked open . . . and it was Iain, the man with the guitar we had met at the harbour on the first evening. It seemed that the rainy nights in the tent had got to him: for the big storm he had found solace in a caravan owned by a fisherman and tonight he had somehow found us.

'When you've been on the island a few times, you get to know where everyone is,' said Iain. I handed him a cup of tea. 'You're a lifesaver. It's pretty treacherous out there. So what have you boys been up to?'

We told him of our adventures at the Singing Sands and of how we now had the better part of three songs under our belt. He admitted that, after nineteen years of playing the guitar, he hardly ever wrote songs, but still got immense pleasure out of playing songs by other people. And he had similar musical tastes to us: he liked Otis Redding, The Ramones, Led Zeppelin and Syd Barrett.

Certain records always make their way back onto my stereo and Syd Barrett's two solo albums, *The Madcap Laughs* and *Barrett*, are played constantly. I've been guilty of mythologising the mentally unwell, or at least have been drawn to their visions of the world, and Syd Barrett's charm is partially down to his unhinged character which, combined with good looks and a dark stare, is compelling. But that's a reason to discover someone, not to constantly go back to his or her work. There is something about those albums that draws you in. The songs are simple and frequently unfocused – some are rough takes with Barrett falling apart halfway through – but the best, like 'Terrapin' and 'Octopus', are childlike works of art.

'I can show you how to play "Terrapin" in five minutes,' said Iain. 'It's really easy.' It was just a few strummed chords starting in E. Barrett had a simple technique for the song: he hit a chord then sang the line, so the words were always trying to catch up with the music. The lyrics could not have been simpler: 'I really love you, and I mean you. The stars above you, crystal blue. Well oh baby, my hair's on end about you', before going into the chorus that features some daydreaming whimsy about 'floating, bumping, noses dodge a tooth, the fins are luminous'. You could see how Syd Barrett would have come up with these: by staring down into a tank of terrapins and using them as the inspiration for a love song. Our own material quickly exhausted, we spent the next few hours playing favourites, drinking whisky, and – in Doyle's case – chopping logs. The songs were a shared language that offered a quicker kind of friendship than talking. We kept going until three in the morning, with the rain lashing the roof and the fire and a bottle of whisky keeping us warm.

For our remaining time on Eigg, there was not much more to do other than argue, explore the island on foot and practise our songs. We spent a day walking up the Sgirr, the volcanic lump of rock at the centre of the island. As we fought through metre-high heather to scramble up the side of the mountain, Doyle's forty-a-day habit got the better of him. 'Better . . . stop . . . to enjoy the . . . view,' he gasped after every ten minutes of climbing. 'Don't want to . . . get there too fast.' At which point he would collapse onto the heather, make some lewd comments about what a good bed it would make for him and a lucky lady, and light a cigarette.

I resisted attempting to compose a song at the top of the Sgirr. On the way back down we passed through a valley, following the course of a stream, which looked like it could have been in the Himalayas. We entered a pine forest that had been severely hit by the storm a few days earlier; many of the huge trees had been uprooted, the ripped bases making crevices in the earth and their fallen trunks forming walkways in the air. We saw a golden eagle flying above the treetops – two were nesting in the forest – and ended up climbing over fences to come down a hill that led to our bothy. The journey was over.

Two nights later we were on the sleeper back to London. We decided to mark the end of the trip by playing Robert Johnson's 'Love In Vain' on our guitars, the space was so small that the only way to do this was to play from our respective bunks, lying down. Doyle showed me how it went.

'It's really simple,' he said. 'It goes like this. No, hang on. It's like this. No, hang on . . .'

We got there in the end.

Chapter Ten

Red Light Fever

A date was set to go to ToeRag Studios in Hackney, east London, and record the single: 19 July 2006, a Monday in four weeks' time. If we couldn't make that the next available booking was not for another two years. 'Bad Part Of Town', augmented as it was by Doyle's riff, had to be the A-side. Then there were the two songs we had written in Eigg: the psychedelic 'Ibid' and the singer-songwriter-like 'Coming Back To You'. There was also an instrumental I had worked on that came out of what Bridget St John had revealed about alternate tunings and finger-picking patterns; with a few alterations to 'Ask Me No Questions' it was possible to create a new piece of music that sounded nothing like the one it was based on. I called it, for no particular reason, 'My Dearest Dear'. It would be good to get 'Ask Me No Questions' down, too – this was the song that had guided the journey more than any other. Liam Watson, our friend who had built ToeRag and acted as producer-engineer on most of the records made there, was surprisingly enthusiastic about my proposal.

'It's going to be great!' he said with guttural enthusiasm, when I called him to ask if we could book a date. ' "The Bad Part Of Town Sessions" will be legendary.'

'Can we do four or five songs in a day?' I asked, seeing no reason why we shouldn't be able to – the average song takes three or four minutes to play. Why should it take any longer than that to record?

'It's a stretch,' he said, 'but we can try. I'm all for doing things fast and not hanging around too long.' He could do it for a few hundred quid, remarkably good value as studios go. There was only one problem. Liam liked to record live, and, as such, he expected any band that came into his studio to be tight. I didn't even have a band yet, and was not convinced that Doyle had been practising the songs since we returned from Eigg. Four weeks didn't give us much time to get it together.

'I'll be your drummer,' said Liam, when I told him about my dilemma. 'You play guitar and Doyle can play bass. You or NJ can sing. What more do you need?'

'The other thing I'm not sure about is the vocal melody to a couple of the songs,' I told him. 'We haven't really worked out a good way for NJ to sing them. The problem is that I haven't got time to learn how to read music or find out how the rules of music work.'

'That's never stopped pretty much everyone else,' he said dismissively. 'You should do what Joe Meek did. He would take a backing track – any backing track, it wouldn't matter which – and hum over the top of it until he found a melody that he liked. Then he would hum it to the band and they would work out a way to play it. That's how he came up with "Telstar".'

'Telstar' by The Tornadoes (Margaret Thatcher's favourite song, incidentally) was an instrumental smash from 1962 that the Welsh producer Joe Meek recorded in the bedroom of his flat in Holloway Road, north London, along with hundreds of other early sixties British beat singles by acts like The

Honeycombs and Heinz. Meek was an inventive genius – he would stamp his foot on the floorboards for a stomping rhythm and experiment with early electronics for space-age sounds – and he was Liam's hero. He was also certifiably insane. Driven crazy by repressed lust for Heinz's Aryan beauty and slender physique, he ended up killing his landlady and then himself. I only had to hope that 'Bad Part Of Town' would not have a similar effect on Liam.

'Sometimes, if I think a band isn't ready to record, I'll spend a week with them in a rehearsal room and help them knock the songs into shape,' said Liam. 'But I have to charge for each day.'

'At the moment,' I said, 'I'll be lucky if I can get Doyle for an afternoon. He's always working.'

'In that case, I might be able to help you come up with a melody,' he said. 'Then I'll get a songwriting credit.'

This didn't sound like a good idea. Doyle and I had written the songs. What if we ended up in debt to Liam because he had given us a few fortuitously placed 'la-la-las'? People have ended up bankrupt over less. We had no choice but to work out those vocal melodies ourselves.

In the weeks following our return from Eigg, a couple of things happened that made it look like there might be hope for the recording after all. One evening NJ and I went over to see some old friends called Fan and Colin, both of whom turned out to have hidden talents. Fan had grown up in a remote part of Cornwall and, forced to make her own entertainment, had picked up a nylon-stringed guitar. Without a teacher and not knowing anyone else who played, she had invented her own style, which was close to the classical technique of giving one finger to every string. Now she could play a few pieces of her own creation that were quite sophisticated, and yet she had no

idea about the basic first position chords that most people learn
in the first few weeks of playing. For a brief moment I wondered
if our record wouldn't benefit from a second guitar line
featuring this most intuitive of musicians. Lovely though it
was, however, I concluded that it was not possible to utilise
Fan's talent, since she had no way of following what other
people would be playing. But Colin revealed a skill that took
the possibility of recording a sixties-style rock'n'roll song onto a
whole new level.

For some bizarre reason, Colin had a childhood obsession
with the Hammond organ. He had never learned piano, but was
given a Hammond by his parents for his thirteenth birthday and
spent after-school sessions learning to play it from then on. He
had an unfortunate weakness for British nineties alternative
bands, like Radiohead and The Wonder Stuff, but luckily he
played the Hammond like he belonged in The Doors or The
Small Faces. The Hammond has a reassuring, warm sound:
always on the edge of kitsch, it has innocence in its whirling,
sustained notes, but a groove too. All the best garage bands had
a Hammond or Farfisa organ to spice up their otherwise
primitive songs. '96 Tears' by Question Mark And The Mys-
terians, an all-time classic from 1966 recorded when its Mex-
ican-American lead singer was only fifteen and the rest of the
band weren't much older, is based around an organ riff.

'Do you know why The Doors never had a bass player?' asked
Colin. 'Because Ray Manzarek played all the bass parts on the
Hammond. Listen to this.'

Colin had recently managed to transport his unwieldy and
temperamental old Hammond from his parents' house to his
flat. He hit a series of pedals to build up a rumbling bass
rhythm and added a melody onto the top of it on the keys. Is
there anyone in the world who doesn't have a secret musical

skill? I decided to teach Colin the parts to 'Bad Part Of Town', not difficult since most of it is in E and C. He took off on the organ, his long fingers looking like they wouldn't be out of place in a seventies horror movie – if he lost a few teeth and wore a black suit covered in cobwebs, Colin could have been playing the church organ while a village beauty is denounced as a witch and burned at the stake, her bodice popping open in ecstatic despair.

'Colin,' I asked him, 'what do you think you'll be doing on the day we go into ToeRag to record our single?'

'I can almost guarantee right now,' he said, still pounding away at the Hammond, 'that, whenever it is, I will be doing absolutely nothing whatsoever.'

So it was set. With Liam as the drummer, Doyle and myself on guitar and bass, NJ singing, Colin on his magic organ and anyone else who happened to turn up on the day on tambourine, there was actually going to be a band. A band that was past its first flush of youth, perhaps, but a band that made music nonetheless. It looked like a long-gestating dream might finally come to flower.

Throughout this journey of learning, the person who I kept coming back to, in terms of imagination, lyrical wit and economy of structure, was Lawrence. And he was closer to living on the streets than anyone else I knew. Then, on a Thursday in May, I witnessed in quick succession the extremes of lifestyle that music can bring. In the morning I went to the house of Andrew Lloyd Webber, the most commercially successful writer of musicals of the twentieth and, most probably, the twenty-first century, to talk about how he approached writing for musicals. I went to Lawrence's place round the corner afterwards.

I have never been a huge fan of musicals, but two have made an impact. The first is *Cabaret*. Christopher Isherwood's Berlin stories, on which *Cabaret* is based, are portraits both of fully realised, acutely observed characters and of Berlin before the Second World War, when the divine decadence of the Weimar era was giving way to Nazi aggression. The film and the theatre production of *Cabaret* work because Sally Bowles is such a compelling character; a lost, spoilt, but unloved rich girl trying to be a femme fatale in a fading, doomed bohemia. Liza Minnelli inhabits the songs so totally that they are camp, glamorous, theatrical, tragic and realistic. In the film Kander and Ebb's songs take place in the plastic reality of the nightclub, which continues to shine and dazzle, as the world outside becomes an increasingly foreboding place. The mood jumps from the high theatre of 'Wilkommen' to the saucy humour of 'Two Ladies' to the lonely hope of 'Maybe This Time', and *Cabaret* achieves what must surely be the goal of all musicals: escapism with depth.

The other musical that I love is *Jesus Christ, Superstar* by Tim Rice and Andrew Lloyd Webber. The portrayal of Jesus Christ as a proto-hippy, complete with Judas as a black militant and Yvonne Elliman's Mary Magdalene as a sexy moonchild is too good to resist. The title track is the kind of the anthem that makes you want to fall on your knees and throw your arms up to the Lord, and 'What's The Buzz?', in which the rather thick apostles bombard Jesus with all manner of inane questions, is an unstoppable slice of orchestral funk. Somehow these two rather posh, rather stiff public schoolboys made a countercultural, religiously questioning masterpiece.

Most of Andrew Lloyd Webber's musicals leave me cold. I can just about stretch to *Evita*, his story of Eva Peron, the less than angelic former first lady of Argentina, but I draw the line at *Starlight Express, Phantom Of the Opera* and all of those other slick but vacuous productions that have been keeping Broadway and London's West End afloat for the last three decades – and made their creator very, very rich indeed.

Andrew Lloyd Webber has a house on Chester Square in Belgravia, west London, with David Bowie and Margaret Thatcher among his neighbours. Many of the white pillared houses – and they really are houses rather than flats, rare in London's most central, most expensive boroughs – have not only Rolls Royces but liveried doormen outside them. I went into Lloyd Webber's house to be met by a frightfully proper butler, who offered a cup of tea with the kind of natural decorum one usually only sees in television adaptations of P.G. Wodehouse novels. The open ground floor, essentially a reception, had a large black sofa with a coffee table with neatly stacked art books on it and, on one wall, a Pre-Raphaelite tapestry that looked like it must be worth amounts I'm not even capable of counting up to. After a while Lloyd Webber's polite assistant – everyone was well brought up in this house – came to take me upstairs, in a lift, to his office one floor up. Lloyd Webber was polite (naturally), rather formal, and with a face that looked like it had benefited from age. He also had a strangely agitated, sweaty air, as if he was about to be found out for something.

Quite often, if I meet someone famous, I find myself stumbling over my words and, out of nerves, forgetting names that I should know, and it isn't unusual for the famous person in question to give me, short shrift and emphasise their superiority, not only over me but over the great mass of humanity in general. Andrew Lloyd Webber did not do this. With perfect grace he found a way of agreeing with whatever inanity spewed from my mouth before explaining aspects of his craft with

eloquence. I put it down to an upbringing in which good
manners are equated with not making people feel awkward. I
managed to ask him how he went about approaching writing
for musicals.

'Music is never the starting point,' he said, going against
what almost all other musicians had said. 'Musical theatre
starts with the story and you have to write what is right for
that; you are its servant. Construction is absolutely vital:
everything must work together and have a reason for being
there. It if doesn't, no matter how good the melody or the
arrangement, it has to go.'

He illustrated his point by explaining the genesis of *Evita*.
Tim Rice had come up with the idea of a musical based on the
life of Argentina's first lady, Eva Peron, and of having the
revolutionary South American hero, Che Guevara, as its narrator.
Lloyd Webber's job was to give some kind of musical sense to
this idea. He remembered going to see the last stage performance
ever given by a drugged and intoxicated Judy Garland.

'She attempted to do "Over The Rainbow",' he said. 'It was
one of the most awful sights I had ever seen. She ended up being
booed off stage, and you couldn't help but feel for this poor
woman as the song that had made her famous, the song that she
would always be associated with, turned on her. I realised that,
if I could do the same thing with Eva Peron, I would be halfway
up the ladder.'

He leaned forward, as excited about the story as if he were
pitching it to a theatre producer for the first time.

'So I came up with the idea of a political speech in which she
was insincere but which was her big moment, which became
"Don't Cry For Me, Argentina",' he continued. 'And the song
turns on her in the same way that Judy Garland's did, because it
is the song that she sings in her final broadcast.'

Lloyd Webber based the framework of *Evita* around this cynical crowd-pleaser of a song. 'Every song I have ever written – or every good one, at least – comes out of trying to capture a dramatic situation,' he explained. 'I think that's the way with musicals. I have often said that you could have "Some Enchanted Evening" by Rogers and Hammerstein, which is one of those rare songs that has a perfect melody, in the wrong moment in *South Pacific* and nobody in the world would remember it.'

I asked him what a perfect melody was. 'They exist,' he said ' "Do-Re-Mi" from *The Sound Of Music* is perfect, whether you like it or not, because no other melodic genius than Richard Rogers could come up with something so blindingly obvious.'

'So where do your melodies come from?' I asked, thinking as I said it of that absence of a vocal melody in 'Coming Back To You'.

He shook his head, and then stared at the floor. 'To tell you the truth, I just don't know. When you come up with a simple melody, your first reaction is to assume that it already exists, and then comes the exciting part: to realise that it doesn't. There are so many melodies out there that nobody has got to yet.'

A lot of people had told me that their best work comes from some cosmic force that they are privileged enough to tap into. I suggested to Lloyd Webber that the best songs really come from hard work and trial and error. 'They do. Did Richard Rogers just sit down and write "Do-Re-Mi" in its entirety? No, because initially it went: "Do *is* a deer, a female deer, Re *is* a drop of golden sun." And somebody pointed out to him, a singer most probably, that that didn't work. Very often somebody else will suggest the slightest alteration to your song that actually changes everything.'

In the late sixties Tim Rice had been fixated on a Bob
Dylan lyric that asked: "Did Judas Iscariot have God on his
side?" So began the idea of doing a musical from Judas
Iscariot's point of view.

'Did Judas have God on his side? Who knows?' said Lloyd
Webber. 'But it was a good angle and quite a controversial one,
if you think about it. Of course nobody would stage it. We had
to release it as an album before anyone would touch it.'

I was only with Andrew Lloyd Webber for forty minutes
before he had to go off somewhere. 'If you have a good idea for
a musical, let me know,' he said breathlessly, before rushing
into another room, and I think he might have been serious –
he did appear to be in a semi-permanent state of panic.
Thinking of how he said that he had no idea of where
melodies came from, and of how it looked like this reality
bothered him, I realised that dealing with something as hard
to hold as melody for a living must be phenomenally stressful.
Each song for a musical, each idea, might be his last. And he
looked like he was coming to that conclusion himself. His
assistant showed me the way out and my brief glimpse of how
the very wealthy lived was over.

Lawrence lived two streets away from Andrew Lloyd Webber. I had been calling Lawrence's phone for the last few weeks
and he hadn't answered, which could mean any number of
things, but I did know that his days in the tiny, dingy studio
flat were numbered. It would be worth a try. I rang the buzzer
on the street, and, to my amazement, a hesitant and shaky voice
answered. 'Will, Jesus Christ!' he said in his Birmingham
accent of permanent surprise. He allowed me in.

Lawrence was indeed about to be chucked out of his flat for
good, and was about to embark on a stay in whatever hostels
Westminster Council's social security department dumped him

in. He was trying to get enough money to put his beloved vinyl records into storage. I had asked him once which record he would grab if his collection were on fire. 'I'd burn with them,' he replied. Now their very existence was threatened. And he looked terrible. He was so thin that you would guess he had stopped eating altogether. At least he had managed to get his possessions into boxes, which were stacked up in the middle of the dark, airless room – he had hung a dirty orange curtain over the window to block out the sun of that bright and warm May morning. The only light came from the television, which was tuned to a chat show that looked like it was filmed in the reception of the corporate hospitality suite of a provincial airport. The room stank of the chemical air freshener that Lawrence insisted on using in his all-in-one battle against more organic noxious smells. The walls were bare, beyond a piece of paper over the television featuring a few words in Lawrence's childish scrawl.

I took a look at Lawrence's emaciated body, the dirty walls, and the sad hesitancy of the boxes stacked in the middle of the room, and came to a conclusion.

Drugs are not the answer.

Lawrence was cheerfully suggesting that his current misfortune was only a slight mishap that would pass soon enough. He started telling me about how some of his junkie friends had broken into a car and stolen a CD and MP3 player that they sold to him for £15. 'Honestly, they're the loveliest kids you could ever hope to meet,' he said. 'They're proper begging street junkies, but they're great guys. I think it's a bit of a bargain for only £15.'

When I first met Lawrence I had decided that I wouldn't make any kind of judgement on his lifestyle, but this was too much. Here was a truly original thinker, and a great songwriter, and a gentle, really rather innocent man, who had got into drugs because, by his own admission, he thought they were cool. It seemed like such a waste and a cliché too: the world was full of untalented people who carve out an identity for themselves by embracing the drugs lifestyle as set out by any number of outsider figures. But Lawrence had a gift that, if only he could get himself together a little more, could be shared with the world. And I don't think the hard reality of the drugs lifestyle suited Lawrence, a childlike, naïve person, at all. I told him as much.

'You're right, and drugs will stop you dead in your tracks,' he said, sitting cross-legged on the floor, looking apologetic. 'It was only because I had done so much work that I got into such a mess. I felt that I could afford to take a few years off.'

He talked about his latest idea for a song, which was inspired by his obsession with the equally thin American celebrity Nicole Richie. 'I was looking through all these celebrity magazines I get, like *Heat* and *Closer*. And they're all calling Nicole Richie a lollipop head, because, while she's thinned down so much, her head has stayed the same size. And I thought, wow, Lollipop Head! That's a term for the masses. They all leave their offices for their dinner and go buy a copy of *Heat* magazine, so, if someone did a song called "Lollipop Head", it would go to number one. Ideally I'd like a woman with a Jamaican accent to sing it, so it would be a bit like "My Girl Lollipop" by Millie. And then Nicole Richie might go out with me. She used to be a junkie, you know.'

I played Lawrence the new version of 'Bad Part Of Town' on his narrow-necked guitar. It sounded awful.

'That riff you've got there,' he said, looking serious, 'is amazing. Because it changes, so you have a second part that answers the first part, which means it's resolved. Loads of songwriters don't even bother to do that: they just repeat the first half. You're already learning songwriting tricks.' (I forgot to mention that it was actually Doyle's riff.) 'That's really good. Who's going to sing it when you go to ToeRag? You?'

'My voice is so terrible that I was thinking of getting NJ to sing it.'

'What?' he snapped, close to animated by shock. 'You can't do that! It's your big song. You have to sing it because this journey of yours demands it. And, besides, it's a man's song. It's about being tough and living in the bad part of town. I like your voice anyway. Who cares if you can't sing for toffee? Honestly, "Bad Part Of Town" is a great song.'

I moved on to 'Ibid'.

'It's funny,' he said. 'Because you've just started writing songs, you've got a strange way of doing it, but can you see what you're doing? When you first came round, you showed me this supposedly intricate stuff on the guitar, but you weren't actually writing songs at all, even though you thought you were. Now you've done a chorus for "Ibid" in G-D-A, which is the most basic chord construction there is.'

'So do you think it works as a song?'

'All the big hooks are in those chords,' he said, by way of reply. 'That's good, because after doing all this strange stuff in the verse you come to the chorus and everyone can understand it. It all adds up to a weird pop song. But, if you're asking me if it's going to be a hit . . . no, it won't. It might appeal to a couple of old hippies, but that's about it.'

Lawrence was so fresh in his enthusiasm and his way of looking at the world, yet he was attracted to the most degraded, sordid aspects of life. And I saw a similarity between the way his mind worked with that of Andrew Lloyd Webber. Lawrence was teaching me that I should follow well-worn structures that have a musical sense. Andrew Lloyd Webber talked about how every musical part should serve the whole. The message was the same. And both were eccentric people whose talent was a product of the fact that their minds worked in unconventional ways. I told Lawrence where I had been prior to meeting him.

'You are joking,' he said, his mouth hanging open. 'That's amazing. I can't believe you actually went into his house. I'd love to do that.'

'I didn't think you'd like Andrew Lloyd Webber.'

'I like anyone who's rich,' he replied, wistfully. 'And another thing. When you go into ToeRag, can I come too? I've always wanted to go there. I won't be any trouble. I won't try and take over. I'll just stay in a corner, taking notes. The most I'll try and do is shake a tambourine and maybe suggest the occasional change.'

Why did everyone want to come into the studio with us? When I did my debut gig I had to practically drag the band on stage, and then they disappeared immediately afterwards so they could catch the last bus home.

After Lawrence expressed astonishment that I had heard a rumour that he was terrified of wood ('That's ridiculous. I love wood'), then talked of his all-consuming terror of dairy products ('Who isn't scared of them? They're horrible'), I told him that I had to go. Every time I said goodbye he pulled out another item of clothing that he was proud of, including a leather jacket with 'kill' spelled out in silver studs on the back. It was rather like Otto when I tried to put him to bed and get him to go to sleep. 'Daddy, I've just got to tell you something!' he always said with the utmost urgency. 'What is it?' I always replied. And the answer would be: 'Um, um, um . . . Spider-man has a web shooter.'

I left not knowing what to think. He was still operating, and still cheerful, in spite of the wreck that drugs had made of his life. Andrew Lloyd Webber had worked hard, and made commercial decisions, and not taken drugs, and made a lot of musicals, and made millions. I wondered if, given a different set of circumstances and greater discipline, Lawrence might have done the same.

I went to a party that night, where I bumped into a friend who was a sort-of boss. He worked with my Hammond organ master Colin and he had heard all about the recording session and single. 'Have you heard my harmonica-playing?' he said excitedly. 'I'm really good! You need me on that session. I could turn your song into a blues classic.'

'I'm not sure if we really need a harmonica player,' I told him.

'I can play anything,' he said, his face wide-eyed with the anticipation of recording joy.

I had to be strong. 'Listen,' I told him. 'We *might* need a triangle player for the B-side. How about that.'

His demeanour turned stern. 'Might I suggest,' he began, 'that you remember which side your bread is buttered on.'

'What do you mean?'

'Take it any way you like. All I'm saying is that me and my harmonica have got a lot to offer the world.'

In the meantime, these songs needed to be ready in time for the session. Lawrence was right: I had to sing 'Bad Part Of Town', however bad my voice was. People kept saying that plenty of great singers couldn't sing – Bob Dylan, Lou Reed – but they could deliver their songs with conviction and I couldn't. Sensible advice came from the Scottish acoustic guitarist Bert Jansch, who had been such an inspiration when

I first picked up the guitar. I loved the way Bert sang. It was quite odd, with lots of rising and falling inflections that didn't follow any particular melody. After seeing him play at a concert, I asked Bert how to approach a song when you can't actually sing.

'The best thing to do is experiment with as many different ways as possible until you find your voice,' he said. 'That's what I did, because there *will* be a way of singing certain words with conviction. What I found is that I could only sing by playing the guitar and using that as an anchor. It can take time to find it, but, if you persevere, the way will show itself eventually.'

A few days later I sang 'Bad Part Of Town' to NJ.

'Obviously you sound awful,' she began, 'but I don't know if it really matters with this. Most of those garage band singers that you like had horrible voices too. A bigger problem is that you're playing guitar with real confidence, but you're singing with so little certainty that it's almost impossible to hear you. You sound apologetic. You can't be apologetic in the "Bad Part Of Town".'

'So are you saying that I shouldn't bother, or I should persevere?'

'I know I'm going to regret this, but I think you should persevere.'

We moved on to 'Coming Back To You'. I remembered what Andy Partridge had said about isolating the notes you sing, of feeling the steps beneath your feet. I knew that it would be good to keep the vocal melody in the key of the song, which, in this case, was D. From there I found three notes – G, E, D – that worked well against the first line. For the second line it went off the scale – F#, E, D – to create a sense of sadness that seemed to make sense against the opening words: 'Because I'm wrong, doesn't mean you're right.' Then I reversed the process. That was the melody of the verse done, and for the chorus the vocals could just follow the chords. But NJ's singing was too pronounced. She was belting out the notes like she was singing a show tune in a piano bar in New York at three in the morning in front of an audience of gay men – which would probably be her spiritual home, but I didn't see that as the right setting for the song.

'You're trying to sing it too well,' I told her. 'The way you're delivering it has no relation to the meaning of the words.'

'What is the meaning of the words?'

'It's about, you know, having an argument, and Peckham, and . . . stuff.' Then I remembered something that bands always used to say in interviews with the *NME* when I was growing up. 'Actually, it kills the song if you try and over-analyse it and explain what every word means. I let my music speak for itself.'

'You don't know, do you?'

'I . . . er . . . I . . . I . . .'

She picked up her book and began to read. 'But,' she said, not looking up, 'you have found a tune for me to sing.'

'What do you mean?'

'Ever since you started trying to write songs, you've been coming up with some guitar parts and some words, but you haven't actually set down a sequence of notes for the singer to reach. Wasn't that what Andy Partridge was telling you to do back in December? For the first time, you have.' She smiled. 'We'll practise this one tomorrow. I want to read for a bit now.'

I am a slow learner, but it seemed that, finally, all this advice that people had been giving me had sunk in. 'Coming Back To You' could be called, without fear of reprisals from the Trades Descriptions Act, a song.

*   *   *

It was emerging that NJ was a far better singer than I had previously given her credit for. But there was still the problem of my own voice to consider, and how I was going to get it around 'Bad Part Of Town'. Professional help was needed.

NJ had a friend called Caroline, the mother of Otto's best friend, who was a music teacher. She lived in north London and was one of the most patient people I had ever met, which perhaps explains how she managed to survive at one of the toughest schools in the country, teaching kids with learning difficulties in a school in one of London's most deprived boroughs (Hackney). Surely there was nothing I could throw at her that wouldn't pale in comparison to what she had to go through on a daily basis with a classful of fourteen-year-old boys. So I gave her a call.

Caroline had one day off. She told me to come at midday; that was when her two-year-old son went to sleep for an hour or so. 'Before we start,' she said when I arrived, 'we need to do some vocal exercises. You sing from the head, the chest and the belly, and I think you're probably a head singer. So I want you to stand up straight – you can't sing properly with your diaphragm all squashed – and take a deep breath through your nose . . . and out through your mouth. Now, repeat after me. La-*la*-La-la-La-laaa.'

'La-*la*-LA-la-La-laaa.'

'La-la-LAAA-LAAA-*la*-laaa.'

'Try again. La-*la*-LA-la-La-laaa.'

'La-*la*-LA-la-La-laaa.'

'Good. Now me-*me*-ME-me-Me-meee.'

Then she told me to sing 'Bad Part Of Town' the whole way through.

'OK,' she said, as it came to an end. 'Presumably you're meant to be sounding tough in this song, but you're singing like you're attending a class in flower arranging. So you need to find the right way to convey the words. And your problem isn't that you can't sing, whatever anyone might have told you – it's that it seems you haven't been taught technique before. At the moment you are trying to harmonise with a chord, which nobody can do because a chord is made up of two or more notes played simultaneously. You can only reach pitch by actually hitting a note itself. So, first of all, let's find out what you're trying to sing.'

Caroline made me break down each part of the song into the root note upon which the chord is based, and then concentrate on that note. She told me to keep the rhythm of the song on the guitar, but to just play notes, not chords, and sing along to them. It took a while to get into it, but slowly my singing did start to improve.

'You see? The problem before was that you didn't have anything to aim towards, so you were floundering around in the dark and going all over the place,' she explained. 'You're singing much better now. Can you hear that? You don't have to have a brilliant voice for this song because what you need to convey is a certain attitude. But you can certainly get through it.'

We went through the middle eight of 'Bad Part Of Town'. Caroline played the piano and sang 'It's not like everyone's bad here' in her high, perfectly pitched voice, and it was like hearing Slade performed by the Royal Philharmonic. She was isolating a melody to the song that was there without my knowing it. With Caroline's help, my voice sounded almost bearable for the first time. It was quite a revelation. Unfortunately, my singing found less of an appreciative audience in Caroline's toddler son who, having been woken up and presumably scared by the strange noises coming from my mouth, had appeared at the bottom of the stairs looking as if the world might end at any minute. It was time to stop.

'You know, Caroline,' I said, as I put my guitar in its case, 'if you ever get sick of school, you might think of becoming a singing teacher to rock bands. You've taught me more than anyone else I've met and you did it in the space it took your son to have his midday nap.'

'Oh, don't be silly,' she said, waving her hand and closing her eyes, and I had a flash of Caroline in front of her school class, getting on with it in the most efficient way and not thinking about herself. 'Come back any time – well, any time on Wednesday between 12 and 12.30.'

I went from Caroline's house to Mara Carlyle's new place. It had been a while since I had seen Mara and her fortunes had taken a dramatic turn for the better. She had a new record deal, lots of gigs, and a flat in the heart of London courtesy of her uncle, a lawyer who spent most of his time abroad and hence wanted his pied-à-terre used by someone he could trust. I wanted her to sing 'Coming Back To You', and who knows? Perhaps she would like to actually record a version of it.

She had cut her hair short and, with her small, lithe body in jeans and a T-shirt, she looked like a countryside tomboy let loose in the city. 'I've decided that I'm either going to live in the middle of nowhere or in the heart of London,' she said, as I marvelled at the Romanesque busts, mahogany desks, and all-round grown-upness of this flat in the Temple courts, which occupied the building where Dr Samuel Johnson once lived. 'So let's hear this new song of yours.' I played 'Coming Back To You' on the guitar and did my best to sing it as NJ had done. Then Mara sang it.

'It's a good tune,' she said, as it came to an end. 'But some of the lyrics grate. "Please don't think you don't have a use,

because I need someone to wax my leather boots" . . . too silly.
If you're trying to be funny, it's not working, and, anyway, it
doesn't scan. It would flow better if you removed "leather". And
I'm not so sure about "rice and fish at the Miracle Pot, it took a
miracle to see what you've got." It reminds me of Pam Ayres. I
feel like a bit of a twat singing it.'

'You have totally ruined it for me,' I told her. 'I was trying to
be heartfelt and now all I can think of is television poets from
Berkshire with rueful expressions. Anything else?'

'The line "please don't think you don't have a use" is a bit
clumsy, isn't it? Two "don't's" with only two words to separate
them. The music is nice, though,' she said, pressing a finger to
her lips and staring intently at nothing in particular. 'The
chorus relates really well to the verse and it steps up a gear in a
very natural way. I like the line "we got soaking wet and now
my boots won't dry", too, because it sounds like a bit of a dig.
When you were playing it, I could hear how it might be nice to
arrange it. I heard backing vocals. It had a Bob Dylan seventies
touch. That's a sign of a good song – if it unlocks your musical
imagination, it is working. I can hear brush drums and some
slide fiddle in there, too.'

This was faint praise. Mara had said that the words sucked
and that the music was nice. I wrote the words and Doyle wrote
the music.

'It's much better than your last one . . . what was it? "Before
Daylight"? It's a proper song and it fits together well. The
problem with your old one was that it was two songs stuck
together. That can work – "Bohemian Rhapsody" by Queen
and "Paranoid Android" by Radiohead are examples of that –
but they are very well thought out and there is a specific
purpose to what they are doing that borrows from classical
orchestral techniques. You still need to be careful about making

the sound and the meaning of the words relate to the way they are sung, though. "Miracle", for example, is not an easy word to sing. You might want to think about that. But, otherwise, you've got a good song here, and you have succeeded in finding the missing melody that seemed to be eluding you last time. Well done.'

'So, do you think you might like to include it on your next album?'

'No.'

'OK.'

I thought I might as well try 'Bad Part Of Town' out on her. I did my best to keep the whole thing in time, remember the words, and, most of all, to take on board the things that Caroline had said. Somehow they all seemed to go out of the window. Mara stopped me halfway through to mutter about having an important date to keep and that she must leave that instant. It turned out she wanted to catch the launderette before it closed.

A few hours later, after Otto made me repeatedly sing the line from 'Bad Part Of Town' 'soon these streets are going to explode' so that he could leap out from behind the sofa and scream, I told NJ that I had made a recording of Mara singing 'Coming Back To You' on my Dictaphone.

'Let's hear it, then.'

We sat motionless as Mara perfectly executed the words, bringing a jazzy undertow to the tune that I hadn't previously known existed. She sang it in a smoky, late-night way, with lots of rising and falling notes. Mara gave space to the lines in a way that gave the whole thing the air of a cool breeze. It came to an end. After about half a minute, NJ broke the silence.

'Well,' she said, 'she does have a lovely voice.'

'You know how she goes up rather than down on the line "the long way round"? It makes it a lot better. And she pointed out the lyrics that didn't work. So I've replaced "rice and fish at the miracle pot, it was a miracle, I saw what you've got" with "rice and fish and a glass of wine, get that for me and I'll be fine." And I've got rid of "please don't think you don't have a use, because I need someone to clean my leather boots" because that doesn't work. Now we have "sit down on the bed, and don't block the light, and then I'll be yours, I'll be with you tonight." '

'But I liked those lines,' said NJ, quietly.

'They seem cheesy to me now.'

'But your new lines are just bland and unimaginative, whereas the old ones were full of character,' she said. 'In the miracle pot line you get the feeling that this woman is really furious with him, so she's saying that it's a bloody miracle that she can see his worth at all. And the line about needing someone to clean her leather boots is really poignant. I agree that it scans better without "leather", but, apart from that . . . no. I liked it the way it was.'

'You hate change. It scares you.'

'That's unfair,' she replied, calmly. 'What you have to understand is that Mara's changes don't work with my voice and it sounds pretentious if I try and copy what she does. Listen, you think I'm upset because you got Mara to sing it, but it's not that. It's just not very nice to be compared unfavourably to someone else. Why don't you let me sing it my way, and then maybe you'll see what I mean?'

This time NJ sang it much more softly, with a hesitancy that brought a new meaning to the words. She didn't emphasise the lines as much as Mara did; she landed on the notes and kept the drama to a minimum. And she was right: with her voice the old words worked better, which made sense, since they were written with her in mind. She was making this song her own. It was coming together.

A few days later we got a babysitter and went to our friend Richard Vine's house. Richard, a quiet, bearded man who has a grin that reminds me of the dog Muttley in the seventies cartoon *Dastardly And Muttley*, had set up a digital home-recording studio in his bedroom from which he had made entire albums. I'm not sure if he ever entertained ideas of being a professional musician or not, but he seemed happy to keep a stable job and make his music without commercial pressure. We planned to record demo versions of the songs that we would, with any luck, lay down for real at ToeRag Studios.

I knew that it was going to be almost impossible to get the band – Doyle, who was addicted to overtime, on bass; Colin, who had a rather unwieldy instrument, on Hammond organ; and Liam, who had better things to do, on drums – together for rehearsals, so I decided to record acoustic versions of the songs that I could then give to everyone in the band to practise to.

It was a Sunday evening and, after NJ's performance a few days earlier, I was excited at the prospect of recording 'Coming Back To You', filled with hope that finally it seemed possible to present a real song to the outside world. But I could not help but feel that Richard had wished he had never agreed to have us round. He had been out late the night before and had a hangover, and mentioned something about a film on television that he was hoping to catch in an hour or so. NJ stood in front of a microphone in Richard's bedroom and I sat on the bed, playing guitar. And as soon as Richard announced that he was recording, everything fell apart. NJ no longer hit the notes and her timing was out. My guitar sounded terrible. It was a disaster.

'I thought that was great,' said Richard with a yawn, looking at his watch.

'It was awful,' said NJ, close to tears. 'I got nervous.'

'What did you get nervous about?' I said. 'We're in Richard's bedroom, not Abbey Road.'

'I just got nervous. Leave me alone!'

It was the fact that we were being recorded that did it. I had heard people talk about this. It's a phenomenon known as red light fever.

'We have to do another version,' I said.

'For this reason I think you're being ambitious in trying to record four or five songs in a day at ToeRag,' said Richard. 'It takes time to get it right.'

That evening we never got it right. NJ's timing got worse. I nodded at her every time it was her cue, but she was lost within two lines. My playing was clumsier than it had ever been – this song that I had practised and practised was all over the place. Richard was getting increasingly impatient, but he restricted his comments to a slight shake of the head when I messed up a guitar line and he even muttered 'sorry' when he did that. We moved on to 'Bad Part Of Town', for which I played the guitar part first then sang over the recording of that. It sounded like I was reading out a quantity surveyor's report.

'That's great,' said Richard. 'Excellent, well done.'

By the time we got to 'Ibid', NJ and I were completely disheartened. Richard suggested some changes to the arrangement that made the song work better – he moved a weird instrumental bit near to the end before the final chorus reached a crashing finale, and told me to play the guitar softer – but we had performed terribly. We couldn't cut a disc with the songs in this state. It was just humiliating.

'Richard was being far too nice,' I said, as we drove back home. 'We were clearly appalling.'

'It's called overstaying your welcome,' said NJ. 'He wanted to get rid of us because we were wasting his time by being so unprepared. What are we going to do?' We're meant to be going into ToeRag in three weeks.'

'There is only one thing we can do,' I replied, taking a deep breath. 'Panic.'

Chapter Eleven

My Dearest Dear

In wanting to write a song that utilised the folk guitar styles that I liked, I had come up with the instrumental 'My Dearest Dear'. Taking Bridget St John's advice and experimenting with different chord shapes until something emerged had created it. But it was currently more of a musical idea than an actual defined song and I wasn't sure how to develop it.

The answer was to go and see Bert Jansch. Since he had given me guitar lessons a year and a half earlier, this taciturn pioneer of folk guitar-driven songwriting and his cheerful wife, Loren, had become friends. There was something admirable about the way Bert is such a curmudgeon who, in his own quiet way, does exactly what he wants and has a lot of fun too. I remember the night he first met NJ. Excited to talk to him after his records had been played on such heavy rotation at our house, she introduced herself by saying how much she loved his version of the old Irish air 'Blackwaterside', to which he made a perfunctory grunt. Then she asked him what he thought of Bridget St John. He declined to give any response whatsoever.

'What did that mean?' NJ asked me later on that night. 'Did he consider her not even worthy of mention, or did he shag her back in the sixties, or has he never heard of her?'

'It's impossible to say. But, if he isn't interested in some-thing, he makes it clear. Which I think he did to you.'

Despite his resemblance to an imperious frog that won't be pushed off its lily pad by the bigger fish in the pond, Bert was a very kind man, and he had dignity. He didn't have to give me guitar lessons for free, after all, but, if he was around when I called on him, he invariably agreed to do so, as he had done with some rather more illustrious players than myself, including the singer Beth Orton and the guitarist Bernard Butler. As you discovered more about the world of musicians who have a grounding in both virtuosity and surrender to the song, it seems that all roads lead to Bert Jansch. He has been an influence on successive generations, from the first wave of guitar gods to modern American folk-influenced musicians. He stayed in his garden flat in Kilburn, with its rows of guitars on the walls and cups of tea brought regularly by Loren, and the world came to him.

I caught Bert at a good time. He was about to go on tour and was feeling positive about the future. Only months after a massive and extremely dangerous heart operation, he was excited to be playing live, making a new album, and coming back into fashion. I asked him how he felt about this new generation of people discovering his songs. 'I've been doing this for so long now that I don't really think about it,' he replied. 'Even when I was young, I knew that popularity would come and go. When I made the first album [in 1965] it sold reasonably well and then didn't go any further. Two or three years later it was reissued and it has stayed in print ever since, so you get used to the fact that young people are going to discover it. I'm the opposite of a one-hit wonder. Because I never had huge success at any one time, I haven't dated.'

It turned out that Bert had been having a songwriting lesson himself a few hours before I came round. He had just bought a

DVD player and had a disc of Big Bill Broonzy in concert. Broonzy was the American country blues guitarist who came to England in the early sixties to introduce a young, eager and earnest generation of white boys to the blues, and Bert used to watch his fingers when he played to learn what he was doing. 'He wore a silver thumbpick, which stood out because he was black,' remembered Bert, on going to see Broonzy play in Paris in the early sixties. 'That's how I learned finger-picking techniques, but, of course, I got a lot of it wrong and, as a result, I never really nailed the way he structured songs out of blues patterns. Now I'm learning from him all over again. So you can always improve, even if you are in your sixties and you have been playing guitar every day since your teens.'

I retuned the guitar to play 'My Dearest Dear' – and I decided that, with Bert, the less said about 'Ibid' or 'Bad Part Of Town' the better. While I concentrated on getting the pattern right for the song, I was wondering what he would say about it. It couldn't be good – he had never bothered with giving false praise before. Often, if someone takes apart your creative efforts, you can dismiss their stings by any number of reasons: jealousy, ignorance, conflicting tastes. With Bert I couldn't do that. I loved his music and respected the clarity of his vision and the integrity of the things he said. If he said that my song stank, it meant that it was reminiscent of a dying fish market.

I went through the strange chords, still not knowing what they actually were, but feeling that a tune was emerging from them. There was a droning sound of an A note that held the whole thing together. Bert wore a wry smile through my playing, which I didn't take as a good sign. When I came to the end of the sequence, Loren rushed in and said, 'I think that's lovely,' shooting Bert a look that could be translated as: 'go easy on him or else.'

After a few seconds of agonising silence, he said: 'That's not too bad, actually.'

'But you need to go somewhere with it,' he continued. 'If that sequence of chords is going to be the verse, then I'd suggest you do a traditional blues pattern for the chorus, which would be the first, fourth and fifth chords in the scale. You could follow them with the seventh chord. You can keep the same finger-picking pattern and it will work well over them.'

I tried it and, sure enough, it did sound like a real chorus. The song was forming and actually having a proper shape. 'Songwriting is aided by following a few basic rules,' said Bert. 'Once you get going, it's up to you to do what you want with those rules, but they can help you find a structure to hang your ideas on. You quickly find that folk music follows predictable patterns. The fun is in being creative over the top of them.'

It is this attitude that is at the heart of Bert's appeal for his fans and of his blasphemy for his detractors. Bert began by playing in traditional folk clubs and pubs, like The Howff in Edinburgh and The Troubadour in London. When he left Edinburgh as a young man in the early sixties, he lived without fixed address, busking in Paris with the American bohemian singer Ramblin' Jack Eliot, doing duets with his equally free-spirited on/off girlfriend, the singer Anne Briggs, and finding places to stay by turning up at clubs, doing his set, then hanging around until someone offered him a bed for the night. And he learned to ignore the rules of the clubs that tried to preserve the folk songs in aspic, which led him to fall out with leaders of Britain's sixties folk revival, like the communist singer Ewan MacColl.

MacColl was the organiser of The Singer's Club, where you were meant to perform only the songs that came from the region you were born in. Bert got chucked out for playing Davy Graham's instrumental 'Anji'.

'The whole thing was ridiculous,' said Bert. 'He was laying down all these rules, but he was a man from Salford pretending that he was Scottish and his wife, Peggy, was accompanying everyone that got up on stage, yet she was American. And he wrote "The First Time Ever I Saw Your Face", which is absolutely lovely but certainly not a traditional folk song in any sense of the word. I've never been interested in that museum aspect of folk. As far as I'm concerned, it should be an honest reflection of your environment, and, if that environment is reflected by rock'n'roll or hip-hop, then that's as valid a form of music as anything else.'

Loren had made some pasta and I had brought a bottle of wine. We sat down to eat at a table that had, for the last few months, been dominated by a 1,000-piece jigsaw puzzle of a Jackson Pollock painting that Bert and Loren, having worked so hard at completing, could not bear to take apart again. 'The thing about Bert is that he's only ever been interested in playing the guitar,' said Loren, as Bert sat over his pasta and poked dispiritedly at an olive. 'He's still completely focused on it at the age of . . . what are you? Sixty-three? And he can be oblivious to everything around him. That's why I think these young people keep coming to seek him out: because he's never embraced image or the business side of things, but concentrated on going deep into the songs. They recognise his integrity.'

They also sought him out, I believed, because they wanted him to teach them how to play 'Anji', 'Blackwaterside' and any other number of songs that he made his own through his creative dedication to them. Perhaps what was most inspiring about Bert was that he had a deep love of the folk-based music he played, but he was not in thrall to it, meaning that he didn't hold a song with so much respect that he couldn't alter it as he wished. It's this combination of freedom and commitment that interested me.

The folk music faithful will tell you that you can't write a folk song, that it has to be passed down, through oral history, from one generation to another, and that your rendition of it should be as authentic – as unchanged – as possible. It's not an argument that can be easily dismissed because it is concerned with paying respect to the past, but it is also paradoxical. As anyone who has ever given or received gossip knows, anything that gets passed orally mutates with each new telling. Folk songs are the same. One of the most famous songs from Black America, 'Stagger Lee Shot Billy', takes on thousands of different forms. The great outlaw hero of the title is variously known as Stagolee, Stagger Lee, Stackolee and Stack. He shot Billy over an argument about a Stetson hat, a cheating move in a game of cards, a woman, or some combination of the three. New Orleans, Memphis and St Louis are among the cities that have laid claim to the scene of the crime; sometimes streets in Missouri are mentioned. The only consistency is that big, bad Stag/Stack/Stagger Lee shot a man, and generally (but not always) gets hanged for the crime.

Disputes about what constitutes folk music are nothing new. The great pastoral English composer Vaughan Williams had a nice definition of it: 'the reaching out to ultimate realities by means of ordered sound.' The early German romantic writer Wilhelm Grimm claimed that the folk song 'composes itself', which is a profound way of describing its nature: it's less about self-expression than memory and shared experience. Cecil Sharp called folk song 'the song that has been created by the common people, in contradistinction to the song, popular or otherwise, which has been composed by the educated.' It isn't a great definition, since it equates 'the common people' with the non-educated, but it does highlight the fact that folk songs generally existed to share stories in communities where literacy was rare. Perhaps another great German writer, Goethe, gave the most honest definition: 'We are always invoking the name of folk song without knowing quite clearly what we mean by it.'

Cecil Sharp was gripped with a fascination with English folk song at a time when it had fallen out of fashion and, mostly through not being written down, was in danger of dying out. The English trait of self-deprecation had resulted in the dismissal of its own traditional music, like the dismissal of the rich heritage of English food that followed, and is only now being rediscovered. Sharp recognised this. He stated that 'in less than a decade, the English folk song will be extinct' – and got to work, chiefly travelling to Somerset to collect songs from the local people who sang them. At the same time Vaughan Williams was coming to the same conclusion about the much-ignored value of English traditional music: 'There, in the fastnesses of rural England,' he wrote, 'was the well-spring of English music; tunes of classical beauty which vied with all the most beautiful melody in the world and traceable to no source other than the minds of unlettered country men, who, unknown to the squire or the parson, were singing their own songs.'

Singing reduced the grind of rural life in the age before consumer entertainment, which is why so many families did it together. I found a book called *A Song For Every Season* by Bob Copper, one of the members of The Copper Family, folk singers and agricultural workers from Rottingdean on the Sussex Downs. Bob's grandfather, James Copper (1845–1924), used to sing his way through every aspect of life, including putting his grandchildren to bed. Unfortunately the lullaby he chose to get them to sleep was 'Admiral Benbow', the story of the British hero of the Napoleonic wars, who had his legs blasted off by chain-shot and ordered that his bloody stumps be placed on the quarter deck so that he could watch the rest of the battle. Unsurprisingly, the Copper family grandchildren suffered frequent bouts of nightmares.

Bob Copper explains how song was so integral to the life of his family, a situation not untypical among farming communities in the first part of the twentieth century. His father, Jim, would hold a candle in the evenings while the women did needlework and grandfather James waxed the family footwear and sang. 'A song seemed to make a task a little lighter and the long winter evening a little shorter,' wrote Bob. 'As Grandad hammered, he would most likely be singing one of his old songs with everyone joining in the chorus.'

My favourite folk album is *Folk Roots, New Routes* (1965) by Shirley Collins and Davy Graham, swiftly followed by Shirley Collins' collaboration with her sister Dolly, *Love, Death And The Lady* (1970). *Folk Roots . . .* presents traditional songs in a pure form and yet shines with the complex and contradictory characters of its two creators. Shirley Collins grew up singing folk songs with her Sussex family, learning the banjo as a teenager to accompany her unfettered voice on faithful renditions of old English songs that were mostly found by Cecil Sharp in the early 1900s. As a young woman, she went on song-collecting expeditions through the southern states of America under the guidance of the American song archivist Alan Lomax, who was also her lover, and she has spent most of her life singing English, Irish, Scottish and American songs in folk clubs and in concerts, in between raising a family. Davy Graham lived a life that, drenched as it was in mysticism, drugs and experimentation, could not have been further from Shirley Collins' reality.

How these two conflicting personalities – the English rose of the folk world and the dark magus of the guitar – ever came together is something nobody can really be sure of, except that it was Collins' then-husband's idea. The result is one of those rare moments of alchemy that, like The Beatles at the height of their powers, come from nowhere, never to be repeated. The first song is called 'Nottamun Town'. Shirley Collins sings about riding a horse 'with not one hair on him but what was called black' and, all of a sudden, this sensible woman, who smiles meekly like a prim, pre-Swinging Sixties mother on the album cover, is a bringer of dangerous, elliptical messages from the distant past. And when the stark naked drummer appears in verse two, she appears to be a conduit for some rather odd sexual fantasies too.

Perhaps the most erotic, most mysterious song on the album is 'Hares On The Mountain'. Shirley Collins sings in her detached, casual way about courting as an animal drive: 'If all the young men were hares on the mountain, how many young girls would buy guns and go hunting? If all the young men were blackbirds and thrushes, how many young girls would go beating their brushes?' Before coming to that, she sings: 'Oh Sally, my dear, I wish I could wed you. Oh Sally my dear, I wish I could bed you.' She smiled and replied 'then you'd say I misled you.'

Inspired by *Folk Roots, New Routes*, I wanted to develop 'My Dearest Dear' into a proper song, maybe even with words, especially now that Bert Jansch had given me an idea for the chorus. So it was fortuitous that a few evenings later our friend Michael Tyack, an early music enthusiast and the leader of the medieval rock band Circulus, should come round for dinner, as he always did when living off Pot Noodles got the better of him.

Tyack was in his usual troubled state. There had been dissension in the ranks, with certain members of the band

not willing to buy into Michael's messianic vision of commitment to the cause while living in near-total poverty. He also had
a tendency to make the band wear preposterous costumes, which
they generally grumbled about rather than openly rejected. His
latest were matching gowns in gold lamé accessorised with
two-foot-long pointed shoes. Being lined on the inside with
plastic, the costumes were extremely sweat-inducing. The
band's crumhorn player, Will Summers, had recently collapsed
on stage in his golden gown during a particularly spirited
rendition of the thirteenth-century monk John of Fornsete's
merry ode to a cuckoo, 'Sumer Is Icumen In', and it had taken
four roadies to get him upright again. In his golden scales, Will
kept slipping through their hands like a wet fish.

Circulus had seven members. Four of them had walked out
soon after recording their second album, led by the keyboard
player, whose chief reason was that he hated it. It could not have
happened at a worse time. The band had been booked to play
various festivals which would build up an audience for the new
record but there was less than half a band to do them. To tide
him through the difficult patch, Michael had set up a side-
project called The Princes In The Tower. Consisting of Will
Summers, a Mexican bongo player called Victor Hugo and
Michael, The Princes were not quite as retro as Circulus (they
were Elizabethan rather than medieval) and they didn't present
such an elaborate spectacle, yet already they were encountering
hostility. It seemed that the Renaissance music crowd didn't
like the way Michael put his lute through a wah-wah effects
pedal.

I played Michael my work-in-progress. 'Yup, it's all there,'
he said, shaking his medieval bowl-cut enthusiastically. 'You've
got a real sense of mystery in the music. Now you just have to
find a way of marrying the words with the melody.'

Earlier that evening I had written some lyrics to the tune and got NJ to sing them. I had a line about liking 'coffee hot and with the milk warmed up'. NJ had her misgivings about the words. I don't know if she was going to find the answers she was looking for from a man who wrote a song called 'Power To The Pixies', but her respect for Michael was such that she would trust his judgement.

'The main thing you have to think about is whether the words scan with the music,' said Michael. 'Often lyrics that look ridiculous on the page can sound poignant and suitable when they have the right melody to carry them through. Let's give it a go.'

For the last two lines of each verse, I just held onto the last chord until NJ had finished singing them because they didn't scan at all.

'These words don't fit and you're going to have to get rid of them,' said Michael. 'Well, you don't have to do anything, but, if you're going to follow a reasonably traditional song structure, then they should go.' And so came another important lesson of songwriting: to be able to discard words or music that you might be rather pleased with.

'Also, Will has a tendency to come up with songs in a key that I can't sing, or he forgets about the melody entirely,' said NJ. 'Can you teach him how not to do that?'

'I'd just come up with a vocal melody that you like, if I were you,' Michael replied casually, looking down at the cigarette he was rolling. 'That's what we do.'

Because of his virtuoso abilities on the guitar and a number of instruments that tended to date back to the Renaissance, I had always assumed that Michael's songwriting process was a carefully thought-out one with plenty of adherence to the complex rules of music. It seemed that I was wrong. He played us one of his new songs. It was the result of asking each band member to come up with two lines each. Michael's contribution consisted of the telephone number of his local rubbish clearance company.

'Why don't we try and come up with words and a vocal melody for this now?' suggested NJ. 'Let's just make it up as we go along and see what happens. This tune makes me think of riding a bicycle in the forest. Maybe we should think along those lines.'

I started up 'My Dearest Dear' on the guitar. After a while, NJ came in with the words 'freewheel fine on the forest floor, branches evergreen.'

'Stop and go and the water flow,' I added. 'Stickleback and stream.'

Michael sang in a high voice about dappled barks, oak trees and applecarts. NJ started to harmonise with him, singing different words over the top. I played the guitar furiously, increasingly excited by this stream of consciousness inspired by the healthy outdoor pursuit of off-road cycling, something I can't say I have ever witnessed NJ doing.

Michael's voice got higher and higher. He started singing about the golden light of creation and the naked tree goddess bearing her fruits upon him with such generosity, which reminded me that he hadn't had a girlfriend in a while. 'This is great!' I said. 'We have to record it.'

I got my Dictaphone and asked NJ and Michael to start up again. After a while they were both singing with their eyes closed, presumably imagining this glorious bicycle ride through a beautiful British forest with not a pylon in sight. Michael began to sing something about mushrooms unveiling curtains of perception. NJ was just making open vowel sounds, swaying from side to side and clapping along as she did so. Suddenly we heard the patter of feet running down stairs. Otto appeared in his pyjamas.

'Mummy, I'm scared,' he said. He looked around the room and waved at Michael. 'I can't sleep. I heard strange noises. I don't like that music you're making. Can I have a glass of water? I'm hungry. Have you got any sweets? Hello Michael. Did you bring me a present?'

NJ took Otto back upstairs to bed and Michael and I listened to the Dictaphone recording of 'My Dearest Dear'. It was, to my considerable surprise, dreadful. Michael had been moaning like a dog howling for its master. NJ had been wailing as if in the throes of exorcism. No wonder Otto was scared. And, as for the words, mystical flights of fancy, woodland imagery and descriptions of bicycle parts don't, on reflection, appear to make happy bedfellows.

'Can't I just leave it as an instrumental?' I asked Michael.

'I think that might be wise,' he replied quickly.

Just before he left that night, Michael had some good news. There was a message on his phone from the keyboard-playing leader of the Circulus rebellion. All was forgiven. He had just discovered that he had been listening to the new album through one channel on his stereo.

A few days later I found Shirley Collins. She was living in the East Sussex town of Lewes, and with a book recently written – *America Over The Water*, which documented her time spent collecting traditional songs in the American South with Alan Lomax – she was happy to talk about her own approach to song. At the age of seventy-one, she was no longer singing. Her great tragedy was that she had lost her voice two decades earlier and had not sung since. But she was still deeply involved in the world of British folk music. 'I don't know if I'll be of much help to you, dear,' she told me on the phone, sounding like a kindly grandmother, 'but why don't you come down here and I'll make us a light lunch. We can talk over that.'

Shirley Collins lived by herself in a small cottage built against the walls of the medieval castle that dominates Lewes, a pretty Sussex town not far from where King Harold breathed his last at the Battle of Hastings in 1066. Such an ancient place was a fitting home for a woman who had always been somehow out of time with the world. Shirley had never been involved in, or had any interest in, modern music, to the extent that she didn't actually like much after Handel. She was the opposite of Bert Jansch: her definition of folk music paid tribute to its centuries-old past and her goal was to keep these songs as she believed they were meant to be kept.

Shirley, who had blue eyes that almost looked like they were made of water and which shone brightly in a wide face under a thatch of curly blonde hair, revealed herself to be a free thinker. She hated religion ('people kill prostitutes and invade countries in the name of God and it frightens me') and was open to new ideas while being steeped in old ones: she had collaborated with a man called David Tibet, who, under the moniker of Current 93, had made a series of experimental albums that reflected his Christian faith and belief in a forthcoming apocalypse. 'Can't say I really understand it myself,' said Shirley, as she put the kettle on.

It was hard to equate this eminently sensible, kind old lady with the dark mystery of the songs that she had sung, but perhaps that was an underestimation of Shirley's own depth. I asked her about 'Nottamun Town'. 'It's an upside-down song,' she said. 'Everything is contrary and that sounds to me like witchcraft, but perhaps I'm being fanciful. The words go: "I sat down on a hot cold frozen stone", and when the singer gets thrown from a horse he says: "He tore my hide and bruised my shirt." It is a riddle.'

I couldn't imagine her hanging out with Davy Graham,

having met him and having found out from experience how unpredictable a character he is. 'He really was the most exquisite guitarist, and the one who took it to another level,' she said of him, 'but I couldn't stand all the drugs. One time we were travelling to a concert and he told me that he couldn't be on the same train as me because of some perceived artistic difference, which I found very offensive. I've never had any time for drugs. I remember one of The Incredible String Band telling my sister Dolly that you haven't seen a tree until you've seen it on acid. She shouted that she had seen more bloody trees than he was ever going to see in his lifetime.'

The more I knew about Shirley Collins' music the more I marvelled at her ability to inhabit songs that she didn't write and express herself through them, which I suppose is the appeal of the traditional song. On the train down to Lewes I listened to *Love, Death And The Lady*. At the time of recording that album, she was in the process of splitting up with her husband, leaving her with two small children to bring up on a minimal income. It was a dark period in her life and the music, none of which she wrote, reflected that. Featuring sparse, cold, monastic piano, harpsichord, sackbut and lute arrangements by sister Dolly, Shirley sings traditional working-class British folk songs, centuries old and none of them authored, with such stark tragedy that you are convinced she must be singing about her own life. 'As I walked out one morn in May, the birds did sing and the lambs did play,' begins the opening track, 'Death And The Lady', sounding more like a medieval funeral procession than a celebration of summer. 'I met an old man by the way.' This is the introduction to one of the most personal, tender and bleak albums of the seventies, featuring songs that gain their resonance from being shared and passed down over centuries.

Love, Death And The Lady is about death, sex, violence,

isolation and loneliness. In 'The Oxford Girl' the singer tells of his murder of a lover in a jealous rage ('I plucked a stick from out of the hedge and I gently knocked her down'). In 'Are You Going To Leave Me?', Shirley Collins contains her passionate despair under a cloak of British dignity as she sounds reconciled to an encroaching misery. As for 'Young Girl Cut Down In Her Prime', it's best not to even go there if you're feeling at all sensitive. It is music from the bottom of a deep well of experience. I asked her how she could bring self-expression to songs that someone else wrote.

'It's not that someone else wrote them, it's that 1,000 other people have sung these songs and had that same experience,' she said, as she gave me a coffee and sat down before a large and uneven mug with 'Shirley' roughly sculpted in clay. 'They are universal songs and themes and they can do for you what you need them to do. And, at their best, the melodies are the equal of anything by Purcell or Handel. When you are singing a folk song, it's not your song. I'm slightly standing outside of it, but I'm totally involved. You are a conduit for all this stuff behind you and you want to take it forward too.'

I told her that, with songs like 'Are You Going To Leave Me?', it sounded like she was singing about her own life. '*Love, Death And The Lady* is a dark album and I was at a low point, so I chose songs that reflected my state of mind at the time,' she explained. 'People have always had hard times, so there are a lot of songs like that in the folk tradition, but there is optimism there, too. I inhabit the songs and all of the people in the songs have a common feeling of what we've all experienced, and it's couched in such perfect language.'

Over a lunch of salmon, bread and salad, Shirley laid out her philosophy towards music. 'Really, dear, I'm the wrong person to talk about songwriting since I've never written one and I

don't like new music,' she said. 'A folk song is passed down
through generations and you can't write one. There isn't a
person living who can write a traditional song. The labouring
classes kept these songs going and preserved them in their most
beautiful forms. They couldn't read or write, but they had ears
for the melodies and words and the ability to write songs like
this has now gone.'

I asked her if there were any modern songs that she liked.
'Who wrote "The Night They Drove Old Dixie Down"? That's
a wonderful song, and Neil Young is rather good too. But
nobody talks to me in the way the old songs do. I compare it to
the difference between the original blues singers and the bands
that copied them in the sixties. When I went to America as a
young woman, I met these wonderful people, like Muddy
Waters and Mississippi Fred McDowell. Then I came back
to England and saw The Rolling Stones on the television doing
the same songs and they looked so silly and preening in
comparison. I never tire of hearing something like "Lord
Gregory", but a pop song bores me by the third time I hear it.'

She pushed the salmon across her plate. 'I do remember a
profound night when I was married and living in Blackheath,
and The Beatles were singing "Let It Be" at the BBC. Even the
doormen were singing along. That was beautiful and overwhelming, but that overwhelming feeling didn't last. Yet I can
still listen to folk songs that I sang as a girl again and again and
again.'

That was all well and good, but I wondered if she could listen
to my songs. Given her views on the impossibility of writing a
folk song, it was probably a good thing I ditched the ridiculous
lyrics and nonexistent melody of 'My Dearest Dear' and kept it
as an instrumental. She didn't have to hear that one. I decided
instead to try out 'Coming Back To You' on her, which was

shaping up to be the most fully realised song in our (limited) repertoire, despite the disastrous attempt to record it at Richard Vine's house. First I played it on guitar, then I played a recording I had made on a Dictaphone of NJ singing it one evening at home, a few days after hearing Mara's version. NJ had sung it naturally, without artifice or nervous effort.

'Well, I think that's quite good,' she said. 'That was a complete song. I couldn't hear all the words, but it followed a nice path. I think you're doing very well, especially as the song grabs you straight away and has that nice blue note in the second line. It had a beginning, middle and end. Yes, I think that's rather fine.'

Whether she was just being polite or not, I didn't care. This was the kind of encouragement that gave me hope at this crucial juncture. And while not being able to give clues as to how to write a song, she did have a lot to say about how to sing one.

'The old songs were written for people to sing in a straightforward way,' she said. 'Any decoration was subtle. Now people are off the tune before they have started the bloody thing, so you lose the shape of it. This sounds vain, but I knew how to sing from the start.'

'How did you know?' I asked.

'Like a bird, you fly straight onto the branch,' she answered. 'Or you lift yourself up to it; you don't just buzz around the note. Your wife has a lovely voice, and she has the kind of straightforward singing style I like. I think you'll be all right.'

I wasn't so sure. The songs were in place, but I was to venture into the studio in only two weeks and the band – Liam on drums, Colin on Hammond, Doyle on bass, NJ on vocals and myself on guitar and vocals – had not had any rehearsals whatsoever, nor were we likely to, given that Doyle and Colin had jobs and Liam was going to France. And I knew from the experience of having him as my upstairs neighbour for five years that Liam was not one to suffer fools. He had high standards, and was rumoured to be something of a tyrant in the studio with those who didn't match up to the level of musicianship he expected in his domain. What the hell was he going to make of us?

I stared bleakly at the neat, ordered homes of southern England as the train rumbled along from Lewes to Victoria, and wondered it if could ever be possible to live up to Shirley Collins' prediction.

Chapter Twelve

Fighting a Losing Battle

'I'll tell you what,' said Liam, when I called to tell him, given that it was going to cost me about a grand to make this single, that it might be an idea to have a rehearsal before the big event. 'I'm going to France in a couple of days. If you can make it to ToeRag the day after tomorrow, we can run through the songs. Be there at five.'

I knew Colin would turn up – he had already professed that he would rearrange his wedding day for the chance of having his Hammond skills preserved on wax – but I wasn't so sure about Doyle, whose current method of avoiding the pitfalls his wayward character led him into was to work crushingly long hours for as many days as he was allowed. It seemed that this time, however, Fortuna was smiling. 'I might just be able to make it, as it goes,' he said, when I called him. 'I'll check with my roster.'

It might be difficult to get a babysitter at such short notice in order that NJ could come, too, but I wasn't so worried about her: choosing a singer who happens to be your wife definitely has logistical advantages. We had practised 'Coming Back To You' and 'Ask Me No Questions' a lot since the debacle at Richard Vine's house. As for the rest of the band, one rehearsal for about an hour is not going to turn you into James Brown and The JBs. But it was better than nothing.

I needed a good person to talk to now that the songs were completed, somebody who knew how songs worked, and how studios worked, and how to make the most of your time there. A few months earlier I had met a guitarist and singer from Sheffield called Richard Hawley who, at the age of forty, was enjoying late-blooming success. He had been in various bands – Pulp was one of them – and released three interesting, if not outstanding, solo albums when, in 2005, he reached his creative maturity with a collection of melancholic love songs called *Cole's Corner*. The title track, named after a place in Sheffield where young lovers would meet on a Saturday night, told the story of being stood up and left lonely and disappointed, and it was a consummate lesson in songwriting: a theme that everyone could relate to with a strong melody held together by subtle orchestration and Hawley's deep and proud but damaged voice. The song had come to him, almost whole, one afternoon when he was pushing his two young children on the swings in a park near his house. The rhythm of the swings began it and everything else followed in the next ten minutes. Six months later, *Cole's Corner* brought Hawley the recognition he deserved.

I had been to Hawley's house and got a glimpse of his character and his world. The Victorian terrace that he lived in had a wood-heavy, homely feel, with shelves of records dominated by rock'n'roll, doo-wop, soul, blues and garage. He made us cheese on toast with Sheffield's own version of Worcestershire sauce. Dressed in denims and with a Brylcreemed black quiff, he was a romantic kind of guy, still living in the place he was brought up in and giving the credit for his musical education to his father and uncle, steelworkers who played in rock'n'roll bands. There was something quietly tragic about him, too; the stoic British man who suffers quietly, drinking in the pub to ease the pain of being sensitive to the things around him. He reminded me of a fairground worker who might read poetry in his caravan when he wasn't putting girls in the family way round the back of the dodgems.

I caught him at the right time. He had just come off a world tour and was spending a few days in Sheffield, doing as little as possible. *Cole's Corner* brought a rise in his fortunes, but it put pressure on him, too: he had to produce a follow-up, and, for the first time in his life, he was expected to create a body of work within a set period of time. And before he buckled down, he was going to spend a few days drinking Guinness. He told me to meet him at a pub called Fagan's in Sheffield, a small, dark, beam-lined womb of a place with no wide-screen television, no fruit machines, and an acoustic guitar that the landlord, a large, easy man called Tom, was happy to lend out to anyone who might want to play on it. Richard was leaning into the bar, a lithe rockabilly spider in his second skin of denim and cowboy boots, a cigarette in one hand and a pint of Guinness in the other. There were a few men in suits who had come out for a lunchtime drink, but otherwise the pub was quiet.

'I'm happy to be of help,' he said, in his Sheffield gravel of a voice, 'but I don't know if I'll be much use, because it's like trying to describe air, and a song is an attempt to make air look solid. In lots of ways I don't even want to know how I write a song. But let's go in here and I'll give it a go.'

We went into a separate room at the side of the bar. Tom passed over his guitar and brought us two pints of Guinness. Apparently Richard had sung 'Cole's Corner' in here, to a packed pub, a few nights ago after turning down a similar request made by the BBC.

'What you have to know,' he began, lighting another cigarette, 'is the mechanics of the song, which you can't get away from. There are three chords that make the basic progression: the root, the subdominant and the dominant – they could be C, F and G – and they are the building blocks of music.'

He took a swig of his Guinness. 'Rock'n'roll is based on that progression, but then so is a lot of classical music,' he continued. 'I was listening to 'The Lark Ascending' by that Vaughan Williams the other day and, even in that wonderful piece of music, you can hear the same basic three chords. There are only twelve notes and the rules of music are not written in some book, man. They're written in the stars.'

Every planet in the universe emits a frequency. When all of those frequencies are put together, they form a chord that is in perfect harmony. And so it is with the song: behind the myriad instruments, rhythms, time signatures, melodies, chords and styles that construct the millions of songs existing out there on our own planet, the vast majority of them follow the same rules. Even John Coltrane failed to discover the chord of H. Richard described the trick of songwriting as 'walking down a well-trodden path and coming up with something fresh, since it always *has* been a well-trodden path. Music is just numbers and letters, man. Never be mystified by it.'

He learned the mechanics of songwriting through rock'n'roll – and rock'n'roll pioneers like Chuck Berry and Bo Diddley followed a path that is grounded in the blues. And one of his favourite songwriters was Lou Reed, who seems to be the choice for people who write songs themselves – Lawrence and Gruff had talked more than once about this grumpy New Yorker's talents.

'Lou Reed always stuck with the building blocks of rock'n'roll, but he found a way to make them ironic,' said Richard. 'Take a song like "Some Kind Of Love" by The Velvet Underground. It has an A drone the whole way through and only one change in the entire song. "Heroin" is pretty much just one chord. There is nothing new under the sun, but there are hundreds of ways of making the same old crap sound fresh. In 1,000 years' time no one will give a shit whether The Velvet Underground wore shades and leather trousers, but "Candy Says", "Pale Blue Eyes" and "Sunday Morning" are statements about humanity and they are beautiful pieces of music that will always be relevant.'

I told Richard that now I would like to present him with my own songs. It has to be said that he didn't seem particularly interested in hearing them. I ran through 'Coming Back To You' without too much difficulty, and got though most of 'Bad Part Of Town', during which he kept staring at the landlord – I think it might have been his version of a cry for help. The rest of the people in the pub, all six of them, would no doubt have heard what I was doing too and my voice, not good at the best of times, sounded even more pathetic than usual. I finished. Richard's silence could be translated as 'no comment'.

'Listening to other people's music knocks me off my radar,' he said, which was as close as I was going to get to a critical dress-down from this clearly well-brought-up man. 'Jimi Hendrix said: "learn everything, forget everything, and play". That's the stage I'm up to now; I no longer want to hear other people's music because it's like gossamer, man: one minute you're so sure of a song and then you hear something great and you're uncertain all of a sudden.'

He was getting agitated at the thought of all that good stuff slipping out of his hands. 'You've been to our house,' he said. 'You've seen how many records I've got. But I've learned that the best songs come to me when I'm distracted, or when I can't sleep in the middle of the night, and sensory deprivation is the best way of finding them. And I'll give you a golden rule right now: always have something to record them on wherever you are, because they're like mercury – they'll disappear as quickly as they came if you don't catch them. They torture me in the night, those ideas. By writing them down they stop being synapses and chemicals bouncing around in your head because you've had too much coffee.'

Having the structure of a song was one thing; creating a great sound was quite another. That's where the studio comes in. *Cole's Corner* has the rich, string-laden quality of a Scott Walker or Roy Orbison album. I asked him how he got that.

'First thing to do,' he said, when I asked him about how to prepare for the studio experience, 'make sure you have breathing space in a song. Two guitars, bass and drums work well because it's a bit like a ham sandwich with some salad and cheese in it: it's balanced. And, in the early stages of recording, you don't need to be worrying about the mosaics on the atrium floor; you just need to think about the pillars holding the building up.'

'But what about all those strings on your record,' I asked. 'How did you know where to put them?'

'A lot of music that sounds complicated is very simple at its core,' he replied. 'Scott Walker's albums sound lush, but when you break the songs down, they consist of just a few chords. Whether it's "Louie Louie" by The Kingsmen or "It's Raining Today" by Scott Walker, songs all serve the same purpose: to get a point across. You need to remember that when you're faced with all this studio wizardry.'

My problem, however, was that I didn't feel that the people playing these songs – myself included – were ready. And the songs themselves were not ready either. The main parts were there, but minor details, like tempo and rhythm, had not really been worked out yet.

'Listen, man, I can walk into the studio with a guitar riff and come out with an album,' he replied, concluding his claim with the spark of a lighter. 'And I haven't got a clue about operating the digital technology they've got now, because that's the engineer's job. I got one of them digital recorders once. Did me head in. I lost more ideas in one month with that bloody thing than I had in the last ten years.'

'So you don't have to have everything fully formed before you go into the studio?'

'I never have anything formed before I go in and it drives the band nuts. We rehearsed eighteen songs for my last two albums. Only one song got recorded and, even then, it changed radically.'

I could only afford one day in the studio. Richard Hawley's approach seemed like an expensive way of working.

'It's not because I work very fast,' he said. 'I have a holistic approach to writing a song and I think about everything, from the moment a melody comes into my head to the type of vinyl being used on the pressing. And I'm a workhorse in the studio – I'll put in hard graft like you won't know to make those fuckers come together. It's like a Rubik's Cube: it takes twists and turns until it makes sense and becomes complete, and when I know it's right, I'll get it all down in one or two takes. Apparently Bryan Ferry used to do about 500 vocal takes for a single song during his days with Roxy Music. That is anathema to me.'

Richard played a handful of songs on the pub landlord's guitar, including 'Everybody's Talkin' ', Harry Nilsson's tune for *Midnight Cowboy*, which so perfectly captures the spirit of a lost innocent that the film is about, and 'Pretty Vacant' by The Sex Pistols, a brilliantly constructed rock'n'roll song that puts paid to the lie that the most famous punk band in the world couldn't play. He described how music was a refuge for shy people: 'Even the most rowdy, gobshite musicians probably got into music because it stops them from behaving in the same way as everyone around them. Me dad were a steelworker and he worked for them bastards for twenty years and all he got for it were a broken back and a broken heart. I make music so I don't have a fucking job.'

By the end of the afternoon, I was in a rare interview/lesson situation: Richard actually wanted me to stay, while I was trying to leave in time to catch my train. On a roll after more than one Guinness, he had a lot to say. He also made me realise that everyone is groping around in the dark when it comes to writing a great song. He had given his piano away because he had got frustrated at only being able to play in the key of C, discovering a week later that Cole Porter could only play piano in C too. He cited Jim Morrison as an example of someone who could create entire songs in his head: although it's hard to forgive him for his awful poetry and weakness for leather trousers, the lead singer of The Doors did come up with masterpieces, like 'Break On Through' and 'The Crystal Ship', in their entirety, without any knowledge of music, before singing them to the rest of the band to play. James Brown would write a song that took a single idea and executed it perfectly for about five minutes before finally bringing in the change and 'taking it the bridge'. And Richard Hawley, who had made this lush, orchestral album, which was so tight and so accomplished, pretty much made it up as he went along.

The next day, at five o'clock, which was the earliest that Colin could get off from work, I took a train to Homerton in Hackney for Double Fantasy's first and last rehearsal at ToeRag before the day of recording. I got the inevitable call from Doyle just as the train pulled into Homerton Station.

'Will, man, I'm not going to make it,' he croaked. 'There's been a fault and I've got to sort it out.'

I can't say that I was surprised. Doyle was failing to show the kind of commitment I expected of him. So what if he was going to fix some points on a railway track, erasing the danger of a train coming off the rails and killing hundreds of people? 'Bad Part Of Town' needed a bass player! I grumbled as I walked down Homerton High Street, a bad part of town itself that was awash with pound shops, pubs with one St George's Cross too many hanging outside them and a lot of angry-looking people wandering around with pit-bull terriers. ToeRag was in an unlikely location: down a residential street of small terraced houses, of the kind built at the turn of the twentieth century for local factory workers and their families. There was a small break in these houses with a narrow, weed-strewn driveway that led to wooden garage doors with two bells on them, marked in a biro scrawl: 'ToeRag: Studio' and 'ToeRag: Office Only'. I rang both of them.

Liam appeared at the door. When he was younger I used to think that Liam looked like one of those eternally cheeky boys who filled the pages of British comics in the fifties, forever putting a drawing pin under Teach, who went 'Yaroo!' and jumped three feet in the air before swiping at the mischievous lad with a cane. With his ginger crop, gappy teeth and protruding upper lip, Liam had always been pure rascal material. Now he looked like the rascal's dad. He was wearing a starched white shirt, braces and enormous tweed trousers, and his hair was slicked back with brilliantine. He had grown a neat beard that met in a point. He led me down a dark corridor to the main part of the studio, which is lined with black and white lino tiles and filled with handsome old instruments, including a backless Hammond organ, battered Vox and Selmer amps, and a red Burns guitar, while the engineer's room is dominated by an eight-track half-inch tape machine and a green metallic

mixing desk built in the late fifties and formerly of Abbey
Road, the legendary EMI studios where The Beatles, among
many others, recorded their great albums on only four, or at the
most eight, tracks.

Sitting by the mixing desk was Edrid Turner, ToeRag's in-
house engineer and sole employee, a fresh-faced young man of
few words, pleasant demeanour and, remarkably, a DNA
structure that was designed for employment at ToeRag. As
he sat on the steps outside the control room and smoked a roll-
up, his narrow features, slightly shaded glasses, starched white
shirt and neat haircut made him look exactly like a studio
assistant from 1963.

'Look at this,' said Liam, giving the mixing desk a stroke.
'It's an EMI REDD desk, which stands for Record Engineering
Development Department.'

I looked at it for a while. 'What does it do?'

'It's a mixing desk. It has these faders here, and you can plug
in tapes from a tape machine or microphones from the studio to
be mixed. When we record your session, for example, there will
be you on guitar, myself on drums, Doyle on bass and Colin on
Hammond. We might want to record it onto the eight-track
machine, but we will need, say, three or four tracks for vocals
and percussion. So, with this, I will mix the microphones used
for the Hammond organ, drums, bass and guitar down to the
amount of tracks I want to record them onto. It looks nice, too,
doesn't it? I'd love to have one of these as my dining table.'

Liam explained that we would play live, and there would be
microphones dotted around the studio. The sound from the
microphones would go into the mixing desk. One thing I did
know is that people recorded the vocals separately. I asked Liam
why this was.

'Who says I do that?' he replied. 'Depending on the music

and the experience and ability of the artist, I might insist on a live vocal. If you think the live vocal works for NJ, we will do it. We'll stick the microphones up and roll it onto a single track. A lot of the best records have been made that way.'

'I'd rather not do my vocals for "Bad Part Of Town" at the same time, though. Singing and playing guitar together is so difficult. Can I do the vocals separately?'

'Of course you can. I like to record live, but you have to go with what is going to work.'

I thought about what Richard Hawley had said about not forming the arrangement of the song until he got into a studio. We couldn't really do that – Liam might lose his temper and end up having steam puffing out of his ears if we went in unprepared – but I had already discovered that, while a song may be fully formed when it only involves the person who wrote it, as soon as other musicians or singers come on board, it often has to be changed. So I asked Liam if the arrangement of the song does sometimes form in the studio.

'Yes, it can,' he said, stroking his ginger beard authoritatively. 'I had a guy in a couple of years ago who had spent years doing crazy demos in his bedroom. There we were in the studio with a drummer, and we had to work out a way of making these songs playable. And with most bands it's very common that I might say that we have to shorten the intro or come up with a new bass pattern or need a new bridge. Even for a band that's really tight, I might say, "there's a little thing in there that ain't quite happening, can't put my finger on it, but I think it's in the rhythm. Can we change this?".'

When I formed a band for the first time a year and a half earlier, as soon as I had succeeded in getting the other members to turn up for practice (a miracle in itself), the arguments would start. I had often heard about producers hating bands and vice versa – Phil Spector pulled a gun on The Ramones for daring to criticise his techniques – and wondered whether Liam ever faced minor disagreements with his charges.

'In those situations,' he began, leaning against his mixing desk with an insouciant air, 'you find out if you can work with those artists on a long-term project or not. I often find that there might be something within the arrangement of, say, the relationship between the bass drum and the bass guitar that sounds wrong to me, and I may have a suggestion that will pick it up a little. Some people will say, "wow, I never thought of that" while others might get upset and say, "yeah, well, what if I like it the way it is?" In the latter situation, I'll try and be professional and get the session done, and probably not work with that band again.'

Liam played me a record by his latest group, a Swedish outfit called Peter Berry and The Shake Set. It was exactly the kind of music he liked: a pastiche of the stiff but slightly wacky early sixties British beat sound produced by groups like Gerry and The Pacemakers, The Big Three and Freddie and The Drea-mers. Liam lived above us at our old flat in north London, and he used to drive us insane by doing 'the Freddie' at three in the morning to his favourite beat records. Would he turn Double Fantasy into a beat pastiche?

'I find that all the best bands are open to suggestion,' shouted Liam over the 'shandy beat' (his description) of Peter Berry and The Shake Set, 'and a lot of the not-so-good artists are harder to deal with. Within the world of alternative rock, certain bands tend to be producer-paranoid; they think you're trying to interfere with their art and that is never fun. You are either the enemy, because you suggest that something might be better, or it's a case of, "Oh, he didn't do anything". So you can't win. But, ultimately, recording is a team effort between the band, the engineer and the producer, with the producer acting like a film director, trying to get the best out of everyone and making them each play their part as best they can.'

Peter Berry and The Shake Set shook their last. I asked Liam how prepared our band needed to be before the big day. (It was just over a week away. The question was hypothetical.)

'It's simple,' said Liam. 'You have to rehearse together as much as possible, and practise to the extent that you don't have to think about it when you record. By the time you get into the studio, you want to be able to play it and not have to change too much. If you're thinking about it, it will come out stilted.'

'What am I going to do if my playing isn't up to the song that Doyle and I wrote?'

'We will use our in-house session musician, Eddie here, to take care of the tricky parts for you,' he replied. 'To some people a session musician is a dirty word; it threatens their integrity. But, if you can't do it, and yet you've come up with the idea, get a session man. Now what happens is that people play the song badly – they fluff notes and so on – and then they have no problem with an engineer fiddling about with the track on a computer until it sounds right. That makes no sense to me. The whole way that audio-technology has developed over the years is that, once it reached a certain point in the early seventies, all advancements boiled down to making it possible for people who aren't very good to record impressive-sounding records.'

'So what you're saying is that modern music has its principles all wrong.'

'Exactly. I've got nothing against technology, but the reason why the best sixties records sounded so good is because they had very talented people playing on them, live in the studio. I don't consider it shameful for a band to have a session musician – The

Kinks, The Byrds, even The Who used them – and, if you're faking it with a computer, what's the difference?'

In the sixties, London, New York and the West Coast had a core of ultra-talented session men – in London future Led Zeppelin members Jimmy Page and John Paul Jones were among their number – who played on the bulk of the pop hits that came out of each city. Jamaica had a similar system. Clement 'Coxsone' Dodd, owner of the ska and reggae birthplace Studio One, employed a handful of musicians to back the singers who booked the studio to record their songs. Cat Power had taken a break from modern trends by recording *The Greatest* with the cream of the Memphis session men and women. It seemed a better way to do things than to use computers to cover up your inadequacies.

Still, I was nobody to judge, as was proven when Liam asked me to demonstrate the songs that I would be playing. Eddie leant me his Yamaha acoustic guitar, which I didn't get on with at all. I muddled my way through 'Bad Part Of Town'. Liam was exchanging glances at Eddie as I played, who kept a respectful silence throughout.

'"Bad Part Of Town",' said Liam. 'Classic mediocre garage.'

I ignored this comment as best I could and got on with it. Liam sat behind the drums for 'Coming Back To You', which I played much better – the song only involved strums and a few hammer-ons and, once you had mastered the chord sequence, you couldn't go too far wrong with it – but Liam insisted on rapping out a military beat that turned this delicate singer-songwriter composition into a comedy number.

'Sounds like The Eagles,' he said, when it came to an end. 'And I don't like The Eagles.'

Eddie nodded almost imperceptibly, and he may have given his chin a couple of strokes.

Then it was time for 'Ibid'. I would like to say that I saved
face with this psychedelic complexity, but it went the other
way. I fluffed the notes so badly that it was unrecognisable. The
chords are arpeggiated – each note is picked out and played
separately – and I couldn't for the life of me get my fingers to
hit the right ones. It was horrific, like a miniature death. Eddie
walked out to give the top of the mixing desk a polish. Liam
stopped me halfway through.

'What the fuck was that?' he shouted. 'You're not seriously
going to lay that one down, are you?'

'This guitar is really hard to play . . .'

'A bad workman always blames his tools. You're going to
have to do some intense practising if you really expect me to
pull you through. That was awful!'

I was saved from further humiliation by the arrival of Colin.
We managed to shift Liam's bulky, battered Hammond out of
the storage room and into the studio and gave 'Bad Part Of
Town' another bash. Slowly it took shape. 'The amount of
beats you end each line with can't be random,' said Liam from
behind the drumkit. 'It doesn't matter what it is, but it
should be the same each time. It helps other people know
what to play.'

'All right,' I said, trying not to sound bothered, 'let's make it
eight.'

We started up again.

'It's a bit boring, isn't it?' shouted Liam, as we went over the
riff again and again.

'I thought we should just practise the main riff for a while,' I
shouted back.

'Just play it as it's written and we can work it out.'

Colin's Hammond organ swirled and grooved. Liam's drums
were heavy and lumpen, but they gave the song a tight rhythm.

My playing, on the red sixties Burns electric guitar, was getting slightly better.

'Why do you need an introduction?' said Liam. 'This is a garage song – you have to get to the point immediately.'

We lost the introduction.

'Why do you need the fourth verse?' said Liam, interrupting the playing again. 'It goes on too long in the same vein with that in there.'

We lost the fourth verse.

'Why do you need to say the line "bad part of town" twice? You've got your message across without repeating yourself.'

We lost the repeat of 'bad part of town'.

When Liam's culling came to an end, 'Bad Part Of Town' went down from being a three-and-a-half minute song to a one-minute-52-second song. 'That's better,' he said, leaning back on his drum stool. 'Most pop songs are far too long anyway.'

Gone was Colin's proposed Hammond organ solo. Gone was the moody intro; now the singing started at the same time as the music. Gone was the final verse about flowers blooming and trees growing on streets where nobody would go – the verse of hope. But this was no place for dreaming This was rock'n'roll.

Liam and Eddie were tidying up the studio while Colin fooled around, trying to find Hammond parts for th' songs. Colin was an easy-going man but a great play didn't take him long to work out the right notes to right style. For 'Ibid' he created a spooky churc' that was entirely fitting for the song. I went casually, not even realising that I was playi' despite the disaster of my first rendition o'earlier.

'Sounds good, lads,' said Liam as

"Ibid" we should just have organ, acoustic guitar and voice. That should work nicely.'

This was the first time Liam had given me some sort of hope that our efforts might not be totally disastrous. 'So do you think there's hope?'

'Well I'm going to be straight with you,' he said with a sigh. 'The words to "Bad Part Of Town" are good and, now that you're playing "Ibid" properly, I can hear something quite good in it. "Coming Back To You" isn't really my kind of thing, but there are some pretty chords in there. But you really need to tighten everything up. You're hitting far too many bum notes and the timing isn't together. If you went to a normal modern producer who uses computer technology maybe you could get away with playing as badly at that, but not here. We're going to record the songs live and you need to know what you're doing rather than making it up as you go along. It's an expensive business and you've only got a day. I can do quite a lot in the mixing to make it sound good. But it boils down to this.' He cut a look that went straight to my eye and let me have it.

'You can't polish a turd.'

Two days later Syd Barrett died. He was sixty and died of complications due to diabetes, ending a lifetime dominated by the suffering that mental illness brings. Barrett was the archetypal sixties acid casualty; a good-looking pioneer who took too much LSD and ended up crunching Mandrax into his hair on live American television before opting out for good, returning to any kind of house with his mother in Cambridge and not making with a put Pinked music after 1972, when he appeared at a local venue their deb band named Stars. In the mid-sixties he had est album together with his friend Roger Waters, helmed *Piper At The Gates Of Dawn*, and wrote fractured, fitfully wonderful songs like 'Baby Lemonade', 'Golden Hair', 'Gigolo Aunt' and 'Love You' on those 1970 solo albums I had listened to so many times: *The Madcap Laughs* and *Barrett*. Syd's slightly sarcastic, slightly mournful laconic English delivery, simple chord arrangements and lyrics that were at once fantastical and parochial (I don't know what a gigolo aunt is, but I can imagine one living in Cambridge and drinking tea) made Syd the main influence, alongside The Velvet Underground, on alternative pop and rock music from the eighties onwards.

I could only guess that Syd might have been a little like Charles, NJ's brother, a gentle, deeply musical soul who suffered from schizophrenia. Charles needed peace to cope with his condition and spent most of his days in his bedroom at his parents' house, writing down his thoughts, praying, listening to music, reading, playing guitar and smoking cigarettes. Schizophrenia seems to strike creative, intelligent, rebellious young men in particular: Charles was around seventeen when he got ill, Syd Barrett in his mid-twenties, although the erratic behaviour started earlier. Once ensconced in a life of seclusion in Cambridge, I imagined that Syd Barrett craved normality as Charles did, but he had the affliction of fame and idol worship to deal with. The world encroached on him. Writers and reporters who did manage to get him to open his door were met with a bald, middle-aged, no longer beautiful Barrett telling them: 'Syd can't talk to you now.'

Charles gets tense at the thought of talking to a friend, a health worker or a member of his family, or his mother and father. For Syd Barrett to have strangers turning up at his house must have felt like being attacked by an octopus, its tentacles creeping around every corner, into every window of his mind.

I had taken the afternoon off work so that Doyle could come round to rehearse. It was a Tuesday and we were recording the following Monday, and this was the only time that Doyle could (or would) come over. I told him about Syd Barrett as soon as I opened the door to him.

'Oh right, well, that's sad I suppose,' he said, lighting a Marlboro. 'Still, we've all got to go some time. How's the old songwriting coming along then? Have you managed to massacre my masterpieces yet? What do you have to do to get a cup of tea round here? Come on Will, sort it out.' Then he got past the front door.

In our house there are three bedrooms. One is for the children, one is for us, and one is the 'study', a.k.a. an all-purpose dumping ground for pretty much everything, including the bass guitar and amplifier I had borrowed from my friend Will and never given back; the Hohner semi-acoustic guitar I had found in the attic, a neglected gem; and the Telecaster and amp I had bought to learn to play electric guitar on. There was even a microphone, so, bar a drumkit, the tiny room had everything you needed to rehearse a band in.

Doyle had just been to see a friend of ours who had moved to Spain, where he had bought a wreck of a farmhouse for next to nothing and was renovating it with his girlfriend. 'He was wearing sunglasses,' said Doyle, shocked. 'What's happening to everyone?' Then he picked up some photographs that had been taken at a festival NJ and I had just come back from. In one I was wearing a k... in another an embroidered suede shirt and wide-brimmed ... hat. 'Jesus Christ!' he shouted. 'You've turned into a hipp... ... th Matt gone all Notting Hill and you turning into a blee... ...wer-sniffer, I'm the only one left to fight the good fight....

'What are you, the... ...ed, doing my best to tune up

the guitars over Doyle's never-ending vocalised thought processes.

He thought about this for a bit, and then said: 'A proletarian.'

'In that case, the bass is a good instrument for you – no-nonsense, sturdy and humble. You can play the bass on the recording.'

Doyle stared at me for a moment. 'I see what's going on,' he said. 'You're trying to turn yourself into the star of this little project. I'm being shunted into the background, even though I wrote half of them songs.'

'*Co*-wrote them,' I corrected. 'Now stop moaning and work out a bass line for "Bad Part Of Town".'

I started playing the song. Doyle came in and made everything sound so wrong that I was wondering if I had lost the ability to play it, but this is the effect of two musical instruments jarring against each other. I kept going while Doyle searched for the right notes on the bass. After five minutes or so he found them and the instruments clicked together.

'What's next?' he said.

'Don't you think we should practise that one first? We've only just got it.'

'Once I've got it, I've got it forever,' he claimed. 'What about "Coming Back To You"?'

I wasn't sure what this song needed. Being in a seventies vein, I suspected it might sound best with an acoustic guitar and a voice, but perhaps a country-rock sound fleshed out by brush drums and a bass rhythm would be good too. I started playing it.

'What's that?' said Doyle, open-mouthed. 'You've completely changed it! I knew this would happen. You can't resist tinkering around. It means that when you're famous you can say, "there was someone that did give me a helping hand on this one in the very early days, can't quite remember his name, but really it was all down to me".'

Doyle was right that it had changed – without my knowing it. This was the song that NJ and I had practised the most, and over the last few weeks little nuances had developed that deviated from Doyle's original plan. I had also added the odd note here and there. But it wasn't *that* different.

'It's unrecognisable!' he shouted. 'You've taken all my best bits and eradicated them. Why have you done this to me? And I suppose you'll be playing it in the studio, won't you?'

'I'll have to. NJ won't be able to sing along to your original version. But I've been thinking . . . this could definitely benefit from having a triangle tinkling away in the background. Why don't you do that?'

'I don't do triangles,' he muttered darkly. 'Or penny whistles, before you ask.'

'Moving on, let's give "Ibid" a go.' Since the abject humiliation before Liam and his silent assistant at ToeRag I had been practising this one intensely. I still fluffed a lot of the notes, but at least you could hear the tune now. I suggested to Doyle, in an attempt to placate him as much as anything, that he play lead guitar while I held down the main tune. I had also removed his introduction, replacing it with an early music piece that Michael Tyack had taught me – and he had learned it by listening to the late twentieth-century master of early music David Munrow – called *La Folia* (The Madness).

'It's confirmed: you are a hippy,' said Doyle. 'That one would go well with patchouli oil and *The Tibetan Book Of The Dead*. And why do you have to go and keep changing everything, anyway?' 'Everything else is the same,' I told him. 'You just have to come up with something suitably psychedelic to make this work.'

He knocked out a few uninspiring runs on the lead guitar before putting it down and saying: 'That'll do. Let's go and have a cup of tea.' We had been practising for approximately twenty minutes. 'I suppose you want me to starve to death as well. How about something to eat?' He lit a cigarette and shuffled off downstairs.

NJ arrived, bringing Otto and Pearl back from school, and I knew that, from then on, any further attempts at trying to make our songs sound even slightly coherent were doomed. Otto, who knows a kindred spirit when he sees one, loves Doyle. He was pulling out his many drawings and paintings of aliens, knights, wicked spirits and robot dogs to present to his dishevelled hero, who in turn offered to take Otto to The Fantasy Centre, the bookshop on Holloway Road in north London that he had spent so much of his own youth in. 'What about our rehearsal?' I shouted, pushing Otto's pictures out of the way. 'This is the only chance we've got! I've already faced Liam's wrath once. I don't want to do it again.'

'We've done it,' he said. 'There's no point in doing any more. I know what I have to play now and, besides, you're bound to change everything when we go into the studio.'

'It looks like there's nothing else I can say, then. But you have to at least help me stand up to Liam. I'm scared of him. It's that slicked-back red hair and pointed ginger beard . . . when he gets angry he looks like the devil.'

'He's probably still trying to get over the death of that guy from Freddie and The Dreamers,' said Doyle.

'I'm paying a lot of money for this session,' I said, wagging a finger at Doyle. 'You'd better turn up on time and, once there, you'd better work hard. Otherwise I'll make you wear my kaftan to your railway depot.'

'Stop acting like such a bleedin' drama queen. I never get anything wrong.'

It was a hot, dry day, and NJ, Otto, Pearl and Doyle sat in the garden. NJ had made mint juleps. Doyle offered some art criticism on Otto's paintings, NJ read Pearl a story, and they shared a moment of uncomplicated happiness. I stood and watched them from inside the house, scowling. My one chance to cut a disc had finally arrived, and it was going to be a disaster.

Chapter Thirteen

Punks Vacate the Premises

The studio was booked from 12.00 p.m. to 8.00 p.m. Pearl finished nursery at 12.30 and Otto finished school at 3.30. A friend who lived nearby would pick Pearl up and take her back to her house, then my mother would come at 3.30 to get Otto, drive to the friend's house and get Pearl, and take them both back home. It was only on the evening before that we found out the friend was going to be in the countryside that day and had neglected to mention this to us. After a handful of slightly hysterical phone calls between NJ, my mother and myself, my mother saved us by cancelling a couple of appointments so that she could look after both children for the whole day.

I spoke to a friend, an American in London called Teri Grenert, who had recorded at ToeRag a number of times with her various all-girl rock'n'roll bands. Liam was a very good friend and the records he produced had a vibrancy that couldn't be found anywhere else, but I had heard that once he got behind those controls, he was a changed man.

'All I would say is, don't make too many mistakes,' said Teri. 'He gets kinda angry when you don't get it right, and when I recorded there he lost his temper when the drummer turned up an hour late. You're paying for your time there, but it's his name that goes out on every record that he produces and he wants them all to be good. And don't expect to get the final word on a song.'

'I've got this one song called "Bad Part Of Town",' I told her. 'Liam told me to chop off the last verse, but the problem is that it actually ends in the middle of a sentence now. I was thinking about fighting him over that.'

'He'll tell you to change the words until they fit his arrangement,' she replied. 'And another thing to remember is that he knows what he's talking about. He's got a great sense of music. If I were you, I'd do what he tells you.'

And, of course, I hadn't heard from Doyle. I called him that morning at eleven, just as we began the drive across East London from Peckham to Homerton. He was asleep.

'Bloomin' eck,' he said. 'Is it today?'

'You'd better be there,' I said, in the kind of stern voice I usually reserve for Otto at his most naughty. 'You *will* be there – at 12 on the dot.'

'I'm on the case, man,' he said, before groaning and turning his phone off. I had a disturbing image of his head rolling over on the pillow, a line of saliva seeping out of his open mouth as he closed his eyes – and closed his mind to recording commitments for the next five hours.

It was one of the hottest days of a particularly hot July – the papers were full of reports of the Underground being hotter than the legal limit for cattle trucks – and we arrived early at ToeRag. Eddie opened the door and warned us that by about four the windowless recording studio did tend to get fairly unbearable. Liam arrived five minutes later, not exactly dressed for the weather in tweed trousers, leather winkle-picker shoes, a cotton shirt, a wool tie and a forties tank top. Eddie made a pot of tea. The dank confines of the studio felt like a masculine world: Liam's fastidiousness meant that every piece of equip-

ment had its place, but the lino floor of the studio, the toilet
with its broken seat and one-hinged door that didn't close
properly, and the sink in the office with its cluster of chipped
mugs did not look like they had been assailed by any kind of
cleaning products for a while. Colin turned up, as genial and as
helpful as ever, and began to practise 'Bad Part Of Town' on the
Hammond. My phone went. It was Doyle, telling us that he was
going to be late. He had just woken up. It had gone twelve.

'What do we do now?' I said, intensely aware that, as the
minutes ticked by, so did the pounds.

'Why don't we do "Ask Me No Questions"?' said NJ.

Although we hadn't been practising this as much as the
songs that Doyle and I had written, we knew Bridget St John's
song pretty well, and it needed nothing more than NJ's voice
and my acoustic guitar. I hadn't planned on coming to ToeRag
to record a cover version, though.

'But it's the song that we should do,' said NJ. 'It's just as
relevant as anything you have written yourself. It's the song that
allowed me to discover that I could sing.'

She was right. More than any other, it had guided me in
seeing how a mood, a spirit, a musical idea and a voice could be
captured simply and beautifully to form a song. And perhaps
more significantly, it had awakened an interest in NJ to express
herself through singing that had lain dormant since she last
sang hymns in her school choir as a little girl.

Since we couldn't do anything else while we waited for Doyle
to turn up – and God knows when that would be – NJ's
suggestion made sense. Liam took us into the studio. I sat down
and Liam placed a microphone very close to the strings of the
guitar, and NJ stood a few feet away to sing into a huge silver
microphone held up by a heavy, wheel-mounted stand.

'This mike will be good for NJ's voice,' he said, as he moved

it into position. 'It's called a C12 by AKG and it's one of the
best ever made, although AKG stopped producing it in 1962.
For anyone serious about microphones, I would heartily re-
commend a C12. The technical term for this microphone is
"knockout". And for your guitar this Neumann microphone,
which has little bit of rust on it that in no way affects the sound
quality, will be great too.'

'So you don't want to use a pick-up?' I asked him. You can
amplify an acoustic guitar in one of two ways: stick a microphone in front of it or attach a pick-up over the sound-hole that
you then plug into an amplifier or a PA system.

'Christ, no! I'd never do that.'

'I remember seeing footage of Tim Hardin playing at Woodstock with just a microphone in front of his acoustic guitar,' I
said enthusiastically. 'It sounded great, and you had this one
microphone getting the sound out to hundreds of thousands of
people.'

'The only problem with Woodstock,' said Liam, 'is that
there were some hippies there. OK, let's see how it sounds.
I'm going to go into the control room. When I tell you, run
through the song.'

NJ was nervous. You could tell by the way her narrow arms
kept shivering. She looked lost, alone by the microphone, and
delicate in her white embroidered dress and long red hair.
Liam's disembodied voice came through the studio speakers
and we began. NJ sang the song beautifully, but she missed
her cues.

'OK guys, that sounded real pretty,' said Liam through the
speakers. 'But NJ, your timing is a bit weird and can you not
open and close your mouth, because you keep making a little
sound when you do. Let's give it another go.'

We tried again. 'Ask Me No Questions' requires intense

finger-picking and I began to experience something I hadn't accounted for: guitar fatigue. I couldn't stop halfway through, because this was the dress rehearsal for the real thing. It felt like running a race with a devil behind you that would jam a hot poker up your arse should you lose momentum. The timing was better, but not perfect.

'I think we're ready,' said Liam. 'This time let's do it for real. This knockout microphone picks up everything. And . . . we're rolling.'

There was nobody in the room. Only Liam was listening to the song. And yet, with the knowledge that recording tape — real tape, not a digital recording that could be wiped out at zero expense — was now passing through the reels of Liam's vintage Studer tape machine, you felt an immense pressure. Again, NJ's timing went off severely about halfway though. My heart sank, as she had been so good up until then. But this was only the first take. Maybe Liam would allow us to have another crack of the whip.

'Pretty good,' said Liam from the control room, 'but I think we're getting a case of Red Light Fever here. Don't worry, it happens to everyone. So we know that we can do this song better. Let's give it another try.'

Whatever Teri had said about Liam's intolerance of shoddy efforts, he was on our side. Perhaps he felt sorry for us, or perhaps he could see that we really were trying our best. A producer's job is a diplomatic one as much as anything. He or she has to coax the most out of the people recording and make them feel that they are capable of producing the goods. In spite of the myriad worries I had been harbouring about not being prepared for the big day, Liam was making us feel like we had something worth perservering with, and worth getting right. It was hugely reassuring.

This time it went unusually smoothly – until NJ hit a wobbly note and lost it from then on.

'One more time, guys . . . OK, take three. We're rolling.'

NJ sang marvellously. She hit her cues, and the feel and the rhythm of the song held up. But this time I messed up. There is a line in the song that goes 'and if you stumble, or if you fall down on your way, I'll be there'. For some reason I stumbled all over my guitar just as NJ sang that line, and, although I picked up the slack, the damage was done.

'Come into the control room, band,' said Liam. 'Let's talk.'

I thought that he would be angry. 'That was real good,' he said, surprisingly. 'The combination of NJ's voice with the C12 mike is, to use the technical term, knockout, and the guitar-playing is flowing well. But the problem is that each take had some big mistakes in it. So I'm going to use a technique that you could find on a lot of the great jazz records: to use the best take, which I think was the third one, and get rid of any out of time or out of tune parts by chopping them out and replacing them with cuts from the other two.'

'It's not cheating,' said Eddie, who was sitting on the steps outside the control room, smoking a roll-up. 'Everything used will have been played live by you, which isn't the case with most bands or singers these days.'

'So leave me to it, and I'll get working on these edits,' said Liam. 'I'll call you when I'm ready.'

'Ask Me No Questions' had taken about three quarters of an hour to set up, rehearse and record. I imagined that Liam would take maybe half an hour to cut the mistakes out of the tape and replace them with better versions, so I went out into the corridor outside the studio where Doyle was now lingering, complaining to Colin about seeing a picture of me in a kaftan. 'What happened to the punk of old?' he kept saying. 'It's a great tragedy. Ah, here's the man himself. At least he's not waving a stick of incense.'

'So you've decided to turn up then,' I said. 'I suppose I should be thankful for small mercies.'

'And I've only had two hours' sleep,' he claimed, flicking his wrists as if to shake him into a waking state. 'I've been working nights. Are we going to record these songs or not? What's going on?'

I told him about what Liam was doing, and that we had decided to do a quick recording of the one song Doyle was not needed on while we waited for him.

'So I'm expendable,' he said. 'If I knew this was going to happen, I would have stayed in bed for another couple of hours.'

An hour later I thought that I had better see how Liam was getting on – after all, we only had two hours per song if we were going to get four done in the eight hours I had paid for. All that had been coming from the control room was the sound of tape being pulled backwards and forwards and a flow of expletives interspersed with five-minute intervals.

'It's sounding pretty damn good,' he said. 'Check this out.'

He played me the first half-minute of the song, now perfectly in time.

'Great,' I said. 'Can we get on with the next track now?'

'No we can't,' he replied. 'That's the first cut. I've got four more to do. Go back to the corridor until I'm ready.'

Colin practised on the Hammond, Doyle tried to remember the bass parts he had come up with for 'Bad Part Of Town' a few days before, and I played the riff on my unplugged Telecaster. Meanwhile, the clock ticked.

'Do you think we're going to get everything done?' asked Colin.

'It's half-past three,' said NJ. 'Liam's been in there for two-

and-a-half hours. I think you might have to forget about
"Ibid".'

'Everyone told me that we'd never record four songs in a day,'
I said sulkily. 'I should have listened to them. As long as we get
"Bad Part Of Town" and "Coming Back To You" done, it will
be all right.' The curses rang out from the control room. A
terrible thought occurred to me. What if we *only* recorded 'Ask
Me No Questions'? The whole adventure would have failed. My
goal had always been to write my own song and record it as a
45, and the only song we had done was a cover version – a cover
version of a lovely song, but a cover nonetheless. I would never
be able to get everyone back in the studio again and I had spent
all my money. We hung around, and I sweated in the airless
corridor, and we waited, and Doyle made not entirely helpful
remarks like 'this will probably be a disaster'.

Then, at half-past four, Liam came out into the corridor,
looking pleased. 'That was tough,' he said. 'You're actually
always slightly changing the way you play the song, Will, so it
was very hard to match up the different takes, but I think I've
cracked it. Come and have a listen.'

We filed into the control room. Liam played the tape very
loud. He had put a touch of echo on NJ's singing, giving it a
spooky quality, and because she had sung so close into a very
high-quality (official term: knockout) microphone, you could
hear every nuance of her voice. It sounded so much better than it
ever had before and, because we had mostly worked out how to
play 'Ask Me No Questions' from listening to a CD of Bridget
St John's version, markedly different from the original. NJ
allowed herself a smile. For once she didn't pull her efforts apart
with self-criticism.

'I think you've done well,' said Liam.

'I'm really happy,' said NJ.

'It's lovely,' said Colin.

'This guy used to be a punk,' said Doyle.

'It's got mistakes in it,' said Liam. 'There are some off-notes and the guitar loses the pattern every now and then, but, personally, I don't think it matters. In a modern studio the producer would probably spend a week fiddling about on computers to get rid of those mistakes. But what we've got here is the capturing of a spirit and a moment in time. It reflects who you are.'

'So does that mean that even the big bands get it wrong and then clean it up afterwards?' I asked.

'They're the worst,' said Eddie. 'A lot of them never learn to play tightly together, at least not in the studio, because they know that the engineer and the producer can sort it out after they leave. They can play terribly and get away with it.'

The bands that have embraced technology and turned it into their art, such as the German electronic pioneers Kraftwerk or the more innovative American modern R&B and hip-hop producers, have made a virtue out of the fact that their music is a product of the age they make it in and it is creative as a result. But I disliked music that aimed to sound like traditional rock or pop as made on real instruments and yet was essentially a computer program. Phil Collins admitted that, because he had made a recent album on computers, it wasn't actually possible for a band to perform it, although it was meant to sound like it was. What sorry state of affairs is that? Technology is, for the most part, accepted blindly as progress whether it causes any improvement for humanity or not.

'So what do we do now?' I said to Liam.

'Now,' he said, 'we break for lunch.'

He took us to a Jamaican café around the corner that he had been going to every weekday for the last five years. It had taken the Jamaican women who worked there three years to say hello to Liam, and another year to crack a smile, and now they actually knew his name. One could only wonder what they made of this post-war throwback turning up each week with a different bunch of hairy freaks, but they made the best salt fish and ackee with rice and peas that I have ever tasted.

Lunch was thankfully short, but it still brought us up to 5.00 p.m., giving us three hours left. If we were going to record only one more song, as seemed likely, it had to be 'Bad Part Of Town'. 'Ibid' wasn't fully worked out. 'Coming Back To You' was nice, but it wasn't much more than two separate chord sequences and it did, I have to admit, have a touch of The Eagles to it. 'Bad Part Of Town' was short, it had rhythm, a killer riff, and lyrics that offered a searing probe into social conditions in contemporary inner-city London. I still didn't feel very comfortable about singing it, but we would cross that bridge when we came to it.

Eddie plugged me into a huge Selmer amp from the early sixties while Colin got the Hammond organ warmed up – this endearingly organic machine takes five minutes to get into the right mood before it can make a sound. Doyle, who has a tendency to get stuck on one note, metaphorically and musically speaking, kept saying to Liam, who was trying to set up all the equipment: 'I saw a picture of this guy in a kaftan. He's become a hippy. It's terrible. I'm the only one keeping punk alive.'

'Punks are horrible,' Liam replied. 'They're smelly.' He went into the control room and announced through the speakers: 'Punks vacate the premises IMMEDIATELY.' Doyle scurried out like a dejected beetle.

He was allowed back in once everything was in place. Doyle plugged in the bass guitar and I tried to explain to him the changes: that the introduction and the last verse had gone but, apart from that, everything remained the same. We would record the music live and then I would sing over the top of that recording, listening to it on headphones. Liam got behind the drums and counted us in. We blasted off.

'Hold it, hold it,' shouted Liam, half a minute into the song. 'Doyle, your bass part is far too complicated and you haven't worked out how to play it properly. You're out of time with everyone else. Will, did you give him the demo to listen to?'

'Yes I did,' I replied, remembering Doyle's insistence that, after twenty minutes of rehearsing 'Bad Part Of Town' at our house a couple of weeks earlier, it was time to lay down tools.

'You need to keep it simple,' said Liam. 'Just stick to the root notes and follow the main chords. OK, 1, 2, 3, 4!'

We went off again. Now the timing confused Doyle. Without the lyrics, it sounded like the main riff went on longer and Doyle kept moving onto the next section a line too early. He was sitting on the floor with his bass, getting increasingly agitated. The temperature in the studio was pushing $40°$ C.

'I'm sure you've got it all wrong,' he said. 'When you come to put the vocals on it you're going to find that it doesn't work.'

He was casting doubt into my mind when previously I was sure that I had it right. I kept explaining to him that, for the first verse, the riff went round twice and, for the second and third verses, it went round three times, but he couldn't appear to accept it. On the fourth attempt, however, we ran through the whole song and just about managed to hold it together.

'You know that phrase, "it sounds like a million dollars"?' asked Liam. 'Well, that sounded like four dollars and ninety-nine cents. Let's do it again.'

'I'm sure it's the wrong timing,' repeated Doyle in a low mutter.

'Stop being a goddam candy-ass,' said Liam. 'One more time and then we'll do it for real. 1, 2, 3, 4!'

It grooved. And our secret weapon was Colin. Colin is an affable, well-spoken chap in a tweed jacket who has the kind of understated charm and social skills that would make him a valuable asset to Britain's diplomatic services, but behind the Hammond he was a changed man. He pounded its keys so hard that the rickety instrument was rocking backwards and forwards like a racehorse pushed to its limit, and he conjured up a swirling, incessant sound that made 'Bad Part Of Town' into psychedelic rock'n'roll, filled with energy and excitement.

Doyle, who is, after all, a good guitarist, albeit not a diligent one, finally got his bass parts down. Liam's drumming was tight but primeval. I was the worst musician in the room, but somehow being propelled along by three other people made me get it right – I had to, otherwise I would be letting everyone else down. My hands were sweating and it was hard to keep going – and we hadn't even got to our first take yet. But I could see NJ dancing to our song in the corner of the studio, and that's when I knew that it was going to be OK.

'How did that sound, Eddie?' said Liam when we came to the song's sudden end – for once, all at the same time.

Eddie was in the control room. He gave a thumbs-up from the other side of the glass.

'This time it's for real, boys,' said Liam. 'I want you to give it your all. This is the bad part of town. You can't fuck around in a place like this. This ain't no place for punks. Hit it!'

We did two takes, both clocking in at one minute and fifty-two seconds. The second take was better, and that was the one we would use without any edits or overdubs. Liam was satisfied. Now it was time for the hard part: the vocals. The big problem was that I had written this tough garage boast, and yet my singing on it always sounded so weedy, even after the help given by my singing lesson with Caroline. Nobody, not even the gracious Richard Hawley, had a good word to say about the way I rendered 'Bad Part Of Town' . . . actually, Lawrence said that he liked it, but I think he was being perverse. I would probably ruin what was now a pretty good tune. Doyle could sing. Why couldn't he sing it?

'No way,' he said, before I had even finished asking him. 'I'm strictly background material.'

We only had an hour and a half left. I couldn't be self-conscious any more.

Liam lined me up against the microphone and explained how I had to follow the backing track as I heard it through the headphones. I asked him if I could listen through to the song once before the tape rolled. 'What's the point?' he said. 'Just go for it. Everyone but Will: out of the studio. Here we go.'

I went for it like I had never gone for it before. I stopped thinking about the fact that I couldn't sing, and that I hated my voice, and sang so loudly that my throat was hoarse by the end of it. For the verse I ended up somewhere between speaking and singing and for the middle eight, which is slightly more reflective, I did my best to remember what Caroline had told me about matching the notes. But the strange thing was that I didn't feel like myself at all. And I completely forgot to sing the third verse about starting a club for disadvantaged teens. The one minute and fifty-two seconds was up before I knew it.

'Now I want to double track the vocals for a couple of lines,' said Liam. 'So, this time, you'll be matching your own vocals.'

He played them back through the speakers. Sure enough, it didn't sound like me, and that was good. Once I had sung over my own voice in the two lines that Liam requested, the song was recorded.

'That had so much soul,' said Liam through the headphones, 'I thought I was listening to James Brown. The raw emotion brought a tear to my eye.'

'Should we do it again?' I asked, assuming that his sarcasm meant it was awful beyond belief.

'No way,' he said. 'Ever heard the phrase, "sounds like a million dollars"? That sounded like a million dollars, with a ten-dollar tip thrown in for good measure.'

NJ, Colin and Doyle came back into the studio. 'That was amazing!' said Colin. 'We were in the corridor, going, "is this really him?"'

'You pulled it off,' said NJ. 'I can't believe it. I would never have thought it possible.'

'Frank Sinatra must be turning in his grave,' said Doyle.

I'm not fooling myself. I can't sing. But, put under pressure, I did what anyone can do: found a way to convey the song with conviction. Tim Siddall, my peak oil and fixed-wheel-bicycle-obsessed friend, had told me that this was all that mattered and he was proved right.

Liam explained that, this being a multi-track recording, he now needed to take the various tracks through the mixing desk to end up with a master copy and he requested that we leave him alone to allow him to do that. We shuffled out into the corridor. I was shaking with the excitement of really surrendering myself to a song for the first time. Doyle was sullen and I knew why: the song that he had contributed the most to was 'Coming Back To You' and we hadn't managed to record it. This meant that the single would now be 'Bad Part Of Town' on one side and 'Ask Me No Questions' on the other. But this was another lesson in the process: as The Rolling Stones once sang, you can't always get what you want. Circumstance had different ideas for Double Fantasy's debut.

Doyle had to leave at 7.00 p.m. to get back to work. I thanked him for all he had done – which was actually a lot – and the remaining three of us waited for Liam and Eddie to emerge. They came out just before 8.00 p.m.

'It's finished,' said Liam. 'And it sounds pretty good. The official, technical term for how it sounds is dynamite. Come in and check it out.'

The music was in time, the tune was catchy, and the song didn't hang around for longer than it was welcome. I wouldn't say that I suddenly had a great voice, but I did sound like I meant what I had to say, and that everybody had better sit up and listen. Liam had created magic out of our simple, un-sophisticated elements. It was some sort of alchemy.

When I learned guitar, I had got a lesson from Roger McGuinn of The Byrds, whose 12-string folk-rock sound I had loved so much since first hearing it as a teenager. One way or another I had stayed in touch with McGuinn, and I had called his house in Florida a few days before going into the studio. He had talked about the moments in The Byrds' career that had made the biggest impression on him.

'I'd have to say that "Mr Tambourine Man", which was the first single we recorded, has a big place in my heart,' he said. 'Our producer, Terry Melcher, rolled out these huge speakers at Studio A in Los Angeles after we finished the session and played the song. We looked at each other and said: "Is that really us? It sounds like a hit!" And it was in mono. Terry didn't believe in stereo. He thought it was a passing fad.'

Terry Melcher sounds a little like Liam Watson. 'Bad Part Of Town' was in mono too. And I knew how Roger McGuinn felt. It was hard to connect the preposterous song I had fashioned over the last few months with the soon-to-be number one worldwide smash hit currently pumping out of ToeRag's speakers.

Liam had mastered it – put the various tracks through a mixing desk and matched the levels – but he suggested that it be re-mastered before it was sent off to the pressing plant to be cut onto vinyl.

'Leave it for a week,' said Liam. 'That will give both me and you a chance to listen to it, and, if there are some notes that are too high or too low, they can be sorted out in the re-mastering.'

'It's a pretty good song,' said Eddie. 'Sounds like British rock'n'roll.'

'I have to say,' said Liam, 'that, when you came in a week ago, I didn't think there was much hope. I resigned myself to the fact that I was doing this as a favour, and I was going to ask you to make sure that I didn't have a producer's credit on the record. But now I think you've got an officially dynamite single. The raw emotion of "Bad Part Of Town" contrasts against the pretty delicacy of "Ask Me No Questions". It's sweet and sour.'

He leaned over his mixing desk, eyebrows raised, and said:

'It's what Double Fantasy is all about.'

Chapter Fourteen

Dragon's Tooth Smashes Through Thunder

'Have you heard the news about Arthur Lee?' I said to Doyle on the telephone. He was working on a rail fault, and in his now-managerial capacity as senior faults engineer, he was showing a novice worker the ropes. 'He's dead.'

It was 4 August 2006. Arthur Lee, whose late-blooming recognition had come only a few years earlier, had died the day before after a bone marrow transplant to fight the leukaemia he had recently been diagnosed with had been unsuccessful. The lead singer of Love had moved back to his mother's old house in Memphis, where he had teamed up with a younger generation of local musicians who were behind a series of benefit concerts for the ailing rock legend. Arthur had not paid medical insurance hence, in the home of capitalism, he would find no support from the state.

'The old boy's finally croaked it, then,' said Doyle. 'No, the wrench, not the screwdriver.'

'First Syd Barrett, and now Arthur Lee. Our men are dying.'

'It's a miracle that either of them got this far. They weren't exactly health freaks, were they? Not that one! I've got to go, Will. This clown is going to electrocute us if I don't watch out. We'll meet up and have a beer for old Arthur some time, eh?'

Doyle's indifference to the deaths of our musical heroes,

which reminded me of the reactions of Bobbie Gentry's family
in 'Ode To Billie Joe', was understandable. His own father had
died a few days earlier after a lifetime of alcoholism had led to
physical and mental collapse. For the last year or so, Doyle's
father had been in a wheelchair, just about capable of stringing
a sentence together, most of his hair shaved off after a particularly nasty drunken fall resulted in stitching across his scalp.
'You've got to give him credit,' said Doyle, on the news of his
father's death. 'At least he stuck to his guns.'

Love's album *Forever Changes* held so many memories. Polly,
my first girlfriend, had no interest in rock'n'roll and preferred
arranging dinner parties for unappreciative seventeen-year-olds
to being in the kind of places where pissing in the urinals rather
than the sink is seen as showing off. But even she loved this
wonderfully elegant, dark, tender and violent piece of music,
and it found a place in her minimal record collection alongside
Hymns We Have Loved and James Last's *Make The Party Last*.
Arthur Lee may have been a difficult man, but, with the help of
the (also now dead) Bryan MacLean, he made an album that was
a gift to the world.

With the death of my songwriting heroes only a few weeks
apart, I couldn't help feel that something – my youth, perhaps –
was coming to an end. And, by coincidence, Top Of The Pops,
the BBC's forty-year-old chart show, which was requisite view-
ing for much of my childhood and adolescence, if only for the
(usually vain) hope that there would be a decent song on it,
broadcast its last show a couple of days before Arthur died. I
missed it.

I got a call from Lawrence to say that he had been thrown out
of his flat and was staying in a hostel in the far reaches of east
London, and he was terrified every time he walked into the
place. 'I'm going to get mugged sooner or later,' he said. 'I'm

too naïve. I don't know anything about being streetwise.' For the time being at least, survival was going to have to take precedence over song writing in Lawrence's life.

The following day I drove to Hayes, Middlesex, to get the record made up at a pressing plant called Damont Audio. Two weeks earlier I had taken the master tapes of the songs that Liam had given me to a re-mastering company where a lacquer, or master disc, was cut. I took the lacquer, sealed in a cardboard pizza box, on a train to Hayes & Harlington Station on the outskirts of west London, where Damont, in existence since 1976, was just about hanging on in there despite the fact that the majority of people in Britain no longer owned a record player. Vinyl was now the preserve of collectors, nerds, the elderly, hopeless romantics and other marginal figures alienated by the crush of modernity.

A friendly woman with large glasses and short brown hair, who had been at Damont since it opened and appeared to be its sole occupant on my visit, showed me Double Fantasy's first and no doubt only seven-inch single, played both sides so that I could check that no hisses and scratches had made their way on there, and helped me load up the six boxes of fifty singles into the boot of the car. I drove back with anticipation, but with sadness too. The adventure was over and so was, I couldn't help but suspect, a chapter in my life.

My father had come to visit us that day. A sagacious, calm man, Nev (as we have always called him) gave up a heady, stressful, hard-drinking and hard-working life at the age of thirty-eight – two years older than me – to pursue meditation and the quest for spiritual enlightenment. He was excited to discover that one of his sons had made a single, so he joined Otto, Pearl and NJ as they sat and waited expectantly as I put the 45 on the turntable. 'Ask Me No Questions' came on first.

'NJ!' said Nev in the kind of wide-eyed state of terminal surprise that we had come to expect from him. 'What a beautiful voice! I never knew you could sing like that. It's marvellous!'

I turned it over and put on 'Bad Part Of Town'. Otto started doing somersaults on the sofa and Pearl ran upstairs to her bedroom.

'Sturch!' he said, using my boyhood nickname. 'All of your life I've been telling you that you can sing, that it's only been your lack of confidence that has stopped you. Now you've finally listened to me and, you know what?'

'What?'

'I wish you never had! It's absolutely awful!'

I sent out the single to friends and the people who had helped me along the way, and even managed to get a few into the record shop Rough Trade in Notting Hill Gate, where I had discovered so many vistas of possibility back in my teens. Those 300 copies would get out there, to attics, charity shops and maybe even a few turntables, and have a life of their own. And I hoped that one day, perhaps when Otto was my age, 'Bad Part Of Town' might end up on a compilation of obscure British bands from the first decade of the twenty-first century. I put the songs up onto the music-sharing website MySpace and got a minor charge of thrill when someone from, say, Sweden would have something nice to say about them. (But then, nobody ever says anything horrible on MySpace because they are all hoping that you will be similarly effusive about *their* songwriting efforts.)

Everyone seemed to love 'Ask Me No Questions', and shared my father's amazement that NJ had been restricting this wonderfully pure voice to the four walls of the bathroom for so long. It was also confirmation that Bridget St John's song was an unfairly obscure gem. There are such things as perfect songs, and 'Ask Me No Questions' is one of them.

'Bad Part Of Town' wasn't received as the stone-cold classic I had hoped it would be, but it did have one extremely enthusiastic fan: Otto. 'It's the best song in the world,' he said during our summer holiday car journey. 'When I'm older, my band is going to do "Bad Part Of Town". I'm going to learn how to play electric guitar and I'm going to do it REALLY LOUD.'

'What's the name of your band?'

'Dragon's Tooth Smashes Through Thunder.'

It was so much better than Double Fantasy. I was almost jealous.

Doyle, NJ, Colin and I agreed that, with the help of Richard Vine and his mastery of digital technology, we would record 'Coming Back To You', 'Ibid' and 'My Dearest Dear'. Every time we made a date something got in the way. It still hasn't happened. We keep promising each other that those songs will make for some good recordings . . . one day.

I thought about the purpose of what I had been doing for the last year. Songwriting is time-consuming, and, ostensibly, not the kind of thing an adult with responsibilities should be preoccupied with, but it makes you yield to expression, and reflection. It renews your focus on the aspects of life that matter. And Tim Siddall, the bicycle-fixated friend who had told me that night in the Hatcham Social that songs were all about expressing a worldview rather than a perfect piece of music, had been inspired by his own words. His new obsession was performing protest songs about the end of the world and the evils of Coca-Cola at a local pub called The Ivy House. 'It's all I need,' he said. 'Doing a couple of songs every Wednesday night at The Ivy House has given my life meaning.' And, although Tim's singing and guitar skills were no better than mine, The Boycott Coke Experience was going down a storm.

To the chagrin of London's hardcore cycling community, writing songs had replaced fixed-wheel bicycles in Tim's one-track vision of the world. 'What's the point in cycling all through the night to go to, say, Brighton, then turning round and going all the way back again,' he said of his former Friday-night ritual, 'unless you're going to do a gig?' He had even thought of the perfect way to combine his former and current obsessions: to perform with a bicycle-powered amplifier. All he had to do now was find someone willing to pedal furiously while he sang on stage.

I was reminded of something that Bridget St John had said on that winter evening in her cramped Greenwich Village apartment, where she had stayed since abandoning any kind of high-profile singing career in order that she could give her daughter a happy and secure upbringing, while never actually abandoning the craft of songwriting itself:

'Whatever your level of success, you will have written songs that mean something to someone. That should be enough.'

Acknowledgements

Thanks to NJ Stevenson, Doyle, Liam Watson and Colin Midson for making Double Fantasy a reality. Thanks to Lawrence for his time, wisdom and encouragement, and to Richard Vine for his bedroom studio wizardry and demo-recording patience. Paul Morrissey, Bob Stanley, Mara Carlyle, Keith Richards, Andrew Loog Oldham, Patti Boyd, Arthur Lee (RIP), Gruff Rhys, Ron and Russell Mael, Matthew Friedberger, Andy Partridge, Gaz Coombes, Ray Davies, Lamont Dozier, Jake Holmes, Bridget St John, Chip Taylor, Hal David, Chan Marshall, Iain from Eigg, Andrew Lloyd Webber, Bert Jansch, Roger McGuinn, Michael Tyack, Shirley Collins and Richard Hawley have all been generous with song-related wisdom.

I would also like to thank Simon Benham at Mayer Benham, Mike Jones at Bloomsbury, William Webb, Lizzie Lyons, Loren Jansch, Kelly Pike, Florence Arpin, Fanny Johnstone, Eddie Turner, Ana Cecilia Martins, Tim Siddall, Noel Summerville, Jonny Trunk and Chris Fowler.

I am indebted to the following books and their authors: *Money, Fortuna And The Sublunar World: Twelfth Century Ethical Poetics and the Satirical Poetry of the Carmina Burana* by T. Lehtonen (Finnish Academy Of Science And Letters, 1995); *The Love Songs Of The Carmina Burana* trans. Ed Blodgett and

R.A. Swanson (Garland, 1987); *Nico: Songs They Never Play On The Radio* by James Young (Bloomsbury, 1999); *Across The Great Divide* by Barney Hoskyns (Pimlico, 2003); *A Song For Every Season* by Bob Copper (Heinemann, 1971); *America Over The Water* by Shirley Collins (SAF, 2004); *Ballad Of America* by John Anthony Scott (Bantam, 1072); *Social Background To Medieval Secular Song* by Bryan Gillingham (Institute Of Medieval Music, 1998); *A Medieval Pilgrim's Companion* by Thomas D Spaccarelli (University Of North Carolina Press, 1999); *Turn It Up! I Can't Hear The Words* by Bob Sarlin (Citadel, 1992); *An Introduction To The English Folk Song* by Maud Karples (OUP, 1973); *English Folk Songs: Some Conclusions* by Cecil Sharp (Methuen, 1954).

For permission to reprint copyright lyrics the author and publishers gratefully acknowledge the following:

Extract from 'Low C', words and music by Daniel Goffey, Gareth Coombes, Michael Quinn and Robert Coombes, copyright © 2005. Reproduced by permisison of EMI Music Publishing Ltd, London WC2H 0QY; extract from 'Ode to Billie Joe', words and music by Bobbie Gentry, © copyright 1967 Northridge Music Incorporated, USA. Universal/MCA Music Limited. Used by permission of Music Sales Limited. All Rights Reserved. International Copyright Secured; extract from 'Terrapin' by Syd Barrett, copyright © Lupus Music Co. Ltd; extract from 'Will You Love Me Tomorrow', words and music by Gerry Goffin and Carole King, copyright © 1960, Screen Gems-EMI Music Inc., USA. Reproduced by permission of Screen Gems-EMI Music Ltd, London WC2H 0QY.

A NOTE ON THE AUTHOR

Will Hodgkinson was born in Newcastle and now lives in London with his wife and two children. He has written for the *Guardian*, *Mojo*, *Vogue*, *Daily Telegraph*, the *Idler* and *Wallpaper**. He is the author of the highly acclaimed book *Guitar Man*.

A NOTE ON THE TYPE

Linotype Garamond Three – based on seventeenth-century copies of Claude Garamond's types, cut by Jean Jannon. This version was designed for American Type Founders in 1917, by Morris Fuller Benton and Thomas Maitland Cleland and adapted for mechanical composition by Linotype in 1936.